ARCHAIC FICTILE REVETMENTS IN SICILY AND MAGNA GRÆCIA

BY E. DOUGLAS VAN BUREN

LONDON
JOHN MURRAY, ALBEMARLE STREET, W.
1923

Printed in Great Britain by
Hazell, Watson & Viney, Ld., London and Aylesbury.

ARCHAIC FICTILE REVETMENTS
IN SICILY AND MAGNA GRÆCIA

TO

PROFESSOR PAOLO ORSI

WHO BY HIS GREAT LEARNING AND PATIENT LABOURS

THROUGHOUT MANY YEARS

HAS POINTED OUT THE PATH

ALONG WHICH I HAVE TRIED STUMBLINGLY TO FOLLOW

PREFACE

THE study of the fictile revetments in Sicily and Magna Græcia during the archaic period affords so vast a field for research that one is almost bewildered at the wealth of material presented to one's notice. The careful excavations of Italian archæologists during the last twenty years have been so fruitful in important results that every year our knowledge of the subject is enhanced by the study and comparison of the finds from various sites and by more accurate information as to the collocation of individual pieces.

Thus far Italian scholars have been too fully occupied with the arduous labour of excavating and publishing the finds from some given site to find time to make more than a cursory comparison with similar discoveries elsewhere. The meticulous investigations of Professor Gabrici at Selinus, the wonderful campaigns of Professor Orsi at numerous ancient cities in Sicily and Magna Græcia, merit the grateful recognition of all scholars for the scientific precision with which the work has been carried out and for the prompt and detailed publication of the results.

The finds from earlier excavations were, alas ! less accurately recorded, and clandestine digging in many places destroyed beyond hope of recovery the ground-plan of important buildings and scattered the objects unearthed to every quarter of the globe, often with a false provenance to conceal the nefarious traffic. Consequently the pieces are scattered among museums and private collections, and it is frequently difficult to procure even a glimpse of them and quite impossible to obtain measurements or photographs.

I am therefore the more deeply indebted to the Museum Directors and private collectors who with such extreme generosity furnished me with information, photographs and permission to examine the material.

My grateful thanks are due to the *Direttore Generale di Antichità e Belle Arti* for his goodness in facilitating my work ; to the *R. Accademia dei Lincei* for allowing me to reproduce numerous illustrations from the *Monumenti Antichi* and from the *Notizie degli Scavi*; to Professor Amelung, First Secretary to the German Institute in Rome, for permission to have photographs; to Dr. Aurigemma of the *Museo Nazionale*, Naples, for information; to Monsieur E. Babelon, *Conservateur du Cabinet des Médailles*, Paris, for assistance and permission to have photographs; to Professor Chr. Blinkenberg of Copenhagen for information about the Lindian Chronicle; to Signor R. Carta for much help and advice; to Cav. Di Cicco, Director of the *Museo Provinciale*, Potenza, for his kind help and for photographs; to Dr. Lili Frankenstein for generously putting at my disposal the results of her study of Tarentine terra-cottas; to Professor E. Gabrici, Director of the *Museo Nazionale*, Palermo, who kindly permitted me to examine the material from Selinus; to Mr. Leicester B. Holland for technical advice; to Comm. Francesco Ierace for allowing me to study the material in his possession; to Dottoressa A. Levi of the *Museo Nazionale*, Naples, for information; to Professor E. Mancini, Secretary to the *R. Accad. dei Lincei*, for his kind help; to Professor Paolo Orsi, Director of the *Museo Nazionale*, Syracuse, for his generous permission to study all the material in his charge, for photographs and for his invaluable help and advice; to Senatore Di Petra for the gift of his monograph on Metapontum; to Monsieur Pottier, *Conservateur des Antiquités grecques et romaines, Musée du Louvre*, Paris, for allowing me to have a photograph; to Dr. N. Putortì, Director of the *Museo Civico*, Reggio Calabria, for permission to look at the objects in the museum; to Dr. Quagliati, Director of the *Museo Nazionale*, Taranto, for allowing me to study the material; to Mr. Lunsingh Scheurleer, of The Hague, for so generously sending me information as to the pieces in his museum and a photograph; to Professor Gorham P. Stevens, Director of the American Academy in Rome, for technical advice; to Monsieur Michel P. Vlasto for his great kindness in sending me information and photographs of the objects in his collection.

TABLE OF CONTENTS

SITES

2

PAGE

CATALOGUE

LIST OF ILLUSTRATIONS

(*At end of Volume*)

LIST OF ABBREVIATIONS

A.B.S.A. . . Annual of the British School in Athens (London).

A.J.A. . . American Journal of Archæology (Concord, N. H.).

Ann. d. Inst. . . Annali dell' Instituto (Roma).

Ant. Denkm. . . Antike Denkmäler, herausgegeben vom Deutschen Archäologischen Institut (Berlin).

Arch. Anz. . . Archäologischer Anzeiger (Beiblatt zum Jahrbuch).

Athen. Mitt. . . Mitteilungen des Deutschen Archäologischen Instituts ; Athenische Abteilung (Berlin).

Atti Accad. Napoli. Atti dell' Accademia di Archeologia, Lettere e Belle Arti di Napoli (Napoli).

Atti R. Accad. . Atti della Real Accademia di scienze, lettere e belle arti di Palermo (Palermo).

A.Z. . . . Archäologische Zeitung (Berlin).

B.C.H. . . . Bulletin de Correspondance Hellénique (Paris).

Bull. Comm. Sic. . Bullettino della Commissione di Antichità e Belle Arti in Sicilia (Palermo).

Bull. Inst. . . Bullettino dell' Instituto (Roma, Berlino).

Byvanck . . A. W. Byvanck, De Magnæ Græciæ Historia Antiquissima (Hague, 1912).

C.I.L. . . . Corpus Inscriptionum Latinarum.

Doerpfeld . . "Ueber die Verwendung von Terrakotten am Geison und Dache griechischer Bauwerke" in 41stes Berliner Winckelmannsprogramm, 1881.

'Εφημ. ἀρχ. . . 'Εφημερὶς 'Αρχαιολογική ('Αθήνησι).

Freeman . . E. A. Freeman, History of Sicily (Oxford, 1891–).

I.G. . . . Inscriptiones Græcæ.

Jahrb. d. Inst. . Jahrbuch des Deutschen Archäologischen Instituts (Berlin).

J.H.S. . . . Journal of Hellenic Studies (London).

Koldewey . . Koldewey und Puchstein, Die Griechischen Tempel in Unteritalien und Sicilien (Berlin).

Mon. Ant. . . Monumenti Antichi della Reale Accademia dei Lincei (Roma).

N.S. . . . Notizie degli Scavi di Antichità (Roma).

Oesterr. Jahresh. . Jahreshefte des Oesterreichischen Archäologischen Instituts in Wien (Wien).

P.W. . . . Pauly-Wissowa, Real-Encyclopädie der classischen Altertumswissenschaft (Stuttgart).

Rev. Arch. . . Revue Archéologique (Paris).

Röm. Mitt. . . Mitteilungen des Deutschen Archäologischen Instituts ; Römische Abteilung (Rom, Berlin).

Smith, *Dict. Geogr.* . W. Smith, Dictionary of Greek and Roman Geography (London).

INTRODUCTION

A STUDY of the fictile revetments of early temples in Sicily and Magna Græcia would appear at the first glance to be a purely technical subject, and of course primarily it is so. But we must seek further in order to understand the construction of the temples thus adorned, why they were built, who were the builders, and something, if possible, of the social and political conditions of the towns in which they stood. Moreover, the question arises whether those revetments were the work of local or foreign craftsmen, and in the latter case, what induced these strangers to come hither ? If they came at the bidding of the ruling prince, that fact would imply intimate trade relations or treaties of alliance with their mother-country, and in this way apparently insignificant details add to our knowledge of those remote times and supplement the meagre information doled out to us by early writers.

Nevertheless, we cannot wander too widely into these enticing fields, and have been obliged to limit ourselves to a brief description of the site where the terra-cottas were discovered and a rapid summary of the history of each township to which the shrine belonged in the endeavour to gain some sort of idea of the social conditions which led to the erection of the temple, its varying fortunes and final destruction or devastation at the hands of marauders.

The beginnings of these sanctuaries are, unfortunately, almost always wrapt in the mists of antiquity, and we can only surmise from circumstantial evidence that they often go back at least to the earliest days of the Greek settlers, if not to an even more remote epoch when native rulers held sway in the land. Certainly one of the first acts of the colonists must have been to construct a home for their patron deity, and as the new cities prospered, the citizens took care to enlarge and embellish the sanctuary. When some personality, stronger or shrewder than his fellows, rose to power, he wished to commemorate his reign and possibly to propitiate the Higher Powers by a building which would beautify the city and be a lasting memorial of his piety. In this connection the glimpses we obtain of half-legendary figures seem to take more concrete form ; Kleosthenes (or Kleomenes), who dedicated the temple to Apollo, becomes less mythical, and Pollis, the connoisseur of wine, assumes the character of one of his successors in office if not by lineal descent.

The native leaders, too, appear in a new aspect as men of some degree of enlightenment, tenacious of their old-time rights and barbaric state, but willing withal to accept certain elements of foreign culture, some little amenities of life, painted terra-cotta slabs to adorn their palaces or antefixes with apotropæic significance to ward off evil. Such an one was the Lord of S. Mauro, the Sikel city whose identity is hidden from us, or his brother chieftain of Monte Bubbonía who possessed a summer palace which is a striking analogy to the Homeric house, and a winter one reminiscent of the great palaces of Crete.

Since the period with which we are engaged terminated with the end of the V. Century, it closes just too early to include the great age of the Sicilian Tyrants, the days when Anaxilas ruled at Rhegium and when the mighty House of the Deinomenidai quitted their native Gela to wield a vast dominion from their stronghold at Ortygia. Their rise, indeed, sounded the death-knell of the art of fictile revetment in the large towns, although it lingered on in rural sanctuaries or less wealthy communities ; for it was the Deinomenid princes, intent upon erecting their splendid temple to Athena, enriched with entablature, water-spouts and roof-tiles of marble, who demolished the earliest terra-cotta-sheathed sanctuary in her honour and laid low the *temenos* and all the little shrines within it.

Some faint idea of the glowing splendour of these archaic temples may be gained from a study of the abundant material found in the *temenos*, Syracuse, and still more from the really stupendous slabs which clothed the rather friable stone of the edifices at Selinus. One cannot but marvel at the fertile imagination of the artists who produced such a variety of forms, designs and colouring in spite of rigid rules which curbed their fantasies and a severely restricted range of colours which limited them to the use of red merging into a reddish purple and black fading into rusty brown on a cream ground, for it was only in the V. Century that the black and dead-white scheme of decoration was introduced.[1] Yet so skilfully did they combine or

[1] The colours used and the technique of painting the slabs have been ably discussed by H. Koch, *Dachterrakotten aus Campanien*, Introduction, who gives the analysis of the various colours and explains the whole method of procedure. Doerpfeld, *Ueber die Verwendung*, etc., treats the subject in some detail on pp. 27–9. R. Bormann, *Die Keramik in der Baukunst*, p. 41, gives a succinct account of the development of this art.

diversify the tones and motives, so cleverly did they gauge the play of light and shade, that all monotony is avoided and at first one hardly realises with what scanty materials such a harmonious blending is effected.

The dating of these revetments is influenced by many considerations. The ultimate basis is naturally the style and technique of the work: the earliest examples are painted only with designs unskilfully drawn and often ill-adapted to the field to be covered. The later pieces show increased ability of draughtsmanship and a happier choice of motives. A still later stage discloses the tentative introduction of relief, such as a tiny band of astragalos; whilst in the final phase the relief is very high and colour is used merely to emphasise the salient points of the design. Where architectural remains have been discovered they furnish evidence as to the date of the building, but that is evidence to be used with caution, since the revetments may belong to the building in its original form, or to the various restorations of different periods. Only in the case of an edifice where all the material found is homogeneous, as at Metaurum, can we define the chronological limits. Sometimes an inference can be drawn from objects found in or near the temples, and in this respect the *favissæ* are of the utmost value, because the types of figurines and *ex-voto* found reveal the duration of the cult and can be dated with considerable precision. Where the evidence is scanty, light is often thrown upon the subject by a comparison with other sites; indeed in certain cases the almost total lack of architectonic terra-cottas is instructive, for it warns us that when those cities were founded, or at any rate when they were sufficiently prosperous to erect sanctuaries, the primitive fashion of fictile revetments had been superseded by temples entirely of stone.

The archaic temples of the VII.–VI. Centuries in Sicily and Magna Græcia belonged invariably to the Doric order, but had certain local or regional peculiarities which differentiated them from those of the Greek mainland. Whether the earliest structures were entirely of wood or were made of sun-dried bricks is still a debatable question. As the Sicilian sandstone is very soft and easily worked, it is not unlikely that it was employed even by the first colonists in a land where trees yielding wood suitable for building purposes were comparatively scanty.

The framework of the roof at least was of wood, and in order to preserve it from the inclemency of the weather, it was necessary to cover it with a light but non-porous revetment such as the colonists had seen used in their mother-country, a revetment of fictile slabs, cunningly wrought and joined together, so that they formed one complete scheme of decoration.

The position of different elements was never arbitrary, for each served some structural purpose, hence the preordained order could not be altered. This fundamental rule is of immense assistance in reconstructing the slabs, for the elements must follow one another in a given sequence, in conformity with the framework of the temple beneath, narrow and simple in small buildings, wide and sumptuous in design where a broad member had to be covered.

Certain members of the revetment were essential, such as the geison, sima, *σωλῆνες* or flat roof-tiles and kalypteres or cover-tiles: others were susceptible of modification and development, namely, the slab which covered the end of the ridge-pole, originally a concave disc painted with geometric patterns like the one from the Heraion, Olympia, and the reliefs or figures in the pediment.

The horizontal geison, covered with its fictile revetment, bounded the lower line of the pediment, the geison and sima combined, with their respective slabs, ran up over the pediment and along the cornice of the long sides. At Temple C, Selinus, and at the Temple of Hera Lacinia, Croton, the sima was surmounted by a perforated cresting which lightened the whole decoration and produced an admirable play of light and shade. The sima of the long sides was generally pierced at intervals by the pipes which discharged the rain-water collected on the roof; in the earlier temples these pipes were tubular in form and the mouth was adorned with a concave disc, usually painted with rosettes. In the later temples the gutters were masked by lions' heads which were treated more and more realistically. Where tubular pipes were employed, a pipe corresponded to each vertical row of roof-tiles from which it drew off the rain-water; hence there was one pipe-mouth between each pair of antefixes; if therefore a length of the sima with two pipe-mouths has been discovered, this rule assists one to calculate the width of the roof-tiles and the probable length of the whole roof. On the other hand, where lions' heads were adopted, one pipe often served to drain two rows of tiles, and the last tile of each row had a shallow channel which facilitated the dispersal of the water.

The roof-tiles were sometimes flat, but often slightly concave and with a complicated flanged edge, by means of which each tile interlocked with the one overlapping it.[1] They were laid on in vertical rows from sima to ridge-pole ; where each tile joined its fellow vertically the joint was hidden by a cover-tile, the semi-cylindrical kalypter. In the simpler types of roof decoration the tiles and kalypteres were merely covered with a wash of red or black paint to render them impervious to weather ; this was the case at Selinus and Segesta,[2] at S. Mauro and also at Sardis, where recent excavations have shown that the same method was employed.[3] The last kalypter of the row was kept in place by the antefix with which it was sometimes moulded in one and which rose above the edge of the sima and offered a semi-cylindrical or semi-elliptical surface for decoration. Nevertheless, in Sicily and Magna Græcia antefixes did not play such an important part as on the temples of Etruria and Latium, for the rich sima and especially the cresting did away with their structural significance. The ridge-pole was covered by a series of large rounded kalypteres and astride these at intervals arose double palmettes springing from Ionic volutes curving in opposite directions. An extra large palmette marked the middle of the ridge-pole to break the straight line of the roof as seen from below.

The outer angles and the apex of the pediment were made fast by solid blocks which supported the akroteria consisting of palmettes, Sphinxes or even a complicated figure group as at *Marafioti*, Locri.

At Gela, Metaurum and Selinus enframed groups or figures were found which seem to have been metopes, but they are too damaged to enable one accurately to determine their function.

Whether the interior of the sanctuary was as richly decorated as the exterior is still a matter of uncertainty ; from the mass of material found, from the varying dimensions of the different zones of ornamentation and from the less weathered condition of some pieces one is led to conclude that there were at least certain friezes or bands of decoration, but our knowledge is still too slight to permit us to dogmatise upon the subject.

It is hard to say where this method of decoration originated, whether in Greece proper or in the Nearer East. Certainly the fictile revetments from sites in Asia Minor, from Neandria in the Troad,

[1] Durm, *Baukunst d. Griechen* (Leipzig, 1910), figs. 172, 176 ; Perrot, *Hist. de l'Art*, vii, pl. xliv, 1–14.

[2] Doerpfeld, p. 17.

[3] T. L. Shear, *A.J.A.*, xxvi (1922), p. 392.

Gordion in Phrygia, Ak Alan in Pontus and, above all, from Larissa in Æolis [1] with their metope-like plaques or continuous friezes have more affinity with the earliest temples in Etruria and Latium than with those farther south where the absence of figurative friezes is one of the most marked features. The nearest parallels to the remains found in Sicily and Magna Græcia are the revetments of the Treasuries of the Geloans and Megarians at Olympia [2] and a few poor fragments from other sites of the Greek mainland. These, indeed, so closely resemble the more western examples as to suggest a common origin, or at least strong artistic currents which, flowing westward, influenced the local productions and, often commingling, resulted in an interesting blending of various streams.

The fragments from Gela, as one would expect, show a marked resemblance to those from the Treasury of the Geloans, who, in all likelihood, prepared the slabs at home and transported them ready made to Olympia; whereas the revetments from Syracuse are of different types, some certainly very similar to those from Gela, but the earliest and also the latest far closer to specimens from the Treasury of the Megarians.

As this is not the place for an historical study I have only given the bare outline indispensable for the discussion of each site and only quote authorities who are well known and easily accessible. Whoever cares to consult these writers will there find a full narration of the events and a complete citation of all the classical authors whose writings elucidate the misty story of those bygone days.

[1] Koldewey, 51*stes Berliner Winckelmannspr.*; G. and A. Körte, *Jb. d. Inst.*, *Ergänzungsheft*, v (1903); Macridy-Bey, *Mitt. Vorderas. Ges.* 12 Jhrg., 1907, Heft 4; L. Kjellberg, *Uppsala Universitets Arsskrift*, 1903.

[2] *Olympia* II, "Die Baudenkmäler," zweite Hälfte, pp. 187 ff., pls. cxvi–cxix.

SITES

SITES

AKRAGAS

AKRAGAS, which became one of the wealthiest and most prosperous cities in Sicily, arose on the south-west coast about midway between Selinus and Gela.[1] It was a colony of the latter city and from it received certain Dorian institutions and Rhodian rites, among the last named being the worship of Zeus *Atabyrios*, whose sanctuary was one of the earliest undertakings of the new citizens. They appointed a certain Phalaris contractor for the work and overseer of the construction, and with the money entrusted to him for the purpose he hired slaves and mercenaries and laid in a great store of wood, stones and iron. On the pretence of guarding these supplies against theft he obtained leave to erect a wall round the acropolis. Then, having fortified his citadel and armed his slaves and hirelings, he seized the opportunity of the festival of the *Thesmophoria*, when all the citizens were worshipping without the city, to set upon the unsuspecting revellers, slay the men and gain the power for himself. The cruelty of his rule became proverbial and many arguments and discussions have arisen about the story of the brazen bull in which he was said to have roasted his victims, the first being the artist Perillos who at his command had constructed the bull.

At length his ferocious conduct provoked an uprising in which Phalaris was slain, and for a time the city enjoyed comparative peace and rapidly advanced in power and prosperity. Two men are mentioned as successively governing Akragas, Alkamenes and Alkandros, but whether as tyrants or chief magistrates is uncertain. About B.C. 488 history is reported to have repeated itself, and Theron, following the example of Phalaris, used the post of overseer for the construction of Athena's temple as a stepping-stone to power. Yet there his imitation of his predecessor ended, for his government seems to have been mild and the city flourished. By his alliance with Gelon of Syracuse he extended his dominions and his prestige was further enhanced by their combined defeat of the Carthaginians in B.C. 480.

A year after his death in B.C. 472 his son was driven out and Akragas was under a democratic government until the Carthaginian invasion in B.C. 406. The

[1] Bunbury, in Smith, *Dict. Geogr.* i, pp. 74–80; Hülsen, in *P.W.*, i, cols. 1187–91; Freeman, ii, pp. 63–81; J. Schubring, *Topografia Storica di Agrigento*, trad. Tonizzi (Torino, 1887), pp. 72–89.

city was renowned for its wealth, power and splendid public buildings, but the luxurious habits of the citizens had unfitted them to resist their foes. The siege lasted for eight months, and then, rather than surrender, the able-bodied escaped to Gela, leaving the sick and helpless to be put to the sword by the Carthaginians who sacked and destroyed the city.

This was a mortal blow from which Akragas never fully recovered. After forming a valuable asset in the wars between the Carthaginians and Romans, it was destroyed a second time by the former and eventually fell under the permanent dominion of the latter.

The temple of Zeus *Atabyrios* or *Polieus* was on the summit of the acropolis, now covered by the modern town of Girgenti. Traces of two ancient temples are discernible, one under the cathedral of S. Gerlandus, the other incorporated into the church of *S. Maria dei Greci*. The second of these has been proved by Koldewey and Puchstein to be a structure of the V. Century[1]; it must, therefore, be the Athenaion of Theron and the remains under the cathedral must be those of the temple of Zeus. Unfortunately the church was here built over the site of the temple, not into it as happened at the Athenaion, Syracuse; thus very little remains of one of the few VI.-Century Sicilian temples for whose foundation we have historical reference.

Architectonic remains of the archaic period from Akragas are almost unknown, but in the temple of Herakles two palmettes were found, adorned in relief on both sides alike and evidently palmettes of the ridge-pole. The temple was of the VI. Century, but these palmettes, judging from the advanced style of the relief, must belong to a restoration of the middle of the V. Century (pal. 10).

At The Hague is a fine antefix from Akragas with a Satyr's head. The work is bold and effective rather than very meticulous (ant. 41, fig. 63). There is a replica of this head in the Loeb Collection, and in that case the provenance is given as "Italy," but as it is identical with the other specimen the obvious conclusion is that it also was found at Akragas, and that both heads adorned the same temple.

It is more difficult to determine the function of a large slab (only the left half preserved) decorated in high relief with a lion rending a bull, an effective and very realistic bit of work. One might be tempted to think it is one of the gigantic *arulæ* so often found in this region ornamented with this very subject,[2] but instead of traces of the side walls to right and left, there is at the back a buttress extending the whole preserved height of the slab, a detail which rather suggests that the relief was the akroterion of some small shrine. It may, on the other hand, have been an ἄγαλμα in some temple precinct, a purpose for which its shape seems better suited (relief 1).

[1] Koldewey, pp. 138–40.

[2] E. Douglas Van Buren, "Terra-cotta Arulæ," *Memoirs of Amer. Acad. in Rome*, ii (1918), p. 7, pl. 16.

AKRAI

AKRAI was reputed to have been founded seventy years after Syracuse, that is, about B.C. 665, by a colony from that city.[1] In spite of its important strategic position it never rose to great prominence and always continued subservient to Syracuse; indeed, in the treaty concluded between the Romans and Hieron II, Akrai was included in the dominions of the tyrant. It remained loyal to Syracuse in the Second Punic War and offered a refuge to Hippocrates after his defeat at Acrillæ by Marcellus in B.C. 214. This is the last time Akrai is mentioned in history.

The town was situated on a lofty hill, and formed an important outpost of the Syracusan territory. But few vestiges of buildings of the Greek period still remain, except the very scanty traces of a temple, apparently Doric.[2] Literary evidence affirms that there was an Aphrodision, the site of which may possibly be identified by the revetment of a small shrine noted by the Barone Judica.[3]

In the museum at Palermo are various fragments of fictile decoration, amongst others a slab of the horizontal geison with: (*a*) recurved tongue pattern on the cymation; (*b*) astragalos in relief; (*c*) guilloche; (*d*) astragalos (geisa 35). A specimen from Selinus is very similar to this piece from Akrai, but upon it two toroi replace the astragalos (geisa 28).

CAMARINA

ONE hundred and thirty-five years after the foundation of Syracuse a colony was sent in B.C. 600 to found Camarina.[4] In B.C. 552 the city was destroyed because it attempted to assert its independence, but it was recolonised by Hippocrates of Gela in B.C. 495. In B.C. 484 Gelon carried off the inhabitants to Syracuse; it was then colonised a second time from Gela in B.C. 461. From that time its history was stormy, until it was finally destroyed by the Arabs in A.D. 853.

Very little is known of the ancient city, and the chief authority for temples existing there is the fifth Olympian Ode of Pindar which hints rather obscurely at an Athenaion, a shrine of the nymph Camarina and possibly a sanctuary of Zeus Soter.

The Rivers Hipparis and Oanis form the boundaries and natural defence of a sandy hill which rises between their lower courses, and this hill is further strengthened in the rear by the marshes which stretch out to the north-east and in front by the sea. The weakest side of the city was towards the east; hence here the strongest defensive works must have been constructed, but now only

[1] Bunbury, in Smith, *Dict. Geogr.*, i, pp. 21 f.; Huelsen, in *P.W.*, i, col. 1192.
[2] Koldewey, p. 75.
[3] *Le Antichità di Acre*, p. 112, pl. xiii, 4.
[4] Bunbury, in Smith, *Dict. Geogr.*, i, pp. 486 f.; Ziegler, in *P.W.*, x, 2, cols. 1801–7.

faint traces of the walls remain.[1] No evidence for the temple of Herakles, conjectured by Schubring to have stood on the highest point of the hill,[2] was found in the later excavations. From the foot of the hill a gradual slope led up to the plateau of the acropolis and, on the other side, fell gently away towards the sea. Here, on the summit of the acropolis, was the temple of Athena, constructed of masses of sandstone, coated outside with a thin layer of stucco; only a portion of the steps and of the south wall are preserved, but the temple was exactly orientated and seems to have been *prostyle*, not *peripterous*, since no columns lay around the ruins. The construction dates it as V. Century.

Most of the other buildings, private houses or small shrines, belonged to the IV.–III. Centuries, but a small rectangular edifice near the mouth of the Oanis is proved to have been a temple by the *favissa* discovered close by, containing quantities of votive offerings, dating from the end of the VI. to the end of the V. Century.

Schubring, upon insufficient evidence, locates the nymph Camarina's shrine at the *Casa Amaiddo*, where he reports seeing "many wrought stones, squared blocks and terra-cottas of every size and kind." Of this abundant fictile material only a few antefixes have come down to us, three types of Satyrs' heads from some small shrine (ant. 40), and a Gorgoneion in low relief (ant. 26). The two female heads illustrated by Kekulé[3] are not antefixes, but votive offerings, and should be compared with those found at the little temple, especially figs. 20 and 25 of Professor Orsi's account.

But the most precious monument which we possess is one which vouches for the antiquity of the temple to which it belonged and helps us to reconstruct a whole series of analogous works now, alas! in an even more fragmentary condition. This monument was fished up out of the bed of the River Hipparis and represents a complete group, a youth on horseback which formed the central akroterion of a sanctuary situated near the river's mouth, most likely a pendant to the small shrine at the mouth of the Oanis. The horse's head is nobly modelled, but the work ends abruptly at a line drawn through the middle of the body (cent. akr. 6, fig. 71). The youth, now headless, wore a tight-fitting chiton and was seated upon a richly embroidered saddle-cloth. At such an early period, the first half of the VI. Century, it would have been too difficult a feat to model the horse's legs projecting unsupported from the base. The horseman was imagined as mounting guard over the shrine and ready to launch himself to the attack against the city's foes. This group explains the fragments of similar groups from Syracuse, Gela and S. Mauro (cent. akr. 7, 9). The only analogous work from Etruria was found at Statonia,[4] where the akroterion embodied a

[1] P. Orsi, *Mon. Ant.*, ix (1899), pp. 201–78, plan fig. 1.
[2] *Philologus*, xxxii (1873), pp. 521 f.
[3] *Terrak. von Sic.*, pp. 44, 60, pl. vi, 1, figs. 92, 93.
[4] *N.S.*, 1898, p. 436, fig.4; E. Douglas Van Buren, *Terra-cotta Revetments in Etruria and Latium*, p. 38.

horse's head and shoulders, but there is no hint of any rider. What this group of the horse and rider developed into is revealed by the splendid akroterion from *Marafioti*, Locri (cent. akr. 13), where the rider is supported by the superb figure of the Sphinx who with monumental pose bears up his weight.

CATANA

EXCAVATIONS have shown that Catana was originally inhabited by Sikels, but about B.C. 729 the Chalkidians, six years after they founded Naxos, sent thither a colony under the leadership of Euarchos.[1] The only event recorded in the early history of the new township is the legislation of Charondas; since, however, his legislation was soon adopted by other Chalkidian cities both in Sicily and Magna Græcia, Catana evidently maintained intimate relations with the colonies of kindred stock. It seems to have remained independent until B.C. 474, when Hieron of Syracuse transplanted all the original inhabitants to Leontini and repeopled the city with new colonists, partly Syracusans, partly Peloponnesians. From that time the exiles were perpetually readmitted and expelled, until in B.C. 403 Dionysios of Syracuse ravaged the city and sold the inhabitants as slaves.

Eruptions of Mt. Etna and earthquakes have destroyed the town too often to leave any trace of the earliest city. Only a few sherds of architectonic terracottas are preserved, but they prove that in the VI.–V. Centuries buildings existed covered with a rich fictile revetment. There is part of a geison slab with the usual guilloche pattern (geisa 10); another piece has: (*a*) convex moulding with horizontal scale pattern; (*b*) immense single guilloche; (*c*) torus with hammer pattern (geisa 46). These two examples belong to the end of the VI. Century, but there are others of the V. Century, an ovolo with egg-and-dart in relief; a second bit with: (*a*) two small toroi enclosing an egg-and-dart moulding; (*b*) double meander (geisa 65); and thirdly a fragment with scroll pattern (simæ 2), a most unusual motive of which the only other example is a fragment from Croton (simæ 1). Besides these there is an antefix with a bearded Satyr running left and another with a Gorgon's head (ant. 48, 15).

CAULONIA

CAULONIA is situated on the shore of the Ionian Sea in the territory of the present-day Monasterace.[2] The ancient city covered an extensive area and was encircled on the three land sides by strongly built walls and towers of defence.[3] Various legends are told of the origin of the city. According to one story it was

[1] Bunbury, in Smith, *Dict. Geogr.*, i, pp. 567 f.; Ziegler, in *P.W.*, x, 2, cols. 2473–7; Freeman, i, p. 372.

[2] Bunbury, in Smith, *Dict. Geogr.*, i, p. 575; Oldfather, in *P.W.*, 21ster Halbband (Stuttgart, 1921), cols. 67–85; Byvanck, pp. 112 f.

[3] P. Orsi, *Mon. Ant.*, xxiii (1916), cols. 686–943.

founded by a son of the Amazon Clite; with more historical probability another account related that it was first founded by a colony of Achæans led by Typhon of Aigion, and later received a colony from Croton. Caulonia, therefore, was founded when Croton had already risen to power, most likely some time during the VII. Century, for the coins show that from the middle of the VI. Century Caulonia was an autonomous city of economic importance.

In B.C. 389 Dionysios of Syracuse invaded Magna Græcia, besieged Caulonia and inflicted a severe defeat on the Crotoniates and others who came to the help of the beleaguered city. Caulonia was compelled to surrender, and the conqueror removed the inhabitants to Syracuse and bestowed the territory on his allies, the Locrians. Caulonia never again attained to her former position, and during the Pyrrhic wars was taken and laid waste by a band of mercenaries.

The heart of the earliest city, spreading round the acropolis, seems to have covered the slopes of the *Collina del Faro*, a slight elevation upon the summit of which a very early building with solid foundations was destroyed when the lighthouse was erected in 1890. Upon this hill there must have been at least one small shrine, for here an antefix was found, a triangular field enclosed in a narrow projecting border, showing in low relief a nude youth riding upon a dolphin and holding in his left hand a small round shield (ant. 55, fig. 68). From the evidence of coins [1] and from the region where the relief was discovered the subject must represent Taras, the eponymous hero of Tarentum, and the small dimensions of the slab (cm. 10 × 20) suggest that it may have adorned a *heroön* dedicated, if not to Taras himself, then to some other θεὸς σωτήρ of mariners, Poseidon or Apollo Delphinios. On the earlier coins the hero is without the shield which was only introduced towards the middle of the V. Century.[2] This detail, taken in conjunction with the artistic style of the relief, enables us to date the work towards the end of that century.

Also to the second half of the V. Century belong certain architectonic fragments of unusual form (akr. bases 1–3, fig. 69). They have a small triangular pediment supported upon a row of dentils, beneath which comes a fascia containing ten narrow concave flutings coloured alternately red and black. In the top surface is a square hole which reveals the purpose of these pieces, for they served as the blocks into which the bases of the akroteria were inserted and were then made fast by a metal nail, the hole for which is visible in the upper part of the pediment. Probably a metal rosette or shield concealed the nail and formed the central ornament of the pediment, a derivation from the archaic slab covering the end of the ridge-pole.

Among the *débris* of houses covering the western slope of the *Collina del Faro* were found scanty terra-cotta remains, all broken. There were, however,

[1] Head, *Hist. Num.* (Oxford, 1911), pp. 53–62; Hill, *Handb. of Gk. and Rom. Coins* (London, 1899), pl. xi, 1.

[2] Evans, "The Horsemen of Tarentum," in *Num. Chron.*, 1889, p. 37, pl. ii.

much damaged antefixes showing at least three varieties of Gorgoneia (ant. 9). They probably adorned some small sanctuary, but to the houses themselves belonged the tiles, kalypteres and pipes found in great abundance (kal. 7), and also the fragment of a geison with anthemia in relief alternating with lotus flowers (geisa 70), below which was a border of complicated meander in relief. This fragment is quite late in style and may be dated V.–IV. Century.

Among the houses, indeed, a fine piece of a far earlier fictile revetment came to light (lat. simæ 14, fig. 6), part of a lateral sima decorated on the cymation with large heart-shaped leaves, alternately red and black, the space between them filled by a small black leaf of like form. Below is a fascia with reversed flabelliform palmettes enclosed within broad bands ending in volutes. Each slab was pierced by two tubular water-spouts, the mouths decorated with tongue pattern (spouts 5). The disposition of the various elements is almost exactly paralleled on the lateral sima of the Treasury of the Geloans at Olympia,[1] where the more perfect preservation of the slabs permits us to reconstruct the whole revetment.

There was also a fragment of a raking cornice, but not from the same revetment, for the style appears some decades later than that of the lateral sima. It consisted of: (*a*) narrow concave flutings alternately red and black; (*b*) a small torus with diagonal bands; (*c*) double meander in relief; (*d*) a convex moulding decorated with scale pattern placed horizontally (rak. cor. 7). This arrangement of the different motives is almost identical with the piece found at Falerii.[2] The narrow concave flutings resemble those of the raking cornice from Metaurum (rak. cor. 6), whilst the horizontal scale pattern recalls the fragment from Catana (geisa 46), and even more closely, since it borders a meander in relief, the geison from *Marafioti*, Locri (geisa 61).

The great temple stood near the sea-shore, but owing to persistent quarrying of the dwellers far and near in a stoneless district, very little of its ground-plan can be ascertained. It was apparently peripteral; the ruins show that it was certainly *in antis*, at least as far as the principal front was concerned: the number of the columns on the long sides and other details can only be guessed approximately. It was built entirely of very fine calcareous stone, apparently brought from the Syracusan quarries, a perfectly comprehensible fact in a district where building stone is unobtainable. The roof-tiles were of marble, but the revetment was fictile. There is no shred of evidence as to the deity to whom the temple was dedicated, but it may be assigned to the first half of the V. Century, for the architectonic terra-cottas agree in date with what we can gather from the architectural remains; they are not archaic, and yield no evidence whatsoever of an earlier shrine upon the site. Indeed, they are so alike in style that it is difficult to understand in what order they were placed upon the temple. The

[1] *Olympia*, ii, pl. cxvii; Doerpfeld, pl. i, 3.
[2] *N.S.*, 1888, p. 421, fig. 5.

lateral sima consisted of: (*a*) projecting border with black meander; (*b*) reversed tongue pattern; (*c*) fascia with anthemia and lotus flowers. At intervals the lions' heads which hid the water-spouts project and cover the whole fascia (lat. simæ 29, lions' heads 6). The raking cornice has: (*a*) border with meander; (*b*) broad fascia with anthemia and lotus flowers in relief, painted red and cream on a black ground (rak. cor. 27). Part of the pipe of a water-spout was also found with a piece of the disc mouth still attached and painted with a rosette. This single object is not sufficient evidence to prove the existence of a wooden temple preceding the stone one, or even an earlier and simpler revetment of the stone building with tubular pipes instead of the lions' heads. It is more likely that it was one of the end gutters behind the angle of the raking cornice (spouts 18).

There is another lateral sima of small dimensions, almost identical in design with the raking cornice. Here, below the fascia of anthemia and lotus, is a band of double meander in relief, the spaces filled by squares. On this sima the lions' heads are set between the two fasciæ and cover the upper fascia partially and the lower one entirely (lat. simæ 30, lions' heads 7, fig. 11).

Lastly, there is a lateral sima quite different in style, for the principal fascia is decorated with flabelliform palmettes separated by lotus buds. The design is massive and rather squat, with none of the lightness usually associated with these motives. Below it is a band of double meander in relief, the spaces filled by large red squares, and this fascia is pierced at intervals by holes for the water-spouts (lat. simæ 31, fig. 12). Possibly this sima belonged to one of the secondary buildings. Apparently at a late period it was difficult to procure the splendid marble tiles, so recourse was had to fictile roof-tiles and kalypteres (tiles 11, kal. 8), like those found among the houses.

When planting a vineyard on a hill called *Passoliera* to the south of the town of Monasterace evidence of the existence of yet another temple was discovered.[1] Only faint traces of the rude foundations still exist, for every scrap of stone had been dismantled and carried off, but in a pit expressly dug for the purpose a wonderful collection of fictile revetments was unearthed, heaped in disorder in an area of m. 6.00 × 7.00, plainly a deposit of disused material from a small suburban temple of the first half of the V. Century, with the addition of a few pieces which go back to the VI. Century.

To the earliest revetment seems to belong a lateral sima with certain peculiarities which mark it out as a combination of the usual lateral sima and pierced cresting (lat. simæ 22, fig. 9). It has: (*a*) tiny torus with diagonal bands; (*b*) anthemia in relief separated and framed by lotus flowers painted dead white with touches of red on a black ground. The anthemia rise above double volutes

[1] P. Orsi, *N.S.*, 1922, pp. 147–9. Professor Orsi promises a complete publication of the finds at Monasterace in the *Monumenti Antichi*; until this appears I can give only a very superficial appreciation of the splendid material.

between each of which is a triangular opening for the water to run away; (*c*) fascia with double black meander in relief, the spaces filled by a cross within a square. This slab at the bottom runs far back at right angles, and the lower surface is painted with a narrow band of black meander which gives the exact projection of the slab beyond the entablature, because only that part which could be seen from below was decorated. The geison was adorned with: (*a*) torus; (*b*) projecting border with elongated meander; (*c*) cymation with Doric leaf enclosed, black on a white ground; (*d*) torus; (*e*) double guilloche, the eyes filled by rosettes (geisa 7). Among the *débris* of the earliest revetment were fragments of numerous large kalypteres of the ridge-pole, richly painted with black meander, tongue, chevrons and other patterns (kal. 6).

Among the finds were two small heads which appear too archaic to have belonged to the temple at all. One is the head of a Siren or Harpy with rather pointed features and almond eyes; her hair is parted and waved back so that it hangs in a solid mass over the beginning of the outward-sloping bird's back (lat. akr. 6). The other is a very archaic antefix with a female head. The features are merely blocked out, the eyes are a triangular swelling, the hair is parted and waved back (ant. 50). The head is much battered, but is of reddish clay in contradistinction to the cream clay usually employed at Caulonia.

The second revetment carried out a scheme of black and dead white. The lateral sima had: (*a*) black meander on a white ground; (*b*) cymation with a very slight curvature decorated with reversed tongue pattern in red and black; (*c*) astragalos painted only in white on a black ground; (*d*) broad fascia with white anthemia springing from double volutes and separated by lotus flowers. The middle vein of the petals and the band uniting the volutes are the only notes of red in this scheme of a white design on a black ground. In the middle of each slab is a lion's head with a double mane, extremely realistic and carefully coloured to give a lifelike effect (lat. simæ 23, lions' heads 8). The raking cornice was composed thus: (*a*) black meander; (*b*) reversed tongue pattern; (*c*) white astragalos painted on a black ground; (*d*) fascia with white anthemia and lotus flowers painted only, light on a dark ground (rak. cor. 22). On the geison was a double guilloche between two toroi (geisa 16). Perhaps to this revetment belonged the palmettes of the ridge-pole, rising in relief above double volutes (pal. 7).

The lateral sima of the third revetment was the evolution of the second, for all details formerly expressed in colour only are here portrayed in relief. It was decorated with: (*a*) projecting border with broken black meander; (*b*) reversed tongue pattern; (*c*) astragalos in relief; (*d*) broad fascia with anthemia and lotus flowers in relief and with a lion's head in the middle of each slab (lat. simæ 35, lions' heads 9, fig. 15). The raking cornice exactly resembled the sima (rak. cor. 26), and the geison was adorned with astragalos and meander, both in relief (geisa 67). Among the most interesting features are the lateral akroteria, large anthemia springing from double volutes between which is a small reversed palmette. The leaves of the anthemia were in strong relief with sharp edges, coloured alternately black, cream and red. These anthemia are moulded with two wings at right angles, so as to fit the corner exactly, the only examples hitherto discovered in this region of such an arrangement of a lateral akroterion (lat. akr. 16).

The roof-tiles of the third revetment have an interesting system of interlocking (tiles 6). Two off-sets are cut on the left side of one tile and two corresponding projections on the right side of the next tile, which consequently fitted over it and interlocked so securely that they could not possibly slip. The tiles overlapped for one-fourth of their total breadth, that is, a tile overlapped its neighbour on the right and was covered by the tile on the left. With this system there were no vertical kalypteres, because there was no exposed juncture.

CROTON

In obedience to the Delphic oracle, Myscellus of Rhypæ led a colony of Achæans in B.C. 710 to found Croton.[1] The city quickly grew in riches and power, and its size may be estimated by the fact that the walls had a circuit of twelve miles. The Crotoniates soon extended their dominion and founded several colonies, amongst them Caulonia. Very little is known of their early history, but the fact that they and their neighbours of Sybaris were reputed the two most wealthy and populous Greek cities of Magna Græcia argues that they remained for long on friendly terms. Yet the Crotoniates were less luxurious than the Sybarites and their devotion to athletic sports enabled them to carry off many prizes at the Olympic games. The arrival of Pythagoras in the city brought about many changes, for he quickly acquired great influence and was allowed to remodel the political constitution. Eventually, however, owing to a revolution, the Pythagoreans were expelled from Croton, and a democratic government was substituted for the previous oligarchic one.

The first fact of historical importance recorded was the war with Sybaris which ended in the utter destruction of that city. This was said to have taken place in B.C. 510, and the next great event was the terrible defeat which the Crotoniates suffered at the river Sagras at the hands of the Locrians and Rhegians, who with a force of 10,000 men routed the Crotoniate army of 130,000 men. This overwhelming disaster seriously affected the prosperity of the city, but it revived and nearly one hundred years later was spoken of as the most populous and powerful of the Greek colonies in that part of Italy.

When Dionysios attacked Caulonia in B.C. 389 Croton, at the head of the Greek cities, moved to the defence of her one-time colony. But the Sicilian tyrant

[1] Bunbury, in Smith, *Dict. Geogr.*, i, pp. 709–13; Byvanck, pp. 77f.; Lenormant, *Grande-Grèce* (Paris, 1881), ii, pp. 1–234.

overthrew the allied forces at the river Helloporus. After his fall, however, Croton appears to have regained her independence, but suffered severely from incursions of the Lucanians and Bruttians. Although after many wars and sieges the life of the city sank gradually into decay, yet it never wholly died out and the place has been continuously inhabited until the present day.

Of the ancient city there is not one stone left upon another, but the site of the acropolis is marked by the castle erected in A.D. 1541 from older material by Don Pedro di Toledo. Even the twelve-mile circuit of the city walls has disappeared.

The famous sanctuary of Hera Lacinia was built six miles distant from the city upon the promontory which now bears the name of Capo Colonna. The date of its foundation is shrouded in the mists of antiquity ; probably a sacred precinct existed there even before the coming of the Greek settlers, for the legends of its dedication by Herakles or the Trojan heroes point to the tradition of a pre-Greek origin. One of the treasures stored in the sanctuary was a bronze cup dedicated by Æneas, and the interior of the temple was adorned by paintings, the most celebrated being the picture of Hera by Zeuxis. Processions in honour of the goddess and athletic contests took place at the annual assembly held here of all the Italian Greeks. Both Pyrrhus and Hannibal respected the temple ; but in B.C. 173 the Censor, Q. Fulvius Flaccus, stripped off half the marble tiles from the roof : yet it still retained many of its treasures when Sex. Pompeius plundered it in B.C. 36.

Only one column still stands, the last vestige of the sanctuary of the end of the V. Century into which the earlier Doric temple of the VII. Century was transformed.[1] This later temple was a hexastyle peripteral building with a double row of columns on the east front and fourteen columns on the long sides ; but from the earliest times the sanctuary had been set within a *temenos* and surrounded by a *peribolos* or enclosing wall entered by an imposing *Πρόπυλον* in the east side, and by numerous dwellings for the priests, small *thesauroi* and other edifices, a veritable little sacred city.

Since the terra-cottas were scattered all around the temple, some at a distance of quite 200 metres, the question arises whether they all belonged to the main building or to other smaller edifices as well. There are three distinct types of revetment, because the primitive decoration was abolished and the material removed, as happened at *Marazà*, Locri.

A slab of the lateral sima is decorated with : (*a*) torus with diagonal bands ; (*b*) fascia with broken meander ; (*c*) cymation with Doric leaf which here becomes almost a lotus bud and dart ; (*d*) torus with diagonal bands ; (*e*) fascia with holes for gutter-spouts (lat. simæ 12, fig. 5). Whether the spouts were tubular or not is uncertain, but, granted the archaic character of the piece, it seems most likely. The design on the cymation has no exact parallel ; the inner leaf dwindling to a

[1] P. Orsi, *N.S.*, 1911, Suppl., pp. 77–124 ; *A.J.A.*, iii (1887), pp. 181 f. ; Koldewey, p. 41.

point is found on the lateral sima of the Geloan Treasury and on one type of revetment from Syracuse (simæ 10), whereas the dart between the leaves appears on the first type of revetment from the *temenos,* Syracuse, and its variants (lat. simæ 16).

A geison slab has : (*a*) fascia with painted rosettes ; (*b*) torus with diagonal bands ; (*c*) guilloche (geisa 38), a scheme which again recalls the first Syracusan revetment or the fragments from S. Mauro (simæ 4). Another small piece has three toroi, followed by a single guilloche (geisa 44). There are other little bits with imbrications, motives of scroll pattern like the specimen from Catana (simæ 2), and two large pieces of a sima decorated with narrow stripes in red and black (simæ 5, fig. 44). The slab from Metaurum (rak. cor. 6), with its narrow stripe-like flutings, is the nearest approach to this uncommon motive. The slab is pierced horizontally for its whole length by a cylindrical hole for the insertion of a metal rod to strengthen the slabs and fasten them together.[1] Two large fragments with : (*a*) fascia with meander ; (*b*) torus ; (*c*) narrow plain fascia, have a perfectly vertical front plane, and may complete the striped sima (simæ 6).

The second revetment is of the transitional type combining painting with relief. There are two pieces which undoubtedly formed one slab of the horizontal geison decorated with : (*a*) plain (?) projecting border ; (*b*) fascia with meander (?); (*c*) ovolo with egg and dart in relief ; (*d*) small torus ; (*e*) small fascia with meander ; (*f*) double torus with chevrons ; (*g*) narrow plain fascia (geisa 54). Numerous fragments of another sima were found scattered around the temple and even at some distance away, a fact which increases the likelihood that this was the lateral sima of the second revetment. These specimens agree with the horizontal geison in having : (*a*) fascia with meander ; (*b*) ovolo with egg-and-dart in relief ; (*c*) small torus ; (*d*) fascia with meander (lat. simæ 27). There is a variant of this sima which, instead of the pronounced curvature of the ovolo, has an almost flat profile and certain peculiarities in the treatment of the egg and dart (lat. simæ 27).

The third type of revetment is in high relief picked out with colour. The lateral sima had : (*a*) fascia with double black meander, the spaces filled by red squares ; (*b*) cymation with Lesbian leaf in relief ; (*c*) astragalos in relief ; (*d*) broad fascia with complicated meander in relief, the spaces filled by a white eight-rayed star on a red square (lat. simæ 32, fig. 13). In the middle of each slab is set a lion's head to mask the gutter-spout, so large that it covers the whole sima (lions' heads 5). These heads were treated with great individuality ; each one is different, but all are modelled in an extraordinarily spirited and natural manner. This is the only example in this region of lions' heads upon a fascia of meander ; they are usually combined with anthemia, and the relief meander is relegated to the horizontal geison, although at the temple of Zeus at Olympia

[1] Cf. W. B. Dinsmoor, "Structural Iron in Greek Architecture" in *A.J.A.*, xxvi (1922), pp. 148–58.

the lions' heads were placed upon a sima decorated with complicated meander below a cymation with painted palmette and lotus.[1]

Above the lateral sima ran a lofty cresting consisting of curved bands from which rise an Ionic palmette followed by a lotus flower (cresting 3, fig. 19), an arrangement which closely recalls the marble cresting of the Telesterion, Eleusis.[2]

The horizontal geison repeats the motive of anthemia alternating with an elaborate lotus flower (geisa 72, fig. 43). The small dimensions of these slabs (height, cm. 22·5) have led to the suggestion that they may have been a frieze running along the outer wall of the cella, like that of the temple of Aphaia at Ægina ; but as the motive only covered one fascia of a revetment slab composed of numerous elements, and moreover, as this motive carries out on the façade the scheme introduced on the cresting of the long sides, one is justified in attributing these slabs to the horizontal geison.

Evidently the Ionic palmette was considered the dominant note of this revetment, for both the central and lateral akroteria were in the form of palmettes modelled in relief and picked out with black and red (cent. akr. 18, lat. akr. 15).

The roof-tiles were of the usual types, but they varied in size and shape, thus showing that they did not all belong to the temple, but that the smaller ones must have come from neighbouring buildings (tiles 9).

Perhaps it was one of these subsidiary shrines which the life-sized Gorgon adorned, a great round mask, treated in the more conventional style of the beginning of the V. Century (ant. 10).

GELA

THE seaport of Terranova on the southern coast of Sicily spreads over part of the once-flourishing city of Gela,[3] founded in B.C. 690 by a colony of Rhodians under Antiphemos and Cretans under Entimos. The township, the cradle of the future tyrants of Syracuse, rose rapidly to power and in B.C. 582 was able to send a colony to establish themselves in the Sikel city of Akragas.

The government of Gela was at first oligarchical, and so continued until a certain Kleandros made himself tyrant and after a reign of about seven years was succeeded in B.C. 498 by Hippocrates who rapidly increased the power and prestige of Gela and brought many other cities under his sway. When he fell in battle before Hybla in B.C. 491, Gelon became ruler and further extended his conquests until he gained possession of Syracuse itself. But this event tended to the decline of Gela, for the tyrant's whole interest was now centred in his new

[1] *Olympia*, i, pl. xvi.

[2] Schede, *Antikes Traufleisten Ornament* (Strassbourg, 1909), pl. iii, 21.

[3] Bunbury, in Smith, *Dict. Geogr.*, i, pp. 983–6 ; Ziegler, in *P.W.*, vii, cols. 946–62 ; P. Orsi, *Mon. Ant.*, xvii (1906), cols. 1–758 ; xix (1909), cols. 89–140 ; *N.S.*, 1907, p. 38 ; Freeman, i, pp. 398–410 ; Koldewey, p. 136.

acquisition, and he transferred half the inhabitants of Gela thither and handed over the remainder to the charge of his brother Hieron. After the expulsion of Thrasybulos, however, Gela regained a certain measure of prosperity and was even able to recolonise Camarina which had been devastated by Gelon. The city flourished until the disturbed period of the Carthaginian invasions, but at last in B.C. 405 it was taken and sacked by the Carthaginians. The Geloans were afterwards allowed to return to their city upon payment of a tribute, but they never regained their former position and after varying fortunes became subject to Phintias, tyrant of Akragas, who compelled them to migrate to the new city he had founded near the mouth of the Himera and razed the walls and houses of Gela. Yet some few inhabitants must have gone back again, for it is related that it was once more destroyed, this time by the Mamertines.

To the east of the town in the *Contrada " Molino a Vento "* are the remains of the V. Century Doric temple. A short distance away, between the temple and the modern city, the foundations of a much more ancient shrine were discovered. This earlier construction must be assigned to the VII. Century from the abundant remains of the fictile decoration which were scattered around. The foundations are all that still exist of the early temple ; evidently it was destroyed by the Geloans themselves in order that their fine new sanctuary might have an unimpeded outlook. The stylobate measures m. 35·22 in length by m. 17·75 in width, and running athwart it were traces of another very ancient little temple, pre-existent to the VII. Century building and absorbed into it.

Owing to this drastic demolition the architectonic terra-cottas are terribly mangled, and only patient research and comparison with finds from other sites have enabled the excavators to gain an idea of the revetment as a whole. A narrow slab with a torus decorated with hammer pattern above a large single guilloche, almost identical with the specimen from Metapontum (geisa 50), is the decoration of the lower surface of a geison casing (geisa 49). Another much damaged fragment has : (*a*) Doric leaf ; (*b*) tiny border with chevrons ; (*c*) torus with diagonal bands ; (*d*) fascia with black lozenges between two black lines (lat. simæ 8). Comparison with other pieces decorated with lozenge pattern from Megara Hyblæa, *Marazà*, Locri, the *temenos* and Olympieion, Syracuse and especially from Selinus (lat. simæ 3) leads one to conclude that here also we have part of a VI. Century lateral sima.

An important fragment, because it gives the inclination of the pediment, is the right-hand angle of the horizontal geison (geisa 1, fig. 31). It consists of : (*a*) convex moulding with diagonal bands ; (*b*) a very simple pattern of black meander ; (*c*) boldly formed Doric leaf, alternately red and black. The design is a little less primitive than the lateral sima from the *temenos*, Syracuse (lat. simæ 1), or that from Granmichele (rak. cor. 1) ; it closely resembles the broken slab from S. Mauro (rak. cor. 10), for in both cases the leaves are no longer square at the top, but slightly rounded, and the meander, although not identical, is of the same irregularly drawn character. The S. Mauro slab is completed by a fascia of chequer pattern, and if the Gela example terminated in the same way, these two revetments must constitute the prototype of the Syracusan chequer pattern revetment (rak. cor. 11).

The Geloan revetment is extremely important because it confirms the use of various elements not often forthcoming from a single temple. Part of a large disc with numerous zones of decoration formed one of the akroteria of the primitive fictile decoration. These concave discs had the appearance of great flowers, especially when, as at Gela, a second, smaller disc was set within the larger one. The zone of rosettes, tongue pattern and whirls were not particularly well suited to the surface to be covered, but the variegated whole must have produced a rich effect. A fragment of a second disc was also found, and here the likeness to a flower was enhanced, for instead of the plain concave shell, it is fluted like the petals of a marguerite. On the reverse side it is painted in the same way and it must therefore have been visible from both sides (cent. akr. 2). The great disc of the Heraion at Olympia is well known,[1] and at Mantinea and Sparta[2] such discs were also found. In Sicily, so far, Gela and S. Mauro are the only places where discs of this kind have come to light, but in Magna Græcia fragmentary examples were also found at Rhegium (cent. akr. 4).

The tympanon was filled by a colossal Gorgoneion (height m. 1·05 × 1·10), every feature simplified and conventionalised until they almost lose any human resemblance, but become terrible in their mysterious significance. The hair and beard curl spirally all round the face, the highly arched brows add to the glare of the lidless eyes. The mouth, with its strong square teeth, fierce tusks and pendent tongue, portends the monster's insatiable lust to devour. Even the flat, highly placed ears resemble those of a beast of prey rather than a human being. Truly an apt symbol of ritual expulsion.[3] There were at least four of these colossal Gorgoneia, one fairly well preserved, the others quite fragmentary (ped. 1, fig. 78). Comparison with the now numerous list of those found elsewhere[4] shows that the nearest parallel is the one from the *temenos*, Syracuse (lat. ark. 10), where the eyes and hair are similarly treated and there is the same dart between the brows, although the Syracusan example has no beard.

We would assign to the second type of revetment the magnificent kalypter of the ridge-pole, richly painted with an assortment of motives and with semi-cylindrical openings at the sides for the insertion of the smaller kalypteres which covered the roof-tiles, a detail which proves that these vertical kalypteres were also rounded (kal. 4, fig. 54). The palmettes in relief which surmounted the ridge-pole were rather small, but there is one larger one which arose halfway

[1] *Olympia*, ii, " Die Baudenkmäler," zweite Hälfte, pl. cxv.
[2] Koch, *Röm. Mitt.*, xxx (1915), p. 88, fig. 42, and p. 94, fig. 45.
[3] J. E. Harrison, *Epilegomena* (Cambridge, 1921), p. 5.
[4] E. Gabrici, *Atti R. Accad. Palermo*, Serie iii, vol. xi.

along the beam (pal. 1). The tubular spouts were finished off with unusually large disc mouths painted with multi-petalled rosettes (spouts 17).

The central akroterion of this later phase was the group of a youth on horseback, unfortunately terribly damaged and only to be reconstructed by analogy with the better preserved group from Camarina (cent. akr. 6). Part of the horse's forehead and back covered by an embroidered saddlecloth remain, besides the rider's thigh, right leg, left foot, the right side of his head and portions of his body and raiment (cent. akr. 7). By themselves these pitiful remnants would be distressingly inadequate, but comparison with the other finds shows that they supply certain details, such as the saddlecloth and the rider's soft boots, which the Camarina group lacked.

Besides these, part of a torso from waist to thigh clad in a *chitoniskos* decorated with red and black chequer pattern, a bent knee and a shin with the top of the *endromis* (lat. akr. 11) are really valuable, because they prove that here at Gela there was a Gorgon running to left, a scheme known to us from the more complete specimen discovered in the *temenos*, Syracuse (lat. akr. 10). It has been argued that the small dimensions of these groups exclude their use architectonically, as all effect of the careful workmanship and gay colouring would be lost if they were placed at even a very moderate height,[1] and this argument has great weight. Nevertheless, the fact that identical groups were found at Gela, Syracuse and S. Mauro, all temples where the youth on horseback formed the central akroterion, suggests that the Gorgon-Medusa composition was as definite a part of the revetment scheme as the akroteria themselves.

The third type of revetment was on a very imposing scale ; here also is the group of the central akroterion, but it has, alas ! been shattered almost past hope of reconstruction, and only our knowledge of similar groups from other sites enables us to obtain some idea of its general appearance. Again we have a youth on horseback, but this time on a colossal scale. So far only fragments of the horse have been verified and among them are the following : two monstrous eyes with part of one brow ; on one of them traces of black paint are discernible ; a colossal right foreleg, the skin dappled in places with brown heart-shaped markings ; the upper jaw with strong, square teeth. Two fragments showing part of the harness probably belong to this group (cent. akr. 11). In this composition the artist no longer limited himself to a schematised rendering of the horse's legless body ; here the whole steed must have been portrayed, prancing forward with one foreleg projecting, a fine conception which reveals to us the forerunner of the group at *Marafioti* (cent. akr. 13).

The mutilated remains of a Sphinx or lioness consist of three life-sized paws with little brown markings to indicate tufts of hair ; pieces of the cream-coloured body with the same brown markings ; part of the belly and teats of the monster with the tufted end of the curling tail ; fragment of a rough mane (?) flowing

[1] P. Orsi, *Mon. Ant.*, xxv (1919), cols. 614–22.

out in striated rays (lat. akr. 5). One cannot be certain whether the monster really formed the lateral akroterion, for which there would be many parallels, or whether it was part of the central group, serving as base for the horse and rider like the Sphinx at *Marafioti*. In the latter case we should have a prototype for the *Marafioti* group, complete in every particular, and one which provides the needed link in the chain of evolution between the halting attempt of the early VI. Century and its splendid fulfilment in V. Century art.

In addition to the foregoing remains, portions of the undoubted architectonic decoration of the temple, the excavations produced a few mutilated human figures, but whether they constituted the pediment group of the east front or were *ἀγάλματα* set up in the sacred precinct, it is hard to decide. Hitherto there has been no absolutely certain example of a fictile pediment group discovered in Sicily, but among the terra-cottas from Gela we note many analogies with the temple at *Garitsà*, Corfu, and this very temple further demonstrates that an elaborate composition was not unknown in pediments of VI. Century temples. These fragments are a woman's neck, a bare foot with upturned toes, part of a shoulder draped with a cream garment bordered with black meander and some long, wavy tresses with a little delicately modelled left ear (ped. 4).

If these are indeed the *débris* of a pediment group, this temple supplies us with the successive phases in the evolution of the pediment decoration ; first, the disc akroterion and the tympanon filled by the Gorgoneion ; secondly, the primitive group of the young rider as akroterion and the Gorgon-Medusa as the lateral akroterion, the first timid attempt at a group in movement ; lastly, the akroterion portraying the rider and steed advancing boldly and the tympanon space filled by human figures in various attitudes. Only a careful study of all the material, at present largely inaccessible, would enable us to reconstruct these groups and so perhaps gain valuable light upon the composition of pediment sculptures in general in the archaic period.

In what was the south-east corner of the mediæval town of Terranova lies the *podere Bresmes*, and excavations there laid bare potsherds, roof-tiles and cover-tiles (tiles 8), in fact all the *débris* of a small edifice in wood, not in stone, situated on level ground in full view of the sea and perhaps a few paces from the earliest landing-stage.[1] It must have been a little *heroön*, dedicated to one or both of the hero founders of Gela, a supposition confirmed by the discovery of a large VI. Century *kylix* with a dedicatory inscription to Antiphemos scratched on the foot.[2] This *heroön* near the seashore recalls the one at Caulonia with the relief of Taras on the dolphin (ant. 55).

The *Predio Ventura* lies in the district of the north-west angle of the mediæval town and here some very uncommon objects were revealed, slabs decorated in high relief which from their shape, size and architectonic framing can only be

[1] P. Orsi, *Mon. Ant.*, xvii (1906), cols. 558–60.
[2] P. Orsi, *op. cit.*, cols. 558–60, fig. 380.

metopes. The earliest in style, a work of the VI. Century, is terribly damaged, but the subject was evidently a Gorgon-Medusa running to left, wearing a *chitoniskos* and soft boots with recurved tongues, and carrying a little Pegasos under her right arm. Her large wings curve aloft into the upper corners of the frame and the whole figure was cleverly adapted to fill the square space (metopes 2, fig. 80). The same conception was portrayed on an akroterion discovered nearly a hundred years ago at Gela (cent. akr. 14). Here the Gorgon, clad in the same fashion, runs to right with her face turned fully to the front. Long " pearl-locks " fall over her shoulders and her sharp tusks and pendent tongue add to the " frightfulness " of her aspect. There seems no trace of Pegasos, but fortunately enough is preserved to enable us to study details of the costume, the soft boots fastened by a side buckle and the corners of the *chitoniskos* weighted by tassels, whilst the whole figure reminds one of the Gorgon from Cumæ advancing in the same attitude and clasping her serpent girdle with both hands.[1]

A very mutilated slab with the lower limbs of a man and woman walking to right is in the style of the V. Century (ped.5). The subject of the relief is obscure, but this attitude of the couple recalls the fragment from Selinus (met. 3) and, still more, the frieze from Teichioussa near Branchidæ, now in the British Museum.[2]

Yet another metope depicts a ritual scene, a worshipper introduced into the presence of the goddess by a priestess (met. 4). The relief is smaller than the previous examples and is of light red clay instead of the cream or greyish clay generally used at Gela ; it is possible that it was a votive offering rather than a metope.

On the farther side of the River Gela, a little way from the sea and almost opposite the ruins of the Doric temple, rises an insignificant hill called *Bitalmi*, a corruption of the name of the little rural shrine of *S. Maria di Bethlem*. Here bits of vases strewed the ground, a very primitive stone statuette and all the *débris* which signified a temple or *ναΐσκος*. It was evidently a stone building, for report states that walls were seen, although all trace of them has now perished, but the complete absence of architectonic terra-cottas argues poverty of construction, because if the shrine had been of wood a profusion of fictile revetment slabs would have been recovered. As it is, only one miserable fragment of an antefix is preserved, too battered to be decipherable (ant. 64). The ceramics and figurines date from the VII. to the middle of the V. Century ; there is not a single one later, and therefore in all probability the temple was abandoned towards the middle of the V. Century. It was certainly not dedicated to Zeus or Apollo, the great gods of Gela, for it was only a humble country shrine, and the offerings, like those from *Pojo dell' Aquja*, Granmichele, appear more appropriate to the worship of Demeter.

Sporadic finds at Gela include the lateral akroterion with the figure of a

[1] E. Gabrici, *Mon. Ant.*, xxii (1913), pl. lxxi, 1.
[2] *Cat. Sculp.*, i, No. 21.

Sphinx or Siren said to have been found on the seashore in 1864.[1] The tranquil face framed by the heavy " layer wig " is well preserved, and so is the recurved wing, but all the body is destroyed (lat. akr. 8). The theme is attempted on the earlier akroterion from Cumæ [2] and is often found on terra-cotta *arulæ* both from Sicily and Etruria,[3] although perhaps the closest parallel is the marble relief of a Sphinx from the Acropolis, Athens, in just this pose.[4] In the museum at Syracuse is the lower part of a triangular antefix with a Gorgon's head, a work of the late VI. Century (ant. 7). Another Gorgoneion is perfectly round, but the *stephané* and earrings are indications of a comparatively late date, the second half of the V. Century, when the monster of earlier days was softened to the " pathetic type " of a later period (ant. 36). There are also two types of Satyrs' heads, both of the V. Century, but not from the same edifice, for one is much smaller than the other (ant. 38, 43).

The Geloan revetments are broken and have lost most of their gay colour, but from what is left we gain some idea of how sumptuous these temples once were. Gela in her palmy days sent forth rulers over other even greater cities, and a memorial of her prosperity was the Treasury of the Geloans at Olympia, a triumph of the native craftsman's skill in fictile decoration. It is surprising not to find more direct parallels between the revetment of the Treasury and those employed in the home-town, but the local Geloan terra-cottas, at any rate, prove that the workmen who made and painted them were quite capable of bringing to a successful issue the even more ambitious scheme carried out at Olympia.[5]

GRANMICHELE

IN the Province of Catania, at a short distance from Caltagirone, is a high hill set in the midst of a vast agricultural region, and on the flat summit of this hill were all the signs of an ancient township, identified with much probability as the ancient Echetla, a Sikel stronghold.[6] The road from the plain climbs upwards and is dominated by the slight elevation to the right of the valley opposite "*Pojo dell' Aquja*," a strong position which must have been the acropolis ; the restricted area (m. 100 × 100) marks it out as such, and the fact that there are no traces of walls does not refute the argument, because the pointed rocks aligned along the crest may have served that function, especially as on the south

[1] Kekulé, *Terrak. von. Sic.*, p. 45, fig. 96.

[2] E. Gabrici, *Mon. Ant.*, xxii (1913), pl. lxxi, 2.

[3] E. Douglas Van Buren, *Mem. Amer. Acad. Rome*, ii (1918), pp. 24–6.

[4] Dickins, *Cat. Acropolis Mus.*, i, No. 630.

[5] Professor Orsi informs me that he hopes shortly to bring out the complete publication of all the terra-cottas from Gela. This work will be eagerly awaited, because Gela, as one of the chief centres of manufacture, may be expected to teach us more than almost any other site about the craft.

[6] P. Orsi, *Mon. Ant.*, vii (1897), cols. 201–74 ; Huelsen, in *P.W.*, v, cols. 1915 f.

side a deep passage had been artificially cut in the rocks to give access to the plateau.

The ground-plan of the buildings has been hidden or wiped out by centuries of cultivation, but great heaps of wrought stones lay around, masses of roof-tiles and kalypteres (tiles I), with potsherds from the household stuff, all mixed with black mould and carbonised remains, sure signs of destruction by fire.

At *Pojo dell 'Aquja* hasty and unscientific excavations wrought havoc with the material discovered, but the enormous quantities of terra-cotta figurines, the *favissæ* of a temple, proved that an ancient sanctuary must have stood on the south-west extremity of the hill. The brief tracts of poorly constructed walls were those of hovels of the Roman age, and had nothing to do with the earlier shrine which, from the evidence of the figurines, must have been destroyed towards the end of the V. Century, never to rise again. Careful examination of the site showed that a landslip of the southern portion of the hill had carried away with it the sanctuary which once stood on its edge, probably outside the walls and overlooking one of the necropoles which filled the valley below.

The importance of the temple is manifested by the remarkable life-sized fictile figures which once adorned it,[1] either as cult statues or as agalmata set up in the *temenos*. The only architectonic terra-cotta found was part of a cornice of reddish clay covered with a cream slip and painted with a Doric leaf in rusty black and purplish red below a projecting border adorned with rudimentary meander (rak. cor. I, fig. 20). The extremely primitive character of this slab is shown by the very simple contour, the irregularly drawn meander, and the leaves which do not diminish towards the base. The nearest parallel is the lateral sima found in the *temenos*, Syracuse (lat. simæ I).

These facts, taken all together, demonstrate that on this spot there was a sanctuary or *temenos* with rich fictile offerings ranging from the VII. to the first half of the V. Century, and an examination of the figurines shows that the material, although in part certainly indigenous, was strongly under Greek influence. To what divinity the shrine was dedicated it is hard to ascertain, but the types of the figurines are almost entirely those associated with the worship of the goddess known to the Greeks as Demeter, although here in a Sikel town there was probably an indigenous mother-goddess, later absorbed into the cult of Demeter.

A short distance away in the *Predio Ventura* vestiges of a treasury came to light, with abundant votive material, purely Greek, of the end of the VI. and beginning of the V. Centuries. Peasants working among the vines unearthed a pit containing the statue of a beautiful enthroned goddess [2] and a large number of

[1] P. Orsi, *Mon. Ant.*, vii (1897), cols. 287–321, pl. iii; xvii (1906), col. 573; *N.S.*, 1903, p. 434; *J.H.S.*, xli (1921), pp. 204 f., fig. 1.

[2] P. Orsi, *Mon. Ant.*, xviii (1907), cols. 135–45, pls. iv, v, and fig. 3; *J.H.S.*, xli (1921), pp. 205 f., fig. 2.

figurines, sure indications of a temple in the vicinity. It is doubtful, however, if the three antefixes found in the locality adorned the temple; more likely they came from the lesser buildings which always sprang up around a place of pilgrimage. One is a very archaic semi-elliptical antefix, crudely painted with two rows of meander in brown outlined with red, separated by red zig-zags (ant. 1). The whole treatment is unique, and this must be one of the earliest examples of a Sicilian antefix.

The other two antefixes form a pair, and both represent a Gorgon's head flanked by two great bearded snakes, a work of the second half of the VI. Century (ant. 24). As so often is the case in Sicily, the extensive cultivation of the area precluded further investigations, but a complete excavation might reveal a whole complex of sacred buildings clustered around the main sanctuary.

HIPPONIUM

The site of Hipponium is known from the descriptions given in the Itineraries and from buildings and other remains found in the neighbourhood.[1] It lay on the west coast of Bruttium, inland from the Gulf of S. Euphemia, a position now occupied by the town of Monteleone. It was a Locrian colony, and the founders must have brought with them from the mother-city the cult of Persephone: the Greek colonists, indeed, maintained that the abundance of flowers in the district proved that this was the place whence Persephone was carried away. Gelon, at any rate, appreciated these flowery meads, for the historian Douris of Samos relates that there was a grove near the city of surpassing beauty and watered by a fountain; in the grove was a spot called the "horn of Amalthea" which Gelon had arranged and embellished. Ruins of the temple were said to have been visible until the XI. Century, when Count Roger of Sicily bore off the columns to build the cathedral of Mileto.

In B.C. 388 Dionysios the Elder extended his conquests in Magna Græcia, destroyed Hipponium and transplanted the inhabitants to Syracuse. Ten years later the Carthaginians rebuilt the city, and under Agathokles it regained a certain prominence, for he realised its importance as a harbour, and constructed a naval station about three miles distant at the present Porto S. Venere. Under the Romans the town changed its name to Vibo Valentia.

The site does not seem to be as prolific in antiquities as one would expect; apparently Dionysios did his work too thoroughly to have left any traces of the city's bygone greatness. Recently, however, remains of a temple have been discovered with a marble revetment, and interesting because it appears to have been of the Ionic order, like the later temple at Locri.[2]

At the *Belvedere*,[3] a lofty site with a fine view, the ground-plan of a Greek temple

[1] Bunbury, in Smith, *Dict. Geogr.*, i, pp. 1070 f.; Weiss, in *P.W.*, vii, 2, cols. 1910 f.; *N.S.*, 1895, p. 97.

[2] P. Orsi, *N.S.*, 1921, pp. 476–80.

[3] *Op. cit.*, p. 480.

has come to light, with chips of columns and triglyphs, showing that the building was of stone. A few terribly damaged architectonic terra-cottas were also found, apparently bits of the lateral sima painted only with a design of lotus and anthemia and with remnants of the lions' heads which once masked the gutter-spouts (lat. simæ 34, lions' heads 17).

It seems most likely that the acropolis was situated upon the hill rising behind the modern town,[1] and here a little shrine with an abundant *favissa* was discovered, but there must also have been a real temple, because here the gigantic Gorgoneion was found, the plastic ornamentation of the tympanon like those found at Selinus and Gela (ped. 1, 2). This mask, however, is rounder, and, as far as one can judge from its damaged condition, it seems more sophisticated than the other examples, so that one would be inclined to date it towards the end of the VI. Century. The monster has three rows of tight curls surmounted by a *stephané* adorned with little serpents. The only eye preserved is well modelled, but the little bit of ear still left shows that these organs were the large inorganic bits of leather of the archaic period (ped. 3, fig. 79). Only one piece of a lateral sima was saved; it is much damaged, but half the large opening for the gutter is well marked. It consists of: (*a*) fascia decorated, seemingly, with anthemia; (*b*) torus; (*c*) egg-and-dart in relief; (*d*) torus; (*e*) cyma recta; (*f*) fascia with complicated meander painted only; (*g*) plain (?) border (lat. simæ 33, fig. 14). The nearest parallel to this sima is the one from Croton (lat. simæ 32).

In the *Museo Civico*, Reggio, are certain architectonic pieces once forming part of a private collection from Hipponium. Amongst them is a small Gorgoneion, about cm. 30 in height, evidently an adaptation from the great Gorgoneion of the archaic temple, for the hair is in tight curls and round the head like a diadem rise a ring of little S-shaped serpents. The pointed tusks are small and only half the chin is covered by the pendent tongue (ant. 29). This antefix may be dated early in the V. Century. Two water-spouts of almost the same period are in the form of well-modelled lions' heads, of different dimensions, but both showing strong traces of colour (lions' heads 15, 16).

Far more interesting are some remarkable antefixes where the field in relief directly caps the rounded kalypter. These antefixes are of two sizes, decorated alike with a lion's head in such low relief that the lifelike effect depended entirely upon the strong colouring. The cream head is set against a black background; the lids with their pronounced black outline leave the round black eyes fully exposed (ant. 2). These unusual heads have no parallels in Magna Græcia or Sicily where animal protoma were not employed for antefixes, but they recall those from Neandria in the Troad, although there one shoulder and paw of the beast were also given.[2]

[1] *Op. cit.*, pp. 481–3.

[2] Koldewey, "Neandria," 51*stes Berliner Winckelmannsprogram*, figs. 66, 67; Koch, *Röm. Mitt.*, xxx (1915), p. 11.

HYBLA

NOT far from Inessa, Hybla, another Sikel town, also lay upon the slopes of Mt. Etna.[1] Down to the time of Philistos the inhabitants were qualified as "barbaric," that is, non-Greek, but they were renowned for their piety; until a late period they maintained the cult of the indigenous goddess, Hyblaia, and even in Cicero's day (*de Div.* i, 39) they were held in high repute as seers and interpreters of dreams. The Hyblæans alone refused to join the common league in which Ducetius strove to unite all the Sikel communities. In B.C. 415, owing to their steadfast alliance with Syracuse, the Athenians wasted their territory as well as that of Inessa.

The site has been identified by the topographical references in ancient authors, by a Roman inscription there found, and now in the *Museo Biscari*, Catania, and by rich finds of Sikel and Greek objects.[2] It is close to the modern Paternò, but the ancient city is now covered by lava streams from the volcano.

A few bits of fictile revetment of the V. Century were discovered. The colour scheme is black and dead white with the design in high relief. Both the raking cornice and lateral sima were decorated with white anthemia springing from double volutes and separated by lotus flowers whose outer petals frame the palmettes (lat. simæ 40). On the horizontal geison a black double guilloche was bordered above and below by a row of astragalos in high relief (geisa 33). This scheme is not unlike the third type of revetment from Caulonia (lat. simæ 35), or that from *Marafioti*, Locri (lat. simæ 26), but as a rule the anthemia fascia of the black and white decoration was united with a fascia of complicated meander. The only other instance of anthemia combined with black double guilloche is the third type of revetment, Metapontum (geisa 58).

INESSA

INESSA, a place of great natural strength, was a Sikel city on the southern slopes of Mt. Etna.[3] After the death of Hieron I, the colonists he had established at Catana, to which he had given the name of Aitna, were driven out and withdrew to Inessa, imposing upon their new home the name of their former abode. Later the town passed under Syracusan dominion, and remained faithful to the Syracusan alliance all through the troubles of the Athenian Expedition, and in revenge for this loyalty their lands were ravaged by the Athenians. Of all Sicily the territory around Inessa was the most fertile in corn, and Cicero mentions the town as one of considerable importance.

[1] Bunbury, in Smith, *Dict. Geogr.*, i, p. 1099; Ziegler, in *P.W.*, ix, 1, cols. 25–7; Freeman, i, pp. 159 f.

[2] *C.I.L.*, x, 7013; *N.S.*, 1903, p. 441; 1909, p. 386; *Röm. Mitt.*, xxiv, pp. 84 f.

[3] Bunbury, in Smith, *Dict. Geogr.*, i, pp. 60 f.; Zügler-Bürchner, in *P.W.*, ix, 1, cols. 1536 f.; Freeman, i, p. 148.

The only terra-cotta recovered from here is the top of a large round antefix, only the staring eyes, wrinkled forehead, tight curls, and *stephanê* of a Gorgon (ant. 35), not unlike the Gorgon from Gela now in the British Museum (ant. 36), and, like it, a work of the V. Century.

LEONTINI

THE Chalkidians of Naxos in B.C. 730, six years after the foundation of that city, sent out two colonies at the same time to found the twin cities of Catana and Leontini, both on the east coast of Sicily, but the latter a little inland, because it was thus better able to dominate the rich plain renowned in antiquity for its fertility.

The position was originally a Sikel fortress ; it stood on a hill, cleft into two separate summits, both forming natural citadels, and between them in the valley lay the town and public buildings.[1]

According to Thucydides (vi, 3), the earlier inhabitants were expelled and the Greeks, taking complete possession, prospered greatly. The government was oligarchical, but about B.C. 608 it fell under the yoke of Panaitios, said to have been the first example of a Sicilian tyrant. After his time the city seems to have remained independent until B.C. 498, when it was subdued by Hippocrates of Gela. Its proximity to Syracuse was a source of danger, and Leontini was constantly at war with her powerful neighbour. Under the Romans it was restored to the status of a municipal town, but seems to have sunk into decay.

From Leontini the only architectonic terra-cotta recorded is an antefix with the head of a Satyr, without framing of any kind (ant. 37), token of the existence in the V. Century of a temple with fictile revetment.

LOCRI EPIZEPHYRII

SITUATED on the south-east coast of Bruttium, Locri Epizephyrii was a very ancient city.[2] There are serious discrepancies between the various accounts of its foundation, for some declared it to be a colony of the Locri Ozolæ under the leadership of Euanthes, shortly after Croton and Syracuse were established ; Aristotle (*RP. Locrensium* fr. 504), on the contrary, says it was colonised by runaway slaves from Sparta. In any case, Strabo's statement that they settled first on Cape Zephyrium and afterwards removed thence to the site fifteen miles farther north where they founded their city is probably accurate.

Zaleucus was reputed to have legislated for Locri, and this is said to have been the earliest written code of laws given to any Greek state. Even if the name of the lawgiver is hypothetical, it must be true that they at least possessed a very ancient code, and Locri was always admired as a model of good government.

[1] Bunbury, in Smith, *Dict. Geogr.*, ii, pp. 158 f. ; Freeman, i, pp. 368–72.
[2] Byvanck, pp. 78–81 ; Bunbury, in Smith, *Dict. Geogr.*, ii, pp. 199–201.

After their great victory over the Crotoniates at the battle of the Sagras, the Locrians increased in power and maintained a close connection with the Greek cities of Sicily, although constantly at feud with neighbours on the mainland. In later times they suffered much from the constant aggressions of the Bruttians, and during the Pyrrhic wars seem to have placed themselves under Rome's protection. Yet at the approach of Pyrrhus they declared in his favour and expelled the Roman garrison. His arbitrary rule soon caused them to repent, and during his absence in Sicily they drove out the garrison he had left behind; but their treachery was severely punished, for on his return he levied great exactions and carried off a large part of the sacred treasure from the temple of Persephone. Still later, bandied about from the Carthaginians to the Romans, the city sank into insignificance, although from the words of Procopius it seems to have existed down to the VI. Century A.D., and probably was finally destroyed by the Saracens.

Vestiges of the ancient city are still visible a few kilometres south of Gerace Marina, perched upon three isolated hills now called the "Castelli"; the most northern *Mannella*, the middle one *Abbadessa* and the southern one *Castellacce*. Each hill was surrounded by walls and thus became an *arx*, as Livy (xxix, 6) mentions. The town spread around the base of these hills and extended down to the seashore, for in another passage Livy (xxvii, 26) states that the Romans sent ships to besiege part of the city. A noticeable depression still marks the position of one harbour, and there was probably a second port as well.

Between the hills ran narrow valleys or gullies opening out on to the sea. These exits were skilfully fortified to bar entrance to them, and farther up the valleys were dominated by the acropoles on the hill-tops which constituted a defence against a foe from the mountains, because they were strongly fortified and could be shut off at will from the city below. The valleys were also provided with elaborate hydraulic works, because the disastrous floods caused by the sudden rising of the mountain torrents were a constant menace.

All along the bed of the torrent to guard against this danger a wall was constructed which also served as a military line of defence; it made a sharp turn, and climbing along the ridge of the hill, either reached the round tower on *Mannella*, or stopped short at the steep cliff where the precipitous nature of the ground rendered artificial defence superfluous. This wall was strongly built and fairly high, but there was evidently a fear that its foundations would be undermined by the quantities of sand and matter brought down by the torrent in spate, and that it might finally yield to pressure. To avoid this peril, a second wall was made behind the first at a distance varying from four to seven metres. It does not seem to have been constructed all at once or in accordance with a preconceived plan, but in short stretches and at various times within a limited period.[1]

[1] P. Orsi, *Boll. d'Arte*, iii (1909), pp. 407–10, figs. 1 and 2.

A road must have run between these two walls, and the bed of the road which ran over sandy shifting soil was reinforced by fragments of architectonic terra-cottas, smashed to bits and laid, not in heaps, but in strata along the line of the road. These must have been the fictile decoration of the earlier temple which rose, four hundred metres distant, in the valley between the hills *Abbadessa* and *Mannella,* on the site occupied by the later Ionic temple, but with a slightly different orientation. Only two terra-cotta fragments were found in the earlier excavations close to or within the temple, instead of the quantities generally picked up all around, and this complete absence of fictile remains on the spot denotes that, instead of being cast aside as usually happened, all the best-preserved pieces were collected and taken away for use elsewhere, whilst the broken bits were reduced to atoms and used to fill in the road, a utilitarian method of disposing of sacred property which we find adopted again at the *temenos,* Syracuse.

Lenormant in 1879 was the first to mention that a large temple platform was being rapidly demolished in the *podere Marazà,* but it was not until 1889 that excavations disclosed the existence of a still earlier structure beneath the late V. Century Ionic temple.[1] It stood at the north-eastern extremity of the city, a few paces from the western wall and also from that which faced the sea, situated upon flat ground a few metres above the level of the sea, which was less than half a kilometre distant. As the Ionic temple partly overlapped the earlier one, it was impossible to uncover the whole area, but part of the cella and the east side of the stylobate were laid bare showing that the latter measured approximately m. 35·30 × 17·06, whilst the cella consisted of a *naos* and *pronaos* without an *opisthodomos.* The number and appearance of the columns are unknown, although a few battered drums were found. The archaic character of the building, the extremely slender basis of the walls (only cm. 55), and the utter absence of a cornice or other stone member of the entablature induce one to believe that the upper part of the temple was entirely of woodsheathed with terra-cotta, many fragments of which were found under the pavement of the Ionic temple. Its orientation was not identical with that of the Ionic temple, for the principal façade did not face directly towards the sea, but towards the entrance to the harbour. Traces of burning seem to show that it was destroyed by fire. The shattered decoration of the west front only has been preserved; apparently the east front was radically destroyed and the soil before it entirely worked over. This earlier temple must have arisen not later than the middle of the VI. Century, as is attested by the type of construction, the architectonic terra-cottas and the abundant votive reliefs from the *favissæ.* These last by their subjects help to prove that this was indeed the celebrated sanctuary of Persephone, and the question is further

[1] P. Orsi, *N.S.*, 1890, pp. 248–62, with plan p. 251; 1909, p. 323; E. Petersen, *Röm. Mitt.* v 1890), pp. 161–227, pl. viii plan; Koldewey, pp. 2–5.

settled by the discovery among the *débris* of a marble basin inscribed with the dedication . . .α Τιμάρεος ἀνέθηκε τᾶι θεῶι.[1]

The fictile revetments are hard to reconstruct, but seem to embody four or even five distinct types ranging from the early VI. to the middle of the V. Century which can be only conjecturally grouped, as all the fragments were terribly shattered and mixed up in inextricable confusion. The clay of these pieces is very well worked, the cream slip exceedingly fine and unusually white in tone and the drawing careful.

The first type is represented by numerous small bits of the lateral sima, amongst them, fortunately, one showing the base of the tubular spout. This sima consisted of : (*a*) Doric leaf ; (*b*) torus with closely set diagonal bands in red and black ; (*c*) fascia with seven black lozenges between the tubular spouts (lat. simæ 2). This sima is very similar to the one found at Selinus to the north of Tower M. (lat. simæ 3), although there the water-spouts projected between every pair of lozenges. There is part of a raking cornice which appears contemporaneous with this lateral sima, a cymation with very large Doric leaf coloured alternately cream and black, in both cases with a red margin (simæ 14). This colour-scheme is most unusual, and I do not know of any other example where one of the leaves is cream ; the red margin, too, is an exception to the general rule that the margin should always be black.

Part of the lateral sima of the second type also exists : (*a*) projecting border with three rows of black chequer pattern ; (*b*) red and black Doric leaf diminishing to a point ; (*c*) band of reversed black triangles, broken at intervals by semi-elliptical openings for the dispersal of the water (lat. simæ 11). In Sicily, at any rate, the chequer pattern is frequently relegated to the fascia below the cymation, an arrangement found on the revetments of the second and third types from the *temenos*, Syracuse (rak. cor. 8, 9) ; but in Magna Græcia it was invariably the practice to place the chequer pattern, which is always black, on the projecting border, for example at Metaurum, where a sima was decorated in this fashion (lat. simæ 10). From Metaurum also comes the only other example of a sima without water-spouts, but with pierced drain-holes, although there the openings are round (rak. cor. 6). The raking cornice has : (*a*) torus with closely set red and black diagonal bands to right ; (*b*) projecting border with four rows of black chequer pattern ; (*c*) cymation with Doric leaf in red and black ; (*d*) torus with closely set diagonal bands to left (simæ 8). The geison was decorated with double guilloche, the eyes filled by a dot within a circle (geisa 5, fig. 36). There is also a large piece of a slab painted with immense black meander, apparently the under-surface of a geison casing (geisa 48). There are numerous bits of rounded kalypteres also coloured entirely either red or black (kal. 9).

[1] *N.S.*, 1909, p. 321. fig. 3 : a nominative Timareos seems to be unknown ; the present form therefore must be a genitive indicating the father of the dedicant, the first part of the inscription being lost. A Locrian philosopher Τιμάρης is mentioned in Iambl., *Vit. Pyth.*, 130, 267, who may be the personage named.

To the third type of revetment belonged a lateral sima with: (*a*) cymation with red and black Doric leaf; (*b*) torus with broad red and black diagonal bands; (*c*) fascia painted with black meander with tubular spouts at intervals (lat. simæ 28). Precisely the same motives decorated the raking cornice (rak. cor. 28), and on the geison were: (*a*) double torus with black hammer pattern; (*b*) fascia with double guilloche, the triangular spaces filled by five-leaved palmettes, the eyes by six-petalled rosettes with a dot in each petal (geisa 24).

Perhaps the remains of the plastic decoration on the west front formed part of this revetment; they consist of a wing having the feathers marked by black lines, the beautifully modelled claws of a bird of prey perched upon a small square base and two bits of an animal's body painted cream and dappled with heart-shaped black markings (cent. akr. 12), exactly like those on the fragments from Gela (lat. akr. 5), and evidently the conventional manner of depicting a spotted beast. The composition was undoubtedly some predatory monster, and the bird's claws in conjunction with the dappled hide suggest a Sphinx, a subject later repeated at Marafioti, but with all the grosser elements eliminated.

Only scattered fragments exist of the revetment of the fourth type, but they imply that the colour-scheme was chiefly black and white. There is a fragment of cymation with Doric leaf in black only (simæ 15) and a lateral sima with: (*a*) plain red projecting border; (*b*) Lesbian cymation; (*c*) broad fascia with anthemia and lotus flowers in relief upon a black ground: the anthemia spring from broad double volutes and all the design was picked out in red; (*d*) large ovolo, alternately black and red (lat. simæ 24). This last element is much broken, but appears to be quite certain, and it may be compared with the second and third revetments from Metapontum (lat. simæ 36, 37). Below the central anthemion on each slab was a hole for the water-spout which seems to have been masked by a lion's head, for a fragment of one such head is extant (lions' heads 13), of excellent workmanship, but on a smaller scale than those from *Marafioti* (lions' heads 14). Fragments of the geison show: (*a*) double torus with black chevrons; (*b*) broad fascia with complicated black meander. At intervals there are round nail-holes to fasten the slabs to the framing beneath (geisa 56). In the arrangement of the various elements this sima closely resembles that of the third type of revetment at Caulonia (geisa 67). The lower surface of the geison casings was richly ornamented with palmettes springing from broad spirals with eight-petalled rosettes in the eyes, all in cream on a black ground. The narrow front border of the slabs had a sketchily drawn single meander in black, the spaces filled by hammer pattern (geisa 52, fig. 39).

The fifth type is quite different in character from any of the preceding revetments. The drawing is rough, the paint lumpy, and the surface has none of the beautiful smoothness so noticeable upon the earlier pieces. All these details and the fact that the designs seem poor copies of those employed for the fourth type suggest that these slabs are portions of a late and hasty reparation, carelessly executed with inferior materials. There is one piece of the lateral sima similar to that of the fourth type, but thicker and more carelessly worked; it is now without any trace of colour (lat. simæ 25). Numerous bits of the geison have: (*a*) double torus with black chevrons; (*b*) quadruple black meander coarsely painted on a cream ground (geisa 69). Various small bits of the lower surface of the casings also exist: a rough floral design in black and white; a pattern of black single meander, the spaces filled by hammer pattern, was traced on the narrow front border of the slabs (geisa 53).

The east ridge of *Mannella* extended into a terrace enclosed by the city walls, thus constituting an acropolis, perhaps under the protection of Athena, as the acropolis on *Abbadessa* was under that of Persephone, for here were the ruins of a small temple dedicated to the warrior goddess, much more modest in dimensions than those of the sanctuary dedicated to her co-protectress of the city.[1] Owing to its situation on an exposed and treeless hillside and to the relentless hunt for building stones by the later inhabitants, scarcely anything is left of the little shrine. A certain number of *ex-voto* were found in the *temenos* bounded by the east wall of the city; and in the middle of the terrace the foundations of the temple are visible, a cella, perhaps *in antis*, but without a peristyle. Possibly the original sanctuary was a wooden one; at any rate, it was adorned with a fictile revetment of which various fragments are preserved, painted, but not in relief. A very few fictile roof-tiles were found; the incised sign Φ was four times repeated on the border of one of them, and evidently indicates the place in the row or the number of the row to which the tile belonged (tiles 2).

In the triangular space enclosed by the torrent and further protected by the wall connecting it with the general plan of defence hundreds of fragments of fictile figurines, reliefs and votive offerings were found, clearly denoting a sacred precinct.[2] Right at the foot of the steep incline of *Mannella* the scanty remains of an edifice were unearthed, but as it backed directly on to the sandy hillside it was impossible to complete the excavation until a retaining wall had been built. In the centre of the building was a square pit, m. 1·12 × 1·49 in depth, surrounded by a double wall of blocks set on end. Evidently the place was a *thesauros* with its *favissæ* especially strongly constructed. The only indications of the appearance of the upper part of the building are certain wrought slabs decorated with an anthemion pattern. A fictile antefix, a female head, was also found within the treasury which may be dated towards the beginning of the IV. Century, but the edifice itself might possibly be assigned to the second half of the V. Century, as the construction, clamps, etc., seem contemporaneous with the Doric temple.

Yet the votive offerings go back to the VI. Century, and in order to explain this chronological hiatus Professor Orsi has suggested that an ancient *temenos*

[1] P. Orsi, *N.S.*, 1909, p. 322; 1911 Suppl., p. 67.
[2] P. Orsi, *Boll. d'Arte*, iii (1909), pp. 410–12, fig. 3; *N.S.*, 1909, p. 321, fig. 2.

existed on this spot, although the complete absence of architectonic terra-cottas implies that no temple existed here. Towards the second half of the V. Century important defensive works were undertaken, and with this scope a clean sweep was made of all the *ex-voto* which were cast into the great ditch near the walls and smashed up finely. At the same time the temple or *thesauros* was built, but whether it contained cult images or only the sacred treasures is an obscure point which investigations have not yet revealed.

In 1830 the Duc de Luynes, during his journey in Calabria, inspected the ruins of a temple at the *Casino Marafioti*. In 1910 these ruins had almost disappeared; the south front of the *Casa Marafioti* was based on the remains of the temple stylobate, and vandal destruction had destroyed everything, even to carrying off to the last stone the steps uncovered by the Duc de Luynes.[1]

On the south-eastern front finds of architectonic terra-cottas were extremely rare; on the western front, on the contrary, they appeared in extraordinary abundance, but reduced to fragments of all dimensions, many of which it has been possible to reconstruct after long and patient study.

Thus we know that the lateral sima consisted of an elaborate motive of reversed palmettes and curving sprays (lat. simæ 26, fig. 10). A very unusual detail was the fact that between each pair of palmettes was a lion's head in high relief (lions' heads 14), but these heads were not pierced, for they do not conceal pipes for the discharge of the rain-water which, in this case, ran away through triangular openings between the palmette stems. Thus the lions' heads upon this sima have no structural purpose, and are simply survivals of an earlier method; they may be said to be a *contaminatio* between the mouth of a water-spout and an antefix, for they really signify the end kalypter of the vertical series which covered the juncture of the roof-tiles. The skilful arrangement and large dimensions of the triangular openings produce the effect of a cresting or grill, enframed and held in place by the border which ran all along the top.

The geison which ran round all four sides of the temple had a broad fascia with complicated meander in high relief bordered by a convex moulding ornamented by single scale pattern placed horizontally (geisa 61), which bears some resemblance to the fragment from Catania (geisa 46), but is much closer to the decoration of the raking cornice from Caulonia (rak. cor. 7).

The raking cornice was enriched with: (*a*) projecting border with complicated meander; (*b*) Lesbian cymation with egg-and-dart; (*c*) white anthemia and lotus flowers alternating upon a black ground (rak. cor. 24, fig. 28). Almost the identical meander border is reproduced on the lateral sima at Croton (lat. simæ 32), and the anthemion motive only differs slightly in details from that employed at Caulonia (rak. cor. 27) or Metapontum (rak. cor. 23).

Large numbers of roof-tiles and kalypteres were excavated, and in some cases

[1] P. Orsi, *N.S.*, 1911 Suppl., pp. 27–49.

the latter were moulded in one with the tile, so that each tile was covered by the convex edge of its fellow on the right (tiles 7).

The really magnificent feature of this decoration was the splendid group forming the central akroterion of the western pediment, for, as at *Marazà*, the east front was totally destroyed (cent. akr. 13, fig. 73). It represented a nude youth on horseback, riding forth from the apex of the pediment. Here, contrary to the earlier attempts to portray the subject, the more highly skilled artist has worked out the whole figure of the horse with one fore-leg extended boldly into the void. Yet what gives stability to the group both æsthetically and materially is the wonderful figure of the Sphinx who reclines under the horse's body and upon her uplifted claws steadied the two feet of the rider. This, indeed, is the climax of the primitive endeavours at Camarina, Syracuse, and S. Mauro, the harmonious blending of the Geloan conception of the youthful rider for the central akroterion and the Sphinx for the lateral one (lat. akr. 5). The nobly modelled figures are in the best traditions of V. Century art; the horse's narrow head with its long muzzle and hogged mane recalls the horses of the Parthenon frieze. Probably a corresponding group arose above the eastern pediment, and the two riders symbolised the Dioscuroi as *θεοὶ σωτῆρες* of the city. This plastic group in terra-cotta was the forerunner of the marble group which adorned the pediment of the later Ionic temple at *Marazà*,[1] but has a breadth and solemnity of treatment which the subsequent composition lacks.

MEDMA

MEDMA lay on the west coast of Bruttium between Hipponium and the mouth of the River Metaurus, the site now occupied by the small town of Rosarno.[2] The name, variously given as *Μέδμα*, *Μέδμη*, or, according to the coins, *Μέσμα*, is said to have been derived from a fountain in the neighbourhood. The city was a colony of Locri Epizephyrii which never attained to much eminence, although it survived more important cities of Magna Græcia, for both Strabo and Pliny mention it as still existing in their day, and the former notes that the town was a little inland, with an " emporium " or port on the seashore.

The modern Rosarno covers the probable site of the ancient town and acropolis, and in the *Piano delle Vigne* were outlying suburbs and sanctuaries.[3] Here, in the *Contrada Calderazzo*, excavations revealed a *favissa* and a few sherds of fictile revetment, evidently derived from a sacred edifice close by, which, judging by the nature of the offerings, was a temple of Persephone; undoubtedly the Locrian colonists brought with them the cult of the great goddess of the metropolis. The *favissa* is chronologically of value, because it is intact, without infiltration later than the V. Century.

[1] *N.S.*, 1890, p. 256, fig. in text; *Röm. Mitt.*, v (1890), pp. 201–27, pl. ix.
[2] Bunbury, in Smith, *Dict. Geogr.*, ii, p. 305; Byvanck, p. 118.
[3] *N.S.*, 1913, Suppl., pp. 55–144, plan fig. 66.

Architectural marble remains are rare in Bruttium, and none came to light at Medma ; even wrought stones are very scarce, because here, as at most other ancient cities, the ruins were the quarry for the whole neighbourhood. A very battered fragment of what seems to be a small Doric capital in calcareous stone was unearthed which established the fact that the temple was of stone.

The architectonic terra-cottas belong to two revetments, an earlier and a later one. The earlier exhibits quite primitive characteristics, simple in form but of rather poor workmanship. A slab, possibly from the raking cornice, has : (*a*) projecting border with reversed tongue pattern ; (*b*) cymation with broken meander ; (*c*) convex moulding with diagonal bands (rak. cor. 14, fig. 27). A single disc mouth of a water-spout was discovered, enough to show that the pipes were tubular in form (spouts 10).

A geison slab of the V. Century falls into a category of revetments with a black and dead white colour-scheme (geisa 71, fig. 42). Whilst akin to the contemporary revetments from Locri and Caulonia, it resembles more closely that from Croton (geisa 72) ; but it is interesting to note that the border of broken meander is the identical motive used on the sima of the earlier revetment.

The central akroterion was a palmette rising from and framed by two branching akanthos stems (centr. akr. 17). This palmette akroterion must be dated in the second half of the V. Century ; it is more realistic than the early V. Century example from Croton (cent. akr. 18), but has still something of archaic stiffness about it. Fictile palmette akroteria are rare in Magna Græcia and Sicily, but in Latium and Etruria they were common, as at Satricum and the temple of Apollo, Falerii [1] ; nevertheless, no example from the western world equals the airy grace of the akroterion from the temple of Aphaia, Ægina.

There were only three antefixes among the *débris*, but they are all most interesting in type and make us regret that almost all the rest of the decoration is lost to us. The first type of antefix represents a female head, modelled in the simplest possible fashion, the eyes painted as round circles within the black, almond-shaped outline of the lids (ant. 51, fig. 65). Her brows, a black line without plastic relief, are so arched that they impart an alert expression to her face, intensified by her smiling countenance. She wears a high diadem ornamented with two rows of hammer pattern.

Antefixes with female heads are rare in Magna Græcia, but may have been a speciality of this region, for two other examples, from the neighbouring Metaurum (ant. 53) and from Caulonia, just across the peninsula, are also of the early VI. Century and are more primitive in type than the female heads of the earlier decoration, Thermon.[2]

The other two antefixes are from the same mould and depict a Satyr running to left and holding aloft a *rhyton* (ant. 47, fig. 64). He is spotted all over with

[1] Della Seta, *Museo di Villa Giulia*, Nos. 10188, 3771.
[2] 'Εφημ. 'Αρχ., 1900, p. x, 2 ; *Ant. Denkm.*, ii, pl. liii, 4 ; Koch, *Röm. Mitt.*, xxx (1915), p. 65.

little tufts of brown hair and wears a quaint little garment like a pair of bathing-drawers and red boots. His head is absolutely bald, but he has a long thick beard, apparently carefully trimmed and pointed ; indeed, his whole appearance as he stands out against the dark background is that of a good-natured, convivial being, full of impish merriment, with certain elements of civilisation which have led him to modify the original coarse habits of his tribe. The only other example of an antefix with a running Satyr is the one from Catana (ant. 48), a much more uncouth creature.

The two types of antefixes cannot have belonged to the same revetment, hardly to the same building, even though their dimensions are not very dissimilar. But that there were other smaller edifices in the *temenos* is shown by the water-spouts masked by lions' heads so archaic in type that they resemble dogs rather than lions (lions' heads 1, fig. 50). The muzzle and ears are both long and pointed, the whiskers are indicated by small holes. These water-spouts agree in scale with the Satyr antefixes, and they may both have adorned the same *thesauros* which their apotropæic character well fitted them to guard.

MEGARA HYBLÆA

ABOUT the year B.C. 730 certain Megarians under the leadership of Lamis founded a new Megara on the east coast of Sicily not far from Syracuse, but on a spot less favoured by natural defences or safe harbours than that selected by their neighbours.[1] As the site of their new city they chose an irregular triangle of land bounded by two streams, a tract which still stretches inland from the lighthouse near the shore to the hill now called *Collina del Cantera*. Megara is of the utmost importance for early Sicilian art, because the objects found there have a precise chronological limit, since the city was destroyed by Gelon of Syracuse in B.C. 482.

That an ancient Doric temple existed at Megara is proved by the fine capital of a column now in the Syracuse Museum. Some forty years ago the foundations of this temple, which must then have been intact, were utterly demolished to provide building material for the neighbouring *fattoria* Vinci.[2] The soil of the district, however, is of such a compact, alluvial nature that the impression of the whole structure was left, demonstrating that it was a peripteral hexastyle temple, length m. 41·40 × 17·55, with a cella m. 28·40 × 7·75. This temple must have been erected in the early VI. or even the end of the VII. Century, and one interesting member of the entablature, found many years ago, is a small archaic metope, so badly hacked about that the figure in relief is quite blurred.[3] It represented a warrior in a large Corinthian helmet who kneels, facing right, and draws his sword. This would not be a unique instance of stone metopes

[1] Bunbury, in Smith, *Dict. Geogr.*, ii, p. 310 ; Freeman, i, pp. 381–8, and Appendix XVI ; P. Orsi, *Mon. Ant.*, i. (1890), cols. 689–950.

[2] P. Orsi, *N.S.*, 1920, p. 331 ; *Mon. Ant.*, xxvii (1922), cols. 153–76.

[3] *N.S.*, 1880, p. 59 ; Koldewey, p. 76.

combined with a fictile revetment, for it occurred on Temple C, Selinus, and possibly on some of the other temples there, although the other cases are less well authenticated.

About m. 20 to west of this Temple A a second building was unearthed, thought at first to be a secular edifice or a *thesauros*, but proved by further excavations to be a temple also. In both these shrines and scattered between them were fragments of fictile revetments, so broken and faded that it is hard to reconstruct the designs or to decide to which temple any given revetment belonged. Yet those found more abundantly in or near Temple A seem to fall into a scheme of development which may be conjecturally grouped into three revetments.

The earliest type has a lateral sima with a torus with black vertical bands above a fascia with elongated black lozenge pattern and traces of the openings for tubular spouts (lat. simæ 6, fig. 3). A fragment, which may be the raking cornice of this revetment since it has certain similar elements, shows a torus with black vertical bands above a fascia painted with single meander, half red, half black, in a most unusual combination (rak. cor. 3, fig. 21). Numerous bits of the geison exist, decorated with a double torus with vertical bands entirely black, the eyes filled by four-petalled rosettes (geisa 2, fig. 33). These pieces are all alike in having toroi adorned with black vertical bands, and the character and technique of the ornamentation are also identical.

The second type is hardly less archaic, but the revetment was on a somewhat larger scale. Only a tiny bit of the fascia of the lateral sima has been preserved, but the design apparently consisted of black elongated lozenges, the space under the lateral rays being filled by Doric leaf. To the right is the opening for the tubular spout with part of the torus which covered the point of insertion (lat. simæ 7, fig. 4). Both this sima and that of the first type furnish good proofs for the belief suggested by the finds at Gela, *Marazà*, Locri, Selinus and Syracuse (lat. simæ 2–9) that the lozenge pattern was used exclusively for the lateral sima. Comparison with the first type leads to the conclusion that the various fragments of a fascia painted with black meander belonged to the raking cornice (rak. cor. 4), especially as on some of the pieces simple lines in red and black are traced on the back, which, therefore, was not attached to a background as would have been the case had the fragments formed part of the geison revetment which, here also, was decorated with double guilloche, the curving bands in red and black, the triangular spaces filled by three-leaved black palmettes, the eyes by four-petalled rosettes (geisa 11). There is, moreover, a fragment of a large rounded kalypter ornamented with simple tongue pattern (kal. 3). The base of only one tubular spout still exists ; the torus which covered the joint is coloured cream and decorated with black diagonal bands and the end of the tube finished in a flat lip adorned with red and black hammer pattern ; the disc mouths had red and black tongue pattern surrounded by a border of red and black triangles (spouts 9, fig. 48). Besides these tubular spouts there are remains of a lion's head gutter which projected behind the angle of the raking cornice. All that is left is the lower jaw with strong white teeth, and a small but valuable part of the mane, because it has a smooth convex surface at the back covered with a cream slip, proving that it was not set flat against the sima like the usual gutter masks, but stood free, a natural feature of the angle gutter which had a greater projection to carry off the water from the pediment (lions' heads 3, fig. 51). Lastly, there is a bit of what must have been the lateral akroterion, a wing with feathers plastically rendered and painted alternately red, cream and black (lat. akr. 4, fig. 75). Remains of large birds or Sirens seem to show that at Palaikastro in Crete the akroteria embodied a similar idea [1]: at Larissa in Æolis,[2] as at Olympia,[3] the wings found, although part of the akroteria, were more probably those of *Nikai*; but in the *temenos*, Syracuse, a wing just like the one from Megara was discovered, and at Corinth,[4] too, a wing came to light, and this assumes a special significance when we consider that Corinth has been named as the fabrication centre of that type of fictile revetment most completely represented in its later phases by the treasury of the Megarians at Olympia,[5] a type to which we should expect the terra-cottas from Megara Hyblæa to conform.

The lateral sima of the third type has a torus with diagonal bands above a cymation with Doric leaf in red and black, each pair separated by a black dart (lat. simæ 13), just like the revetment of the first type from the *temenos*, Syracuse (lat. simæ 16). There is a fine fragment of the raking cornice with: (*a*) torus with black diagonal bands; (*b*) projecting border with double black meander, the spaces filled by an eight-petalled cream rosette on a black square; (*c*) cymation with very large black Doric leaf (rak. cor. 5). On this type the meander has been restricted to the projecting border and the general colour-scheme seems black and cream. Numerous fragments of the geison with guilloche on a very large scale, the curving bands in red and black, the triangular spaces filled by immense cream three-leaved palmettes with a red sheath and set upon a red ground, and the eyes by four-petalled cream rosettes on a black circle. The lower surface of the casing was adorned with bold black meander (geisa 18, fig. 34). The colouring seems to indicate that a second type of tubular spout discs belonged to this revetment, for they are ornamented with cream rosettes on a black ground (spouts 9). Finally, there exists one antefix only, treated rather curiously with an incised design apparently representing palmettes rising from spiral bands. Roughly scratched at the back is a similar motive of anthemion leaves (ant. 58).

Temple B seems to have been a rectangular building measuring about m. 46·50 × 28·70, but the ground-plan has been so badly destroyed that it is

[1] *A.B.S.A.*, xi (1904–5), p. 303.

[2] Koch, *Röm. Mitt.* xxx (1915), p. 7. We are informed that Professor Kjellberg's account of these most important excavations will shortly appear.

[3] *Olympia*, iii, p. 37.

[4] Koch, *op. cit.*, p. 82, fig. 38.

[5] *Ibid.*, p. 111.

very difficult to trace it accurately. Within what must have been the *pronaos* a great mass of proto-Corinthian and Corinthian potsherds were heaped, and mingled with them were a few broken fictile remains. There were two paws of a lion or feline, one somewhat larger than the other, portions of two legs of an animal, part of the body or tail and bits of waved tresses (lat. akr. 3). Whether these miserable remnants once formed part of an akroterion depicting a Sphinx or were *ἀγάλματα* in the temple precinct it is impossible to say, although the shattered bits of a female figure of the type of the *Korai* of the Athenian Acropolis, found here in 1893, incline one to the latter supposition. There were also a quantity of very thick curved roof-tiles (tiles 3), with a raised border at one side and an inset on the lower surface of the opposite side which fitted tightly over the raised border of the next tile, so that the two interlocked.

METAPONTUM

THERE is no doubt that Metapontum was a Greek city founded by Achæans, but tradition bestowed upon it an even more remote past, relating that the earliest colonists were followers of Nestor, or, more definitely, of Epeios, and in proof thereof the Metapontines preserved in the temple of Athena the tools he used at Troy when making the Wooden Horse.[1] Yet the name seems to be Messapian in origin and the place may have been a Messapian settlement before the coming of the Greeks. In Metapontum the doctrine of Pythagoras obtained an immense following, and down to the time of Cicero the tomb of the philosopher was shown there. The city grew wealthy and also luxurious, until the inhabitants became notorious for their effeminacy.

In B.C. 212, after Tarentum was taken, Metapontum sided openly with Hannibal, who occupied the city with a garrison. But he was obliged to withdraw his men after the decisive battle at the Metaurus and evacuate all the inhabitants to save them from the vengeance of Rome. Pausanias mentions that in his day the city lay in ruins; at any rate its glory was departed and such life as still existed there was humble and insignificant.

The Duc de Luynes was the first to undertake investigations of importance at Metapontum,[2] and the best specimens from his excavations are now in the *Bibliothèque Nationale*, Paris. Many years later La Cava continued the work,[3] but it has never been carried out with the scientific and methodical care which has made the researches at other places in Magna Græcia, for instance at Caulonia, Locri and Medma, of such far-reaching results for our knowledge of the early history of the region.

The remains of the temple at the locality called *Chiesa di Sansone* were

[1] Bunbury, in Smith, *Dict. Geogr.*, ii, pp. 346–8; Byvanck, pp. 71–3.
[2] *Métaponte* (Paris, 1833).
[3] *Topografia e Storia di Metaponto* (Napoli, 1891).

identified by a dedicatory inscription to Apollo Lyk(eios).[1] Nothing but the foundations of the temple were discovered and not a stone of the super-structure. There was, however, abundant material of the fictile revetment, which falls into three groups, quite distinct, but each type the logical sequence of the preceding one.

The first, but scantily represented, is archaic in character, conforming chronologically to the architecture of the building. The geison has: (*a*) egg-and-dart in high relief; (*b*) small astragalos in relief painted yellow; (*c*) complicated meander, painted black in broad simple fashion and with the spaces unfilled; (*d*) Lesbian sima in low relief; (*e*) torus with broad diagonal bands (geisa 55).

The second group is much more completely preserved. The lateral sima and that sheathing the raking cornice, which have a very pronounced contour, are alike decorated with: (*a*) projecting border with double black meander, the spaces filled by a red square; (*b*) convex moulding with reversed tongue pattern, alternately red and black; (*c*) fascia with anthemia and lotus in low relief (lat. simæ 36, fig. 16). Here the lotus flowers are small and restrained and do not arch over the anthemia. On the lateral sima the middle of each slab is occupied by a lion's head masking the gutter-spout (lions' heads 10). These great heads are very realistic and cover the whole extent of the fascia, entirely concealing the design underneath.

The casing slabs of the horizontal geison were three-sided; the top surface was plain, since it was not visible, the front and under surface were adorned with a series of motives, the development of those used for the first revetment (geisa 57). Those on the front consisted of: (*a*) egg-and-dart in relief; (*b*) small astragalos in relief, painted red; (*c*) fascia with complicated meander, painted only in cream on a black ground, the spaces filled by a cream star on a red square; (*d*) convex moulding with leaf and dart pointing upwards; (*e*) torus with diagonal bands. This torus is three-quarters in the round and with its fellow, ornamented with bands running contrariwise, it borders the double guilloche of the lower surface. The bold egg-and-dart of this revetment have some affinity with a fragment from Tarentum (simæ 20); the contour of the lateral sima is like the one from Locri (lat. simæ 24); but the effect of the whole is a daring innovation, an extensive use of elements in relief which vary the colour-values by increased play of light and shade.

The third group is very similar, but instead of a cream ground, the decoration is black and dead white. The lateral sima has a much less pronounced contour, the design is richer, but the effect is not so striking as the bolder simplicity of the second group (lat. simæ 37, fig. 17). The motives are the same, but here the tongue pattern, which is not reversed, is very square in form and there are nine tongues to each slab instead of six as on the earlier revetment. The lions' heads are almost identical and so is the anthemion pattern. These slabs have an inset

[1] Koldewey, pp. 38–40.

at the sides, instead of the *anathyrosis* of the former type. There are four fragments of this sima in the *Cabinet des Médailles*.

The three-sided casings of the horizontal geison have also very similar motives, egg-and-dart, astragalos and complicated meander, but this time the last named is in relief, painted white on a black ground (geisa 58). Below it is a white leaf pattern on a red ground, like a Lesbian sima but without the dart. The lower surface is again enriched with double guilloche, but here the curving bands and the eyes are entirely black, and it is only the three-leaved palmettes filling the triangular spaces which are picked out with red. This revetment is not so sombre in tone as the one from Hybla (lat. simæ 40), or that from *Marazà*, Locri (lat. simæ 24); there is no motive which is without some touch of red, and as the white patterns are usually in relief, they stand out the more boldly from the dark ground. In the *Cabinet des Médailles* there are thirteen pieces of the front of this geison and four of the lower surfaces; in the museums of Potenza and Naples are many other fragments.

There is one slab with large single guilloche in red and black and a narrow border of black hammer pattern (geisa 50); this may be the lower surface of a geison casing, but it is more likely part of the front surface, as it closely resembles a fragment now in the Palermo Museum which is itself painted underneath with a band of black triangles (geisa 41).

The celebrated triangular kalypteres reported to have been found at this site are purely hypothetical. Certain fragments were conjecturally restored in that shape upon the basis of marble kalypteres found in Greece; but such a form is unknown in Magna Græcia for the kalypteres of the ridge-pole, although in a few instances the vertical kalypteres tended towards this triangular shape. One writer copied from another and similar kalypteres were evolved for Temple C, Selinus, after the model of the supposititious Metapontine tiles.[1]

There was a second temple at Metapontum, now called the *Tavole Paladini*, but evidently a small early Doric peripteros with 6–12 columns. On this spot both the Duc de Luynes and La Cava found bits of fictile revetment which they stated to be of the same type as those from the temple of Apollo, but of smaller dimensions. These fragments certainly have a superficial resemblance, but the revetment as a whole appears to be very rich and quite unique in character. The most prominent feature is the marked projection and overhang of the upper member of the entablature. Thus the upper portion of the lateral sima projects until it forms a sort of canopy edged with a projecting border, on the lower surface of which is a pattern of black meander; the roof of the canopy is adorned with red and black chevrons, and then at right angles comes the sima proper with: (*a*) projecting border again decorated with black meander; (*b*) cymation ornamented with hearts alternately red and black, all outlined black; (*c*) torus;

[1] Duc de Luynes et Debacq, *Métaponte*, pl. viii; Perrot, *Hist. de l'Art*, vii, pl. xlv; Hittorff, *Recueil*, v, pl. 41, F. ix; *Arch. polychrome*, Atlas, pl. vi, 10.

(*d*) fascia with lotus flowers and palmettes painted in cream on a black ground (lat. simæ 38, fig. 18). The absence of any indications of tubular spouts or lions' heads to carry off the water seems to imply that the projecting canopy was surmounted by a pierced cresting through which the water escaped. There is, however, a very beautiful trough-shaped gutter, decorated on the lower surface with a graceful palmette and spiral motive and on the right side only with a complicated black meander. The fact that this gutter evidently projected to an unusual length and that it is painted on one side only shows that the other side was invisible and that the gutter was placed behind the right angle of the raking cornice to carry off the water from the slope of the pediment (spouts 21).

The raking cornice resembled the lateral sima in having: (*a*) projecting border; (*b*) cymation with red and black hearts; (*c*) fascia with black meander; (*d*) small torus; (*e*) very large convex moulding. The lower surface of the slab runs back for a considerable distance, but is undecorated (rak. cor. 31).

One interesting find was a foot, half life-size, in calcareous stone, possibly from a metope,[1] an important discovery because it implies that on this temple stone metopes were combined with a fictile revetment as at Megara and Temple C, Selinus.

There is another revetment, evidently from quite a tiny *ναΐσκος*, the reputed provenance of which is also Metapontum, and here again we find the extreme projection of the upper member. The lateral sima was on a very small scale and consisted of: (*a*) a projecting border having the front surface painted with black meander, the spaces filled by a white star on a red square; (*b*) the roof of the canopy set at right angles and decorated with complicated meander painted only, the spaces again filled by a white star on a red square. Then follows the real sima slab from which project at intervals small lions' heads treated in a somewhat stylised manner with pointed muzzles and open jowls (lat. simæ 39). The little piece of this sima in the Naples Museum is rather blurred and only reveals that the ground of the fascia was dark; but in the museum at Potenza is the mould used for the sima, and this shows that the fascia was enriched with lotus flowers and anthemia in low relief.

A second fragment, apparently the lower surface of the geison casing, brings out even more strongly the archaic character of the decoration (geisa 19). On it, between two toroi with diagonal bands, running to right in both cases, is a double guilloche, the curving bands coloured alternately black and red; the triangular spaces are filled by a three-leaved cream palmette superposed on a ground alternately black and red, the eyes are four-petalled rosettes. It is noteworthy that the motives on this revetment are those used again at the Temple of Apollo and at the *Tavole Paladini*, but on a minute scale, stiffer and more primitive in design.

But the most astonishing thing about this revetment is a narrow slab with

[1] Duc de Luynes, *Métaponte*, p. 45.

figures in high relief illustrating the struggle between Herakles and the ἅλιος γέρων. The hero, clad in a short red chiton, grapples with his opponent, a bearded ancient whose writhing coils fill the whole left side of the slab. The squat figures are coated with a thick layer of colour to conceal the coarse nature of the clay beneath. The scene recalls the group from Assos,[1] or the poros group from the Athenian Acropolis.[2] Unfortunately there seems no record of how or where this precious fragment was discovered. Whether it was an isolated scene depicted over a doorway or part of a frieze portraying the labours of the hero is impossible to determine without more complete knowledge of the provenance; but the fact that the convex moulding borders the top and bottom of the slab only suggests its function as a frieze, for were it an isolated slab the border would almost certainly frame the sides as well (frieze 1).

In answer to enquiries of the Direction of the Naples Museum the Dottoressa A. Levi has most kindly informed me that these pieces have no number in the Museum Inventory; since all unnumbered terra-cotta fragments in the Naples Museum are from Metapontum, the inference is that these fragments also were found there, the more so because they have always been placed in the same case with pieces of that undoubted provenance. The similarity of design with the remains from the temple of Apollo and the *Tavole Paladini* is certainly a strong point in favour of the attribution.

During the early excavations various fragments were discovered and removed without any precise record of the spot whence they came. Amongst them is a small piece of a sima with: (*a*) much broken torus; (*b*) projecting border with broken meander painted yellow; (*c*) cymation with Doric leaf in red and yellow alternately outlined with black (simæ 12, fig. 47). The introduction of yellow seems to relegate this sima to the V. Century, and its small scale implies that it belonged to a building of modest proportions. There is besides part of a geison with a blurred guilloche pattern which differs slightly from the types known at the temple of Apollo. Part of a disc of red clay embellished with an incised pattern of double tongues addorsed was once covered with a cream slip, but no trace of colour is now visible (cent. akr. 5, fig. 70). The disc may not have been architectonic. It is akin to the examples from Rhegium (cent. akr. 3, 4) both in technique and dimensions, but until a more complete specimen is brought to light it will be difficult to determine their precise purpose.

An object of greater interest than these broken slabs is a fine antefix of the V. Century in the shape of a female head which rises above a low base. The head stands out quite free from any background and shows a pensive face with rounded chin and full lips firmly closed. Her parted hair is waved back and hangs loosely over her shoulders. Her eyebrows are painted only, but her eyes are shadowed by heavy lids. She wears a diadem set with rosettes in relief alternately with

[1] Collignon, *Hist. de la Sculp.*, i, p. 185, fig. 86*a*; Perrot, *Hist. de l'Art*, viii, p. 259, fig. 101.
[2] Perrot, *op. cit.*, p. 537, fig. 274.

what appears to be a lotus bud. Round her neck is a heavy twisted necklace resembling a torque, set in front with a massive ornament in relief. The head is full of dignity and grave charm and is well preserved, except that it is broken at the back (ant. 54, fig. 67).

METAURUM

THE city of Metaurum was situated on the west coast of Bruttium on a terrace which lay at a short distance from the sea between the rivers, the Petrace (the ancient Metaurus) and the Budello, where is the present town of Gioia Tauro.[1] Metaurum was reported to be a colony of the Locrians, or, according to another version, originally of the men of Zancle but later occupied by Locrians. It was chiefly famous as the birthplace of the poet Stesichorus, a claim contested, however, by Himera.

A little to the east of the city in the *Contrada Monacelli* architectonic terracottas were discovered, evidently the remains of a sanctuary of which no further trace now exists.[2] Possibly it was abandoned at an early period, for the fictile revetment is archaic in character, but assumes an additional importance from the fact that it is entirely homogeneous, and betrays no signs of even partial restoration later than the VI. Century.

An unusually long slab of a raking cornice had: (*a*) projecting border with narrow, closely set concave flutings, alternately red and black; (*b*) torus with diagonal bands; (*c*) fascia with guilloche (rak. cor. 6). In each slab two round holes were pierced to permit the dispersal of the water which was further facilitated by a grooved channel at the back of the sima. The design round the edge of the holes is in no way blurred or interrupted, showing that no pipes ever debouched from the holes. The only other sima at all comparable to this is one from *Marazà*, Locri (lat. simæ 11), where the holes are semi-elliptical. The narrow flutings are uncommon, but recall the earliest revetment from Croton (simæ 5).

A portion of the lateral sima shows: (*a*) torus with diagonal bands; (*b*) four rows of black chequer pattern; (*c*) bold Doric leaf (lat. simæ 10). Here again in the fascia of chequer pattern above the Doric leaf we find a parallel to *Marazà*, although the shape of the Doric leaf is nearer to the fragment from the *temenos*, Syracuse (simæ 10). Twelve pieces of the tubular spouts disclose the fact that they were of very simple type, merely a pipe unadorned with a disc mouth (spouts 2).

Only one small lion's head of very archaic type was found among the other remains (lions' heads 2). The pointed muzzle is conventionally decorated with incised lines forming a Rhodian rosette to indicate rolls of flesh; the jowl is open and pierced to allow the water to flow away. The work is very fine and is covered

[1] Bunbury, in Smith, *Dict. Geogr.*, ii, p. 348; Byvanck, pp. 118 f.
[2] P. Orsi, *N.S.*, 1902, pp. 128 f.

with a highly polished cream slip. This head appears to be absolutely of the same period as the water-spouts, and since there is no sign of more than one revetment upon the temple, and as one head only was found, we are led to conclude that this was the decoration of the last water-spout of the lateral sima, placed just behind the angle of the raking cornice, so that it drained the water which collected at the back of the pediment, and thus was used contemporaneously with the tubular spouts which carried off the water along the length of the lateral sima.

One of the most precious members of the revetment is an antefix, a female head, apparently set against a semi-elliptical background (ant. 53). Every detail is rendered with meticulous care ; her oval face is framed by the heavy masses of hair, banded smoothly over the top of her head, bound above her ears and twisted round in ever-increasing braided coils, producing almost the effect of a " layer wig." Even in its present condition, with no trace of the polychromy which once adorned it, this little head possesses an extraordinary charm and attractive freshness, for the expression is neither simpering nor morose, the opposite faults into which primitive artists were so liable to fall, but is gay and innocent, just ready to break into a smile. It is noteworthy that among the very limited number of sites from which come archaic antefixes with female heads, three, Caulonia, Medma and Metaurum, are reputed to be Locrian colonies, and although at Locri itself no such antefixes came to light, still both *Marazà* and *Marafioti* produced splendid groups of figures in the round. Hence it may have been Locrian influence which induced the craftsmen of Metaurum to attempt fictile metopes, three of which are still preserved, at least in part, one depicting a two-horse chariot, another the hind quarters of a horse and the third the paws of a feline walking to right (met. 1). Yet it is not certain if these metopes belonged to the temple, for they were not found with the other architectonic material, but farther west in the locality called *S. Maria*. It is rumoured that in this locality portions of a group have been found which represented a youth on horseback (cent. akr. 10), similar to the compositions found at Camarina, Gela, and Locri.

A fragment of a geison slab with complicated meander in relief is of poor workmanship and cannot have belonged to the archaic temple. Together with a small, realistic, but coarsely worked lion's head spout, it must have formed part of a small shrine of the late V. Century (lions' heads 19).

MONTE BUBBONÍA

IN the province of Caltanisetta, not far from Caltagirone, Monte Bubbonía, a lonely hill, rises between two affluents of the River Gela. This natural fortress was strengthened by the addition of a wall around the highest part of the summit, thus forming an acropolis, below which stretched an extensive Sikel city.[1] Within the acropolis was a long narrow building (m. 50 × 7·50) which the analogies of

[1] P. Orsi, *N.S.*, 1905, pp. 447–9 ; 1907, pp. 497 f. ; *Mon. Ant.* xx (1910), col. 744.

the Sikel towns at S. Mauro and Pantalica show to have been the prince's palace ; yet this building is less rude than the other two examples, and the curious construction, partly of blocks, partly of stones squared in the Greek manner, denotes that this *ἀνάκτορον* was built for the Sikel chieftain by, or at least under the instruction of, Greek master-masons.

At the foot of the hill a vast edifice was discovered, a series of spacious rooms grouped round one or more rectangular courtyards. This fine building is reminiscent of the Cretan palaces, and Professor Orsi has named it the " winter palace," again upon the analogies of S. Mauro and Pantalica where such dwellings in sheltered spots offered a more suitable winter residence than the military strongholds on the wind-swept mountain-tops which conformed more closely to the type of the Homeric house.

The ground-plans of the private houses were strewn with both Greek and indigenous objects of the VI.–V. Centuries and prove that the place was indeed a Sikel town, but influenced by the Greek culture whose point of dissemination was Gela.

Upon the acropolis the battered fragment of an antefix came to light, just half the forehead and hair of a Gorgoneion (ant. 3), and in the " winter palace " a similar piece was discovered, this time all the forehead and thick hair framing it, but showing traces of fire as if the building it adorned had been burnt down. These two pitiful relics at least testify that in the early VI. Century the Sikel prince endeavoured to give a touch of refinement to his native dwellings by decorating them with tile ends in the Greek manner.

NAXOS

NAXOS on the east coast of Sicily, between Catana and Messana, was acknowledged to be the earliest of all the Greek cities in Sicily.[1] One story relates that a certain Theokles, whose ship was driven by adverse winds on to the coast of Sicily, returned to his native Chalkis in Euboia and gave a glowing report of the fair and fertile land he had thus accidentally discovered. As a result he was sent forth at the head of a body of Chalkidian settlers to found a colony there. Another version makes him an Athenian by birth, but this less credible account may have been a later invention ; the name of the new city, however, taken from the Greek island, may imply that the colonists were not all of one stock, but that amongst them were at least a contingent of Naxians. We have no account of the actual voyage, choice of site or early history of the pioneer venture. The spot chosen, on the southern horn of the Bay of Tauros, appears to have been inhabited by Sikels, for the tradition was long maintained amongst them that this was the first of their cities to be reft from them by the new-comers.

The enterprise was so successful that six years later a colony was sent forth to found Leontini, which was shortly followed by Catana, but what little we know

[1] Bunbury, in Smith, *Dict. Geogr.*, ii, pp. 404 f. ; Freeman, i, p. 136.

of the history of Naxos is a record of disaster. Herodotus says that it was besieged and taken by Hippocrates of Gela, and it was later in the possession of Hieron who removed all the inhabitants to Leontini and brought in fresh colonists from elsewhere. During the Athenian Expedition the Naxians sided with the invaders, which brought upon them the enmity of the Syracusans. In B.C. 403 Dionysios seized the town by treachery, sold the inhabitants as slaves and razed the walls and buildings. From that time Naxos has never again been inhabited.

Yet the site of the city is clearly marked, for there are traces of the ancient road which lead up to it, the lines of the walls are still partly preserved, and the present landing-place is probably on the same spot as the ancient haven. Near the city was the altar of Apollo Archegetes, where it was customary for envoys to offer sacrifice before sailing to Greece on any sacred mission. Close to the town walls was an Aphrodision.

The site of Naxos has produced no store of decorative terra-cottas, owing most likely to the total destruction of the city and to the constant cultivation of the soil throughout a period of several hundred years. A few antefixes are all that are forthcoming, Satyrs' heads of the V. Century. One specimen has the rough hair and beard, the furry, pointed ears and staring eyes of the savage type (ant. 45), and is near akin to a head from Gela (ant. 43). Another shows a more sophisticated being with refined features, beard arranged in seemly strands and hair bound with a fillet (ant. 42). Apparently no architectonic slabs were ever found here.

RHEGIUM

THE important city of Rhegium, established in a commanding position near the south end of the Bruttian peninsula, was said to have been founded about B.C.717 by Chalkidians under Antemnestos in obedience to the behest of the Delphic oracle.[1] A body of Messenian exiles joined themselves to the Chalkidian settlers, and these Messenians, although not numerous, comprised many of the leading families, so that down to the time of Anaxilas the presiding magistrate was always selected from amongst their number. This aristocratic government soon extended its rule over the smaller towns in the district, but does not seem to have founded any colonies of importance. The Rhegians reached the apex of their glory in the reign of Anaxilas who made himself master of Zancle on the Sicilian coast opposite and thus held command of the Straits. When he died in B.C. 476 he left his power to his two sons, but in B.C. 461 they were expelled from Rhegium, which remained independent until, after a terrible siege of eleven months, it fell under the sway of Dionysios of Syracuse in B.C. 387. Those wretched inhabitants who survived the horrors of the siege were sold as slaves

[1] Bunbury, in Smith, *Dict. Geogr.*, ii, pp. 703–6; Philipp, in *P.W.*, zweite Reihe, i, cols. 487–502; Byvanck, pp. 82–4.

and the city was utterly destroyed. Yet such a valuable position could not be left unoccupied, and in spite of fierce wars and violent earthquakes life has gone on there continuously until this very day.

Rhegium has been too constantly overwhelmed by disasters due to nature and to man to have preserved any traces of the earliest Greek city, but in the VI. Century a temple must have stood in the grounds of the Villa Griso-Laboccetta, for there remnants of the fictile revetment were unearthed, much damaged and reduced to meagre dimensions, but apparently all of one period and exceedingly interesting on account of the varied and skilful arrangement of the motives employed.

There do not seem to have been any fragments which can be definitely claimed as part of the lateral sima, but one magnificent piece and many small bits of the raking cornice exist which show that it was decorated with : (*a*) projecting border with black double meander ; (*b*) cymation with red and black Doric leaf diminishing to a point and separated by a black dart (rak. cor. 2). This sima is moulded at the back with a forked support like that from the *temenos*, Syracuse (rak. cor. 11). The designs of the front face remind one of the lateral sima from Croton (lat. simæ 12) ; they are in no way unusual, but the freshness and vigour of the drawing impress one forcibly.

Pieces of what was apparently the geison have : (*a*) palmettes enclosed in bands which form a pointed arch above and end below in volutes, the eyes filled by four-petalled rosettes ; (*b*) torus with black diagonal bands ; (*c*) fascia with black double meander, the spaces filled by a cream star on a black square (geisa 62). Other slabs of the lower surface of the geison casings have a border on the front face with double black meander alternating with a cream rosette on a black square ; the lower surface is painted with large black double meander (geisa 51).

The kalypteres of this temple were very fine, the rounded top ornamented with boldly traced double meander, the sides with red and black tongue pattern ; the outer edge was finished off with triple toroi (kal. 5). Besides these, there are at least three large discs of the akroteria, painted with zones of tongue pattern, stripes and kindred designs (cent. akr. 3), similar to those found at Gela (cent. akr. 2) and at several Greek sites. Evidently double meander was the favourite motive of this revetment, for we find it on each member in turn, now simple, now interrupted by cream stars or rosettes, but always present in some form.

It is not easy to determine the position occupied by the splendid relief found with the other architectonic remains of this temple. The lower border is intact which gives the whole width, m. 1·00, of the slab, but the top part is broken and most of the right side, so that the present height is m. 1·25, but it must have been at least m. 1·35–1·40 when complete (ped. 6). It seems too large for a metope of such an early period and too high for a frieze. The only alternative is the decoration of a tympanon, for which, however, the subject is not very appropriate, for there is no central point to the composition ; yet that may be a mark of its early date. It represents two women with linked arms dancing to right. Unfortunately their heads are broken off, but their long waved tresses hang over their shoulders and they are clad in the peplos with long *apoptygma* worn by so many of the little bronze figures of that period which have come down to us. Their movements are full of a rhythmic *abandon*, yet without the orgiastic touch noticeable on the relief from Teichioussa in the British Museum.[1]

One magnificent piece of architectonic terra-cotta was found during the excavation of the Odeion (geisa 6, fig. 37). Of course it had nothing to do with that much later building, but as it was discovered at a distance of not more than m. 150 from the *fondo già Griso-Laboccetta* it is possible that it belonged originally to that building. It is the portion forming the left angle of the frontal geison, for although the left corner and all the lower part of the slab are destroyed, yet the upper edge, cut on the slant to fit below the slope of the raking cornice, is perfectly preserved. The ornamentation consists of: (*a*) projecting border with a large single guilloche in red and black; (*b*) Doric leaf alternately red and black and separated by a reversed three-leaved palmette; (*c*) torus with red and black diagonal bands; (*d*) fascia (broken) with uncertain pattern. The most remarkable thing about this geison is marks on the lower fascia of the insertion of two water-spouts, but the traces are too obliterated to determine whether the spouts were tubular or masked by lions' heads. As water-spouts in such a position can have served no practical purpose, they must have been dummy spouts, introduced to make the frontal geison conform to those of the long sides.

Close by were found four fragments of the discs of tubular pipes, all of the same design, a rosette in red and black surrounded by a circle of black triangles (spouts 19).

From the hill above the city called *Collina del Salvatore* came Greek vases, vessels for domestic use and, together with them, architectonic slabs finely worked and decorated with anthemia in relief, work of the V. Century (simæ 19).

When digging the foundations for the new Prefecture evidence of the ground-plan of a Greek temple of the first half of the V. Century was discovered below the Roman baths. Two splendid tiles came to light, moulded with a raised margin on each side, and painted beneath with an anthemion pattern (tiles 12).

From time to time sporadic pieces were found; of one, an immense Gorgoneion, only the right half of the forehead and eye-socket remain (ant. 16). Two other objects are of exceptional interest. One is an antefix, a small female head in very slight relief. Her reddish-brown hair is in crinkled waves, her brows a sharply defined ridge above eyes rendered by a black circle between almond lids outlined black; her mouth is straight, but her red lips are so fully in relief that they almost pout; on her head is a *stephané* enlivened by a red line (ant. 52). In the few instances in Magna Græcia or Sicily where a female head adorned the antefixes, the treatment is so individual that one can never be said to resemble

[1] *Brit. Mus. Cat. Sculp.*, i, No. 21.

another. In contrast to the heads found in Etruria and Latium, where the moulds for certain types were carried from place to place,[1] in this southern region each local artist seems to have originated the type he desired and worked it out with loving care ; hence we get the severe aloofness of the head from Tarentum, the archaic strivings of the Caulonia example, the frank friendliness of the Medma specimen, the appealing charm of the Rhegian head and, the finest of all, the dainty grace of the beautiful little lady from Metaurum (ant. 49–53).

Lastly we must mention an unique piece, an extraordinary gutter-spout in the form of a sea-monster. The modelling is very fine and the monster, with his pointed snout, little sharp eyes, spiky crest and alert expression, is precisely the fabled guardian of Andromeda (lions' heads 25). A somewhat similar sea-monster appears on a revetment from Cære,[2] but otherwise I can cite no analogy in the archaic period among the fictile revetments of either Italy or Greece, and the only parallel known to me is a gutter-spout in exactly this form from Larissa in Æolis, now in Constantinople and still unpublished.

S. MAURO

A FEW kilometres to the south of Caltagirone rise a group of five little hills crowned by the ruins of an anonymous Sikelo-Greek city.[3] These nameless peaks are identified by numbers ; thus Hill I–II was the "sacred hill," Hill III the acropolis, and on Hill V, divided from the acropolis by a deep ravine, were the remains of poor Greek habitations of the VI.–V. Century, roof-tiles, potsherds and all the accumulated rubbish of daily life. Right on the surface was a fine fictile Ionic palmette, yet this, owing to its utter dissimilarity to the rest of the material found here and the complete absence of other fictile decoration, cannot have originally belonged to this spot, but must have been brought over from the sacred hill opposite.

Hill III is divided into two summits, the smaller one covered with rude Sikel hovels ; the larger, on the contrary, shut off by a stout wall, constituted a strong military position and enclosed a rectangular building, evidently the abode of the native prince.[4] This *ἀνάκτορον* measures m. 8·00 × 15·80 × 7·50, and was divided by a transverse wall into two chambers which, on the analogy of the Homeric house, may be called the *megaron* and the *thalamos*. On the east front the side walls were prolonged into *antæ*, thus forming a little *prostas* before the entrance. On the surface of the soil the plough turned up a few bits of fictile decoration, and these, strangely enough, were Greek in character, for it raises the question whether this Sikel prince was pleased to use a few Greek slabs to give

[1] E. Douglas Van Buren, *Figurative Terra-cotta Revetments in Etruria and Latium*, p. 20, Type xviii, p. 21, Type xx, p. 23, Type xxvii.

[2] Arndt, *La Glyptothèque Ny Carlsberg*, pl. 173.

[3] P. Orsi, *N.S.*, 1903, p. 432 ; 1904, p. 373 ; *Mon. Ant.* xx (1910), cols. 728–850.

[4] *Op. cit.*, cols. 736–46, fig. 4, pl. iv.

a partial embellishment to his dwelling, or whether Greek master-masons in the service of the Sikels constructed, or better, directed the construction of the building, as was the case at Monte Bubbonía. Yet the poverty of construction and the fact that the foundations of the *anaktoron* rest upon a *stratum* of soil containing stone implements and prehistoric potsherds and that the two higher *strata* were impregnated with ceramics of all three Sikel periods lead one to conclude that the palace was built in the VII. Century by indigenous workmen and that the Greek slabs were perhaps added later as a pleasing adornment ; but since there is no trace of any Greek ware such as proto-Corinthian, it must have been abandoned about the time of the coming of the Greek settlers. Two points argue in favour of the identification as the prince's dwelling : it is the only imposing construction in this village of hovels, and in it were found the bronze tablets which, if intact, would be an invaluable document for the history of the period.

Four broken bits of architectonic terra-cottas were found on the hill of the *anaktoron* and two cover-tiles painted brown (kal. 1). Right on the surface was a triangular antefix with a Gorgoneion (ant. 6) ; the top is broken but the three "pearl-locks," sharp tusks and pendent tongue date it towards the end of the VI. Century.

The summit of Hill I–II is a level stretch m. 100 × 50, and here were fictile fragments piled in heaps to make a boundary line, roof-tiles, *pithoi*, *pinakes*, etc.[1] Peasants reported that during fugitive explorations on this spot painted slabs and even large fictile figures had been found, but all were scattered. Now there is no trace of the temple which must once have stood here ; it was impossible even to verify if the stylobate was of stone, as it almost certainly must have been, and there was not even any authentic account of walls in position, only of certain squared blocks of stone carried thence and used to build two small houses. The blackened soil tells a tale of a sanctuary burnt down and abandoned, for evidently the district was entirely untouched until Byzantines or Arabs began to cultivate it, and with their coming must date the first dispersal of the fictile revetment. Another long period of neglect followed, for it was only a few years ago that the land was again brought under cultivation, entailing a second scattering of the precious remnants. All that were saved were a couple of basketfuls which were brought to the Syracuse Museum, where lengthy and laborious study resulted in the piecing together of a sufficient number of the shattered atoms to reconstruct the lateral sima.

In the basin between the two hills a small Greek house was uncovered, with many roof-tiles and other objects.

The revetment slabs from the temple were of yellowish clay mixed with lava particles and they are almost invariably beautifully made and fired. After being submitted to a preliminary firing, the slabs were covered with a cream slip upon which the design was drawn with great ability and freedom ; the

[1] *Op. cit.*, cols. 775–8.

outlines were sometimes incised to give a surer guide to the painter, who skilfully diversified his limited range of three colours, motives in black and red on a cream ground, and then the slabs were fired a second time. They were joined together by a system of interlocking edges and were fastened to the wooden framework beneath by metal nails, the holes for which are still visible on many pieces; to ensure the correct placing of the slabs, numerical signs were scratched or painted on the back.

There are two pieces of a sima which do not absolutely join, but undoubtedly are parts of the same slab; they are decorated with the following design: (*a*) torus; (*b*) very simple black broken meander, (*c*) cymation with square-shaped Doric leaf in red and black; (*d*) convex moulding with chevrons; (*e*) four rows of chequer pattern arranged in alternate red and black diagonal lines (rak. cor. 10, fig. 24). The simple meander and square Doric leaf resemble the angle of the horizontal geison from Gela (geisa 1), whilst the diagonally set chequer pattern reminds one of the raking cornice of the revetment from the *temenos*, Syracuse (rak. cor. 8), and, indeed, the similarity of the whole design inclines one to believe that this also was a raking cornice. The question has been raised whether the small dimensions of this sima, cm. 24, do not indicate that it formed part of the interior decoration; yet it seems to be of a more archaic nature than the sumptuous revetment of the transitional period with the richly decorated spout discs. That is indeed so intricate that it is hard to believe it was the first decoration employed and that it was not preceded by a simpler revetment, quite conceivably on a more modest scale. The existence of an earlier revetment is further vouched for by other elements, decidedly too archaic to conform to the later transitional type. One of these is part of a large concave disc which must have had a diameter of cm. 55·5, ornamented with a zone of tongue pattern in red and black (cent. akr. 1). This was part of the smaller disc placed inside the outer one which sealed the end of the ridge-pole. The piece is valuable, because it shows how the larger disc radiated out behind the smaller one, thus supplying just that link left without proof by the fragments from Gela (cent. akr. 2).

Another miserable fragment is of the greatest importance (cent. akr. 9); it is the under part of a man's knee, rather more than life-size, in very high relief, and is all that has been so far found of what was evidently a group of a youth on horseback like those from Camarina and Gela.

A recurved wing moulded double, the feathers rendered by broad splashes of colour without plastic relief, is the best-preserved piece of a number of fragments evidently belonging to one group. It is impossible to ascertain whether the left side of a very archaic face was in the round or in high relief, because the whole of the back of the head is missing. There is, however, another little bit which suggests the hair of a Gorgon in pearled strands radiating out from the centre and two pieces of imbrication, seemingly part of the chiton covering the thigh of a large figure. Quite certainly in the round were the muzzle of a little horse and the head of a small serpent (lat. akr. 12, fig. 77). None of these pieces fit together, but the clay is the same, and a consideration of them as a whole induces one to believe that originally they composed such a group as the Gorgon-Medusa from the *temenos*, Syracuse (lat. akr. 10), and that in this case also the monster, clad in an embroidered chiton with serpent girdle, moved swiftly in the ancient running scheme, supported by her strong pinions and clasping under her arm the little Pegasos.

Yet this group must have been an advance upon the one from Syracuse because it was completely in the round and needed no slab as background. So far nothing has been discovered to prove definitely whether these Gorgon-Medusas were part of the architectonic decoration of the temples or were *ἀγάλματα* set up in the *temene*: yet it is significant that each time they have come to light in close proximity to a temple, amid the remains of the fictile revetments and in all three cases, at Syracuse, Gela and S. Mauro, at sites where the youthful rider incorporated the central akroterion.

A square fragment, presumably the base of an antefix, has a lower border with broken black meander ; the design above is completely obliterated (ant. 62).

The lateral sima of the transitional revetment was extraordinarily rich (lat. simæ 19, fig. 8) : it was executed principally in colour, but the astragalos which bordered it at top and bottom testifies to a very restrained introduction of relief. The motives were : (*a*) cream astragalos in relief ; (*b*) projecting border with double black meander, the spaces filled by a red square ; (*c*) cymation with lyre-shaped Doric leaf, alternately contrasted, the reversed one being filled with a cream palmette on a red ground ; (*d*) torus with black diagonal bands ; (*e*) fascia with four-rayed black lozenges, each united at the point to its fellow. From this fascia the water-spouts projected, two spouts to each slab, spaced in such a way that the interval between disc and disc corresponded to their diameter. The tubular pipes were cm. 22 long and were adorned with a concave disc enriched with a variety of patterns, rosettes, rays, whirls, all beautifully adapted to the field to be covered (spouts 20, fig. 49). The geison consisted of : (*a*) torus with red and black bands ; (*b*) double guilloche ; (*c*) cream astragalos in relief (geisa 23).

There are, moreover, a few pieces of more doubtful destination ; some are decorated with rosettes, the cream astragalos again appearing on the border : this repetition of the motive found on the lateral sima suggests that these are fragments of the raking cornice (simæ 4). Rosettes are introduced on the lateral sima from the *temenos*, Syracuse (lat. simæ 16), but the best parallels are the revetment of the temple to north of the Gorgon Temple, Corfu,[1] or the splendid sima from Delphi.[2]

Numerous pieces of small palmettes rising from double volutes show that they were attached to a moulded base which fitted over the ridge-pole kalypteres

[1] Doerpfeld, *Athen. Mitt.*, xxxix (1914), p. 166, fig. 4.
[2] Koch, *Röm. Mitt.*, xxx (1915), fig. 47.

(pal. 2, fig. 52). One palmette of larger dimensions marked the middle of the ridge-pole.

The function of one small palmette is uncertain (pen. pal. 2); it is only cm. 8 in diameter, but it is unusually thick, cm. 7·4. These measurements suggest that it may have served the same purpose as the little palmettes which hung from the raking cornice of the revetment from the *temenos*, Syracuse (pen. pal. 1).

Curved roof-tiles and kalypteres were found among the material from the temple (tiles 4); they were all smashed to bits, mostly painted black, but some of the kalypteres were adorned with various patterns and finished off by a thick torus.

The excavations revealed a gradual change in the ethnical character of the anonymous city at S. Mauro: Greek settlers made their way into the Sikel stronghold, but whether by peaceful penetration or by force of arms there is nothing to tell us, for although the traces of burning on the acropolis might imply a violent assault, yet fire must have been no uncommon accident in these villages of thatched huts. The temple, however, with its sumptuous decoration, the *ἀγάλματα* of the *temenos* and the rite of cremation all prove the introduction in the VI. Century of quite a new current of civilisation, bringing its own religious ideas, expressed in the medium of its own art. Probably the fictile slabs were not of local manufacture; the numerals scratched on the back of each slab indicate that they were brought from a distance, most likely from the neighbouring Gela, which must have been a great centre for the fabrication of this type of decoration, since the Geloans took pride in adorning with the finest fruits of their handicraft the Treasury which they dedicated at Olympia.

SELINUS

SELINUS, the outpost of the Greek world against the Phœnicians, became one of the most important cities in Sicily. It was founded about B.C. 630 by a colony from Megara Hyblæa under the leadership of Pamillos, a native of the elder Megara, accompanied by a contingent from thence.[1] Having passed by several more promising positions, the settlers established themselves upon the slight elevation between two sandy, swampy valleys, through each of which a stream flows down to the sea. Theirs was the most western of all the Greek colonies and their advanced position soon brought them into hostile contact with their neighbours, for their boundary towards the north-west touched the Phœnicians at Mazaros, and extended as far north as to bound the territory of the Segestans with whom, as early as B.C. 580, they had already fallen out.

Vague allusions to Selinus are all we know of its early history, but the oligarchical government was transformed into a despotism and about B.C. 510 Selinus was ruled by one Peithagoras, from whom it was delivered by the Spartan Euryleon, whose subsequent attempt to seize the power for himself ended in his

[1] Bunbury, in Smith, *Dict. Geogr.*, ii, pp. 956–9; Freeman, i, pp. 418–29; iii, pp. 451–71.

defeat and death. The struggles and enterprise of the Selinuntines brought them great wealth and power ; they possessed one or more havens at the mouths of the two streams and maintained a fortified mercantile station at Mazaros.

It was the renewed strife between Selinus and Segesta in B.C. 416 which led to the Athenian expedition into Sicily, for the Segestans appealed to Athens to aid them against their foes who had sought the powerful help of Syracuse. Nevertheless, beyond sending forces to assist the Syracusans, Selinus does not seem to have played any great part in the war ; but when the Athenians were defeated, the Segestans, in despair at their unprotected condition, called in the Carthaginians. Owing to the rather grudging help granted them, the Segestans were not able to defeat the Selinuntines, but in the spring of B.C. 409 the Carthaginians sent over an army of 100,000 men, against whom the Selinuntines, in their unprepared state, were powerless. The siege of Selinus only lasted ten days, but even after the walls were taken by assault, the citizens defended themselves bravely and street fighting continued from house to house. Out of all that numerous population only 2,600 men under the command of Empedion escaped to Akragas. Soon after Hannibal razed the walls, but permitted such inhabitants as survived to reoccupy their town as tributaries of Carthage. Selinus never recovered from this crushing blow, but gradually sank under the dominion of Carthage and was finally destroyed in B.C. 250.

As the city increased, the original settlement on the Western Hill became the acropolis, constructed on a wide terrace sustained by a vast embankment built up of squared blocks and containing temples and other edifices of an official character.[1] There are still traces of the earliest town walls, for the best-preserved stretch starts from the outstanding tower on the northern front of the acropolis, and after running north-east for about m. 50 ends in a re-entrant which perhaps indicates the position of a gate.

On the Eastern Hill was another group of sacred buildings ringed with walls of rectangular blocks which served to strengthen the scarped side of the hill. Farther to the west was yet another *temenos*, entered by *Propylaia* and surrounded by large stretches of walls which enclosed the temple of Demeter *Malophoros* with its rich *favissæ* containing objects ranging from the VII. to the V. Century, altars, houses for the priests, wells, water-conduits and *stelai*, a little sacred city complete in itself.[2]

Beyond the city several necropoles spread over the hillsides, because in the VI.–V. Century the primitive necropoles at Galera and Bagliazza were abandoned in favour of a new district to the west of the city.

The excavations at Selinus have been carried on intermittently for a great number of years. Owing to the devastations wrought by human foes and by seismic disturbances, the material was scattered and confused to a degree which

[1] Hulot et Fougères, *Sélinonte* (Paris, 1910), pls. i–iii.

[2] *N.S.*, 1898, pp. 258–60 plan, fig. in text (Salinas) ; 1920, pp. 67–91 (Gabrici).

rendered the work most delicate and arduous. Unfortunately the earliest excavations were conducted with little scientific precision, and the masses of fragments brought to the museum at Palermo were thrown into heaps without any record of their exact provenance. To Professor Doerpfeld and his collaborators we owe the first attempt at reconstruction upon a really accurate basis, and now Professor Gabrici, who for some years has been carrying out most careful investigations on the site, promises us the complete publication of all the fictile remains. This important work should throw a flood of light upon many dark problems and furnish new criteria for a study of the whole field of terra-cotta revetments. In the meantime I can but give a brief and necessarily inadequate summary of the marvellous treasures which Professor Gabrici's exhaustive treatise will more fully reveal.

Temple C was a large Doric peripteros with 6–17 columns,[1] but it was not the earliest edifice which existed on the spot, for under the pavement were traces of a smaller building, slightly differently orientated, which must have been one of the first undertakings of the colonists and of which nothing but the ground-plan now remains. Yet possibly to this primitive building belonged certain bits of archaic fictile revetment which certainly have nothing to do with the splendid decoration of Temple C and yet appear like forerunners of the motives there found. Among them is a small piece of a sima with recurved square leaf-pattern above a fascia with addorsed lotus flowers enclosed by intertwining stems (rak. cor. 19). The cymation is low, the lotus pattern compact, with none of the graceful flow of line found on the revetment of Temple C. The motive seems a development of that found on the first revetment, Syracuse (lat. simæ 15), but more archaic than the one from the Hall of Echo, Olympia.[2] Then there is a tubular water-spout with disc mouth painted with a rosette (spouts 16); the small diameter, m. 0·125, shows that it must have come from an edifice of modest dimensions. An antefix with a palmette in low relief may be tentatively ascribed to this building; it is of the archaic pattern, directly capping the master-tile (ant. 56).

Probably to this revetment one should attribute the splendid relief which filled the tympanon, a monstrous Gorgoneion which has been most cleverly reconstructed by a comparison of the few fragments which remain with the examples from Gela and Hipponium (ped. 2). The face is very broad with round eyes, a deeply recessed mouth furnished with tremendous tusks and a pendent tongue. The hair round the forehead ends in symmetrically arranged curls; it is bound just below the large flabby ears and hangs over the shoulders in innumerable little "pearl-locks." The beard is rendered by a series of tiny spirals traced all round the cheeks and chin. As far as one can judge from the miserable fragments which remain, this VI.-Century head seems less archaic than

[1] Koldewey, pp. 95–104, pl. xii, figs. 71, 76; Hulot, *op. cit.*, pp. 216–30.
[2] *Olympia*, ii, pl. cxvi, 5.

the Gorgon-Medusa from Syracuse ; yet it would have appeared an anachronism if combined with the developed V.-Century revetment of Temple C, whereas it agrees chronologically with the simple tubular pipes and stiffly designed motives which we have assigned to the little sanctuary of the first colonists. The exact position of these Gorgoneia has been much discussed ; some authorities consider them to have been akroteria, a development of the concave discs of the primitive period. Yet not only are the discs and these monstrous Gorgoneia almost, if not absolutely, contemporaneous, but also, as Professor Gabrici points out, the latter are entirely unsuited to fulfil the function of akroteria, because it would be impossible to support a thin slab, m. 2 in height, at such an elevation unless it were fastened to a solid background for at least two-thirds of its height. Upon the summit of a temple, especially in such a windy place as Selinus, a slab of that nature would not have lasted many days.

Most likely there were several complete renovations and partial restorations of the revetment of Temple C, but two types can be distinctly made out, an earlier one with thicker slabs and a more compact pattern, and a later one with a free, flowing outline. None of the slabs are preserved in their entirety, but what their height must have been can be gauged by the blocks of the substructure which measure cm. 51, thus demonstrating that the sima and geison combined must have measured not less than cm. 53.

To the earlier type belong slabs of the lateral sima with cymation with square Doric leaf recurved, alternately red and black, followed by a double guilloche between two toroi (lat. simæ 20). The curving bands of the guilloche are black, the eyes also are simple black spots and four-leaved palmettes fill the triangular spaces between the bands.

To this sima corresponded a cresting of palmettes and lotus flowers addorsed and alternately reversed, similar in design to the cresting of the second type, but much heavier and more compact in outline (cresting 1) ; here also the water ran away through holes pierced in the cresting which obviated the functional use of water-spouts and antefixes.

The raking cornice consisted of : (*a*) Doric leaf ; (*b*) torus ; (*c*) fascia with anthemia and lotus flowers addorsed and linked together by spiral stems (rak. cor. 20). This graceful motive recalls the sima from the Treasury of the Megarians, Olympia, but is much lighter and airier and more closely resembles the one from Lusoi in Arcadia.[1] The curved support at the back of this cornice is painted with a large simple leaf-pattern like the examples from Rhegium (rak. cor. 2) and Syracuse (rak. cor. 11). The motive of the lateral sima was carried out on the horizontal geison, thus producing a uniform geison design which ran right round the building as at *Marafioti*, Locri.

A quantity of roof-tiles and rounded kalypteres were found in the west portico of Temple C. Among the latter were small kalypteres which covered the junctures

[1] *Oesterr. Jahresh.* iv (1901), p. 62, fig. 132.

of the roof-tiles in vertical rows and others of unusually large dimensions which covered the ridge-pole ; the body of these latter kalypteres was adorned with meander and other patterns and finished off with a triple torus elaborately ornamented with bands and chevrons (kal. 13). Two kalypteres of this type were found in the necropolis of *Manicalunga*, where they had been used to cover burials : one is now in the museum at Palermo ; another in a collection at Castelvetrano, where there is also a flat roof-tile possibly from this revetment.[1] Astride these kalypteres rose small palmettes in relief, painted on both sides (pal. 5). Some little palmettes, decorated in relief on one side only, have a curved base and show points of attachment which suggests that they were pendent palmettes and hung from the lower surface of the geison (pen. pal. 3).

The second revetment was a repetition of the first, carried to a higher point of development. The reconstructions of both Cavallari and Doerpfeld have been proved by later excavations to be erroneous in certain particulars : the former introduces tubular water-spouts which were rendered superfluous by the pierced cresting ; and the latter does not differentiate between the two types of revetment which are blended together in his reconstruction.

The lateral sima consisted of : (*a*) square Doric leaf, alternately red and black, the recurved top being painted in the contrasting colour ; (*b*) torus with red and black bands ; (*c*) double guilloche, the bands all black, the eyes a red dot and the triangular spaces filled by five-leaved palmettes, the first, third and fifth always coloured red ; (*d*) torus with bands. The lower surface of the sima slabs is painted with a strip of single guilloche with a border of cream meander, the spaces above filled with red, those below with black (lat. simæ 21).

The raking cornice had : (*a*) cymation with Doric leaf ; (*b*) astragalos in relief ; (*c*) anthemia springing from double spirals and separated by lotus flowers whose petals overarch ; (*d*) astragalos ; (*e*) simple black meander. This cornice is painted at the back with a simple leaf-pattern (rak. cor. 21). No other specimens from Sicily or Magna Græcia have quite such airy grace as the anthemion pattern here used ; the motives from Locri are heavy in comparison, only slabs from the Treasuries at Olympia furnish close parallels, and they belong to the later revetments with a white design on a black ground.[2]

The geison repeated the motive of the lateral sima, square Doric leaf above double guilloche (geisa 34).

A stately palmette rising from double volutes formed the central akroterion of this revetment. The palmette is modelled alike on both sides and its height was cm. 39 × 36 (cent. akr. 16). It is the only floral akroterion so far known in Sicily ; but at Medma (cent. akr. 17) and at Croton (cent. akr. 18), where both the central and lateral akroteria were of this type, fine specimens were found of this form of akroterion, a form so common on the marble revetments of later buildings.

[1] *N.S.*, 1884, p. 336, pl. vi, *a*, *d*.
[2] *Olympia*, ii, pl. cxxi.

The lion's head built into the material to west of Temple C and a couple more of these heads discovered in the later excavations on the temple site are water-spouts of the V. Century and undoubtedly part of the decoration of this temple (lions' heads 12) ; the fact that they are so few in number and that lateral water-spouts were not needed on this revetment indicates that the only position they can have occupied was the angle behind the raking cornice like the one from Metaurum (lions' heads 2).

During the excavations upon the acropolis innumerable pieces of fictile decoration came to light ; they vary in design, in scale and even in technique, for some are masterpieces of this art, whilst others look like late and hasty reparations. One slab, probably a raking cornice, has : (*a*) torus with black vertical bands ; (*b*) projecting border with black broken meander ; (*c*) cymation with red and black Doric leaf tapering to a point and separated by a black dart ; a band of black chevrons, outlined only, is painted below the cymation ; (*d*) torus with closely set black diagonal lines (simæ 13). The pointed leaf separated by a dart is a fairly common motive, but the only other examples of a true chevron pattern are the earliest revetment from S. Mauro (rak. cor. 10) and a lateral sima from Gela (lat. simæ 8). Another sima can be reconstructed from two fragments which give : (*a*) projecting border with three rows of small black chequer pattern ; (*b*) red and black Doric leaf diminishing to a point and separated by a black dart ; below the cymation is a painted band of broken meander, the upper ones red, the lower black ; (*c*) torus with red and black vertical bands (geisa 64). On another little fragment of this motive the three rows of chequer pattern appear on the projecting border, but the Doric leaf had merely a thin black outline and no dart (simæ 9). Chequer pattern on the projecting border was rare in Sicily ; indeed the only other example seems to be the revetment of the fifth type from the temenos, Syracuse (simæ 10), but it was frequently found in Magna Græcia. The meander is also of an unusual character, but at Selinus it was evidently a favourite device of the artists to experiment with this motive, for every possible variety and combination are to be found, at any rate amongst the simpler types, for the later complicated motives used at Metapontum, Locri and elsewhere are rare, with the exception of one tiny bit which, by analogy with the meanders from Metapontum and Croton (geisa 58, lat. simæ 32), seems to have been a quadruple meander (geisa 66). One small fragment has : (*a*) astragalos in relief ; (*b*) double meander, black superimposed on red ; (*c*) torus with vertical bands (geisa 63) ; this meander resembles the revetment of the fifth type from the Olympieion, Syracuse (rak. cor. 29).

Endless fragments of geisa show a wealth and variety of motives which almost baffle description : sometimes the eyes of the guilloche are filled by a black dot (geisa 29–32), at others by a red one (geisa 34). In other cases the guilloche is single, the eyes filled by four-petalled rosettes (geisa 41, 42), one specimen on a very large scale has multi-petalled rosettes (geisa 43).

Really astonishing are the enormous slabs measuring respectively cm. 61 and cm. 65 × 92 and decorated, the first with double guilloche, the curving bands in red and black, the triangular spaces filled by five-leaved palmettes, the eyes by five-petalled rosettes (geisa 22), and the second with double guilloche with five-leaved palmettes and seven-petalled rosettes; this latter casing is painted on the lower surface with a narrow band of broken black meander finished off by a torus with red and black diagonal bands (geisa 26). One other geison was even more colossal, but is now reduced to tiny pieces: it consisted of a double guilloche, the eyes filled by eight-petalled rosettes which alone measure cm. 8·5 in diameter (geisa 27). Perhaps these immense slabs belonged to the same revetment as the monstrous kalypter, which is on so large a scale that one is filled with amazement at the size of the temple whose ridge-pole was covered by such a stupendous cover-tile (kal. 12).

The most beautiful of all the revetments is one with a very unusual design. Here the Doric leaf is reduced to a red filling outlined by a broad black horseshoe-shaped band ending in spirals; between each pair of these motives, which are rather widely spaced, are graceful red and black seven-leaved anthemia, the middle leaf surmounted by a big red bud sheathed in a black calyx. This bud reaches the same level as the top of the horseshoe arch and, like it, is detached from the background, so that the whole top line of the slab is in the round. Below this design is a band of astragalos in relief moulded round on to the lower surface of the casing, which is decorated with broken meander in red and black between two rows of astragalos (rak. cor. 32, fig. 30). Relief and painting are so skilfully blended on this revetment that it gives an extraordinarily rich yet graceful effect to the design.

Another work said to have come from the acropolis is a large round Gorgoneion, the antefix or akroterion of an edifice of small dimensions. The mask is of the conventional type common to the middle of the V. Century (ant. 17).

The semicircular Tower M was united to the north front of the acropolis by a wall.[1] Beyond it was a wide ditch on the farther side of which materials from many different edifices strewed the ground and were built into the walls of later buildings. Among the *débris* were a few bits of terra-cotta, two fragments of geisa with guilloche (geisa 25, 30) and part of a lateral sima, interesting because it is archaic in character with: (*a*) square Doric leaf; (*b*) torus with diagonal bands; (*c*) fascia with black lozenges (lat. simæ 3). Between each pair of lozenges is the hole for the water-spout, which was in the simple form of a short, rather stumpy tube painted black. The lozenge motive is similar to that found at Gela, Megara Hyblæa, *Marazà*, Locri and Syracuse.

Connected apparently with Temple D (sometimes called that of Zeus *Agoraios*), an early Doric peripteros with 6–13 columns, were scanty remains of fictile decoration. Koldewey and Puchstein have demonstrated that the stone blocks

[1] *N.S.*, 1894, p. 211, fig. 11.

of the horizontal geison can never have had a terra-cotta revetment [1] which must have been limited to the lateral sima and the roof. On the east side of the temple, amongst the lowest deposit of material, Cavallari unearthed a sima which recalls the one belonging to the second revetment of Temple C with its lacy anthemia and astragalos in relief (simæ 7). Besides this, on the west side of the temple two fragments of palmettes were discovered, painted on both sides and fastened with long nails to the support beneath. These were palmettes of the ridge-pole (pal. 6), but no kalypteres seem to have been preserved.

Professor Gabrici's meticulous researches and his painstaking shifting of the confused evidence for the previous excavations have led him to the conclusion that the reports of earlier authorities as to various revetment fragments discovered at Temple F on the Eastern Hill were due to a misconception and that, as a matter of fact, all these pieces were unearthed upon the acropolis and were mainly bits of the sima and cresting of the second type of revetment of Temple C.[2] One writer copied from another without due enquiries as to the truth of the statements, and the conclusion of Koldewey and Puchstein that the pediment blocks at least could never have had a fictile revetment is the first hint of doubt as to the real provenance of these pieces. With them disappear also the triangular kalypteres, reconstructed in accordance with the specimens from Metapontum,[3] but in reality fragments of the immense rounded kalypter of the temple on the acropolis.

The *temenos* of Demeter *Malophoros* at Gággera to the west of the city was entered through *Propylaia*, and within the *temenos* immense deposits of votive offerings were discovered, but curiously scanty remains of architectonic fictile decoration.[4] The most important of these were slabs with figures in relief, apparently metopes from some small building. One relief depicts the bare feet of three persons walking to right ; on another is the body of a man from waist to thigh, clad in a full *chitoniskos* ; he appears to be in violent action and was, most likely, a warrior about to strike his fallen foe : a third fragment reveals only an arm grasping the right arm of another figure, this last wearing a chiton with short sleeves (met. 3). These metopes resemble those found at Gela, especially the slab with feet walking to right (ped. 5). Besides these metopes there were two large Gorgoneia which probably decorated the pediment of some small building in the *temenos* (ant. 23).

A survey of all the material from Selinus demonstrates that the likeness which has been so often pointed out between the decoration here employed and that of the Geloan Treasury, although it does indeed exist, is scarcely as striking as the many

[1] Koldewey, p. 109.

[2] Serradifalco, *Ant. della Sic.*, ii, pl. xvii, B, D, E ; Hittorff, *Arch. polychrome*, Atlas, pls. vi, 16, x, 4 ; Koldewey, p. 130.

[3] Hittorff, *Recueil* (Paris, 1870), pl. xlvi, 9 ; Perrot, *Hist. de l'Art*, vii, pl. xlv.

[4] *N.S.*, 1898, pp. 258–60, plan in text (Salinas) ; 1920, pp. 67–91 (Gabrici) ; Hulot, *op. cit.*, pp. 264–6, with plans in text.

noteworthy differences. At Selinus the cymation has not the pronounced curvature noticeable on the simæ of the Geloan type. Instead of the torus and projecting border above the Doric leaf, the examples from Selinus have a narrow band of single guilloche supporting the pierced cresting, itself the distinctive feature of this type of decoration. Owing to this cresting with its facilities for the dispersal of the rain water, there is no need for water-spouts, and consequently no need for the narrow fascia below the cymation where they are generally placed. This fact implies a radical change in the arrangement of the various elements with a corresponding decrease of functional purpose. Possibly this reduction of the area covered by the fictile revetment was hastened by the fact that at Selinus almost from the beginning metopes in stone formed an integral part of the entablature.

Not only is the profile of these slabs different and more nearly in one plane than that generally used, but the leaf-pattern on the cymation is also frequently quite unlike the usual Doric leaf, diminishing towards the base or frankly heart-shaped. These perfectly straight-sided leaves approximate more closely to the flutings of the fictile revetments in Latium and Etruria and, like those examples, the leaves are recurved and show that each one was painted at the back in the contrasting colour. This particular leaf, found in Sicily only at Selinus and Akrai, recalls the archaic sima of the seventh type from Syracuse and both may have derived originally from Corinth, for it appears again at Corcyra,[1] a Corinthian colony, and also at the neighbouring Troizen in Argolis,[2] where only a small torus separates it from the double guilloche of the geison, exactly as at Selinus.

The influence of the Corinthian cycle may be traced also in the patterns of lotus flowers and palmettes found at Selinus in all stages from the archaic to the fully developed style, patterns which are a constant feature of the decoration of early Corinthian ware. As used on a large *deinos* now in the Louvre,[3] it is almost identical with the motive of the revetment from the primitive building under Temple C : the craftsmen of the fictile revetments, however, followed the ceramists in making the design less compact and more graceful at each attempt until at last they produced the rhythmic flow adorning the sima of the second revetment of Temple C.

History furnishes a clue to the derivation of some of the motives adopted, for Selinus was a colony of Megara Hyblæa with certain adherents from the older Megara. Now from the Treasury of the Megarians at Olympia comes just such a pattern of lotus flowers and palmettes addorsed as that of the earlier revetment of Temple C ; there again, moreover, a cresting with palmettes rose above the sima,[4] but at Olympia the work was later than at Selinus and may be dated

[1] Doerpfeld, *Athen. Mitt.*, xxxix (1914), fig. 4.
[2] Ph. E. Legrand, *B.C.H.*, xxix (1905), p. 271, figs. 3–4.
[3] Pottier, *Vases Ant. du Louvre*, p. 81, pl. lxi, E 874 ; Perrot, *Hist. de l'Art*, x, pl. ii.
[4] *Olympia*, ii, pls. cxix, 4, cxx, 3.

about B.C. 500.[1] Yet the analogies show that both the Megarians and their daughter colony drew from the same source, although the latter had incorporated certain elements and technical methods derived ultimately from the Corinthian cycle, but imparted to them by Syracusan or, more likely, by Geloan workmen.

SYRACUSE

An interesting story is related of Archias, the son of Euagetes, who, in expiation of homicide and in obedience to an oracle, was forbidden to return to his native Corinth but set out at the head of a band of followers to found new colonies for the mother-city. The expedition first founded Corcyra, and then, passing on to Sicily, chose a place marked out by nature as the home of a great city, the rocky island of Ortygia on the east coast.[2] One account states that the Pythia, when consulted, indicated the spot to which they were to direct their steps ; yet these legends have a later ring and it is probable that Archias, one of the ruling House of the Bacchidai, was sent forth with instructions to found a colony somewhere on the Sicilian coast, although the choice of the exact spot was left to his discretion. This was the earliest Dorian colony in Sicily and second only to Naxos in seniority of Greek cities. Nevertheless it was not the first settlement on Ortygia, for that had been long inhabited by Sikels, whose primitive dwellings were brought to light in the very centre of the present town, under the *cortile* of the archiepiscopal palace.[3]

The position chosen by Archias and his followers was a rocky island, detached from the mainland by a narrow channel of water, and forming the northern horn of an immense natural bay or haven, almost round in shape and encircled by long, low hills ending in steep bluffs, a haven renowned in history as the Great Harbour.

On the farther side of the island of Ortygia lies the Little Harbour, a mere outlet of the channel which severs the island from the mainland. Beyond the Little Harbour the ground slopes upward from all sides until it reaches a certain elevation to north-west where Dionysios later constructed his rock-hewn fortress of Epipolai.

The primitive city was confined to the island, which was furnished with a copious spring of fresh water, made famous by the legend of Alpheios and Arethousa.

The earliest history of the Greek settlement is non-existent, as was usually the case with these colonies. Apparently the descendants of Archias and his followers divided up the land among themselves and became an exclusive class of landowners, the Geomoroi, an oligarchy who lorded it over the subordinate

[1] Koch, *Röm. Mitt.*, xxx (1915), p. 51.

[2] Bunbury, in Smith, *Dict. Geogr.*, ii, pp. 1055–69 ; Freeman, i, pp. 328–67 ; ii, pp. 8–49 ; B. Schweitzer, " Geometrische Stile in Griechenland," *Athen. Mitt.*, xxxiii (1918), pp. 8–43.

[3] P. Orsi, *Mon. Ant.*, xxv (1919), cols. 480–1, fig. 72.

population of later comers with an admixture of non-Greek elements. The earlier possessors of the soil were now employed as husbandmen for the new lords and were therefore relegated to the farms and country estates outside the city. For the Syracusans soon began to enlarge their borders, and sent forth colonies which would consolidate their position by acting as outposts. Thus in B.C. 665 they founded Akrai, a site of military importance in the mountainous region inland to the south-west, and this was followed by numerous other foundations.

Vague allusions scattered here and there throughout classical literature seem to refer to a dynasty or series of tyrants. One of the earliest of these is Pollis, casually mentioned two or three times as the introducer into Sicily of a special kind of wine named after him, *πόλλιος*.[1] Most of these authorities refer to him frankly as king (*βασιλεύς*) of Syracuse, but one writer speaks of him, apparently by a clerical error, as the Sikyonian tyrant.[2] He is twice mentioned as an Argive, which looks as if he were one of the earliest colonists, a man of Argos who associated himself with the Corinthian expedition and by degrees obtained the leadership in his new home.

But one of the most important sources of information is the Lindian Chronicle, which records an offering made by him to Lindian Athena.[3] The beginning of each line is broken, but there are strong grounds for believing that the inscription has been correctly restored. As restored it runs : " Pollis, uncle of the Syracusan tyrant . . . . .eus, dedicated images which are called Dædalian, upon which was written : ' Pollis, the son of Sosilas, dedicated to Lindian Athena, he and his two sons, these Dædalian works.' As Xenagoras says in the first book of his chronological treatise." Thus the inscription reveals several important facts about the life of Pollis, for it gives his father's name, alludes to his two sons and mentions his kinship with a tyrant the genitive of whose name ended in *eus*. As there are at least eight spaces to be filled by the missing name, it is perhaps not too hazardous to supply Kleosthenes, who, since he set his name as dedicator upon the temple of Apollo in the VI. Century, cannot have been a mere private individual.[4] The inscription would then run : " *Πόλλις ὁ Κλεοσθέν]ευς θίας.*" [5]

A more dubious reference to a Syracusan tyrant is furnished by the pseudo Aristotle, who relates [6] that Diomedes hung a bronze necklace inscribed " Diomedes to Artemis " round the neck of a stag to which it adhered. The stag was afterwards found by Agathokles, King of the Sicilians, who dedicated the necklace

[1] Athen., i, 56, 31*b* ; Ælian, *Var. Hist.*, xii, 31 ; Julius Pollux, *Onom.*, vi, 16.

[2] *Etymologicum Magnum*, 197, 36 ; Freeman, ii, pp. 8–10, 431–6.

[3] Chr. Blinkenberg, " *Die Lindische Tempelchronik,*" xxxi, in *Kleine Texte für Vorlesungen und Uebungen*, No. 131 (Bonn, 1915).

[4] See p. 77.

[5] Κλεοσθένης, in the Dorian dialect of Rhodes, would have the genitive Κλεοσθένευς. Professor Blinkenberg kindly informs me that there is certainly space for 14, and possibly for 15 letters before ευς.

[6] *de mir. auscult.* 110, tr. L. Dowdall (Oxford, 1909).

in the temple of the goddess in Apulia. Does this legend rest upon an exaggeration of the story of that Agathokles who undertook to build the early temple of Athena?[1] We are told that when it was decided to build a worthy home for the goddess, a certain Agathokles took the contract for the work. He, however, chose out all the best wrought stones to build his own house, paying into the temple treasury the value of the material. But the stones had been consecrated to Athena's use and swift retribution overtook the sacrilegious man; he and his house were consumed by a thunderbolt. The Geomoroi sat as a court to try the case because the heirs pleaded that, as Agathokles had paid full value, he was guilty of no offence. Nevertheless the Geomoroi judged otherwise and confiscated his property to the commonwealth, but the site of his house was set apart as a hallowed spot. It sounds as if his story was another version of the history of Phalaris of Akragas. Possibly he was guilty of more than the sacrilegious act; he may not only have wished to make himself tyrant, but even succeeded in doing so and temporarily wielded such power as to give some colour to the exaggerated legendary appellation of "King of the Sicilians." His fate seems to confirm this conjecture, for had his offence been merely impious, the Geomoroi would have been satisfied with the divine vengeance or at least have made restitution to Athena from the dead man's estate. Instead of that his property was confiscated to the commonwealth—a proceeding paralleled after the expulsion of the Tarquins from Rome. In the account of Diodorus we have, in all likelihood, a version of the affair as presented by Syracusans of a later age who wished to efface the memory of the earliest tyrants. It seems strange that "King Agathokles" should dedicate the necklace in an Apulian temple, but there must have been constant intercourse at that period with the Greek settlers on the mainland, both friendly and the reverse. Perhaps, too, a necklace which once belonged to Diomedes would be thought most appropriately offered in a sanctuary of the district largely colonised by the followers of Diomedes.

Syracuse in its early days was torn with internal strife and eventually one party, the Myletidai, were banished and took refuge at the Syracusan colony of Casmenæ. About B.C. 500 the democratic party within the city drove out the Geomoroi, and shortly afterwards the ambitions of Hippocrates, tyrant of Gela, caused him to invade the Syracusan territory. He defeated the Syracusans at the battle of the Helorus in B.C. 492, and encamped near the temple of Olympian Zeus, but refrained from doing any damage there. In this desperate plight Syracuse was saved by the intervention of the mother-city, Corinth, with whom she had always remained on good terms, and owing to the mediation of Corinth and Corcyra a treaty was concluded whereby Hippocrates withdrew his forces, but the territory of Camarina was ceded to him. At his death, the master of his horse, Gelon the son of Deinomenes, made himself master of Gela,[2] and when the exiled Geomoroi appealed to him, he willingly undertook to lead them back to

[1] Diod. (ed. Vogel), viii, 11. [2] Freeman, ii, pp. 173–222.

Syracuse. In all likelihood he advanced at the head of a considerable force; at any rate, the democracy at once submitted, and in B.C. 485 Gelon became ruler of Syracuse. He at once set about making his new acquisition a city of foremost importance, and entrusted Gela, his native city, to his brother Hieron, who succeeded him in the lordship of Syracuse also when he died in B.C. 478. Hieron was a great patron of art and letters, and during his reign Syracuse was visited by Æschylos, Pindar, Bacchylides and many lesser poets.

Under the Deinomenidai, Syracuse rose to supreme power and importance, but her history is no longer local, but part of the Greek world in general. Our concern is with the earliest period of the city's story, and the great constructions of Dionysios, the activities of Agathokles, go beyond the limits of the subject. After the city was captured by Marcellus it sank to the level of a Roman provincial town. In A.D. 878 it surrendered to the Saracens after a siege of nine months; the inhabitants were put to the sword and the fortifications razed. From this disaster it never really recovered, although life has gone on there continuously and the first constructions of the primitive settlers are now covered by the dwellings of their descendants, a fact which adds to the difficulty of archæological research upon the spot.

The island of Ortygia was dedicated to Artemis and her sanctuary was one of the earliest buildings in the city; it was probably near the fountain of Arethousa, but all traces of it have now disappeared.

Still more important was the temple which crowned the highest point of the new city, the Athenaion, renowned in antiquity for its splendidly wrought doors of gold and ivory, and for the shield which gleamed upon its summit and served as a beacon to mariners sailing in and out of the harbour. To-day the Athenaion has become the Cathedral of Syracuse, but the magnificent Doric columns are still visible, engaged in the side walls of the church.[1] The edifice to which belonged the sumptuous accessories noted above was that erected in the V. Century by the Deinomenidai; but on the same spot and with almost the same orientation there was an earlier shrine and about this pre-Deinomenid temple the story of Agathokles is related.

Only a small part of this early sanctuary is preserved, because it was destroyed by the Greeks when the sons of Deinomenes built the later temple, and by the Byzantines who erected a church on the spot.[2] The ground plan and extension are hard to define, because the long west side was entirely demolished and the principal façade was also destroyed by the work of installing the great *cloaca*, which was made to pass right in front. It seems to have been very long and narrow, a temple *in antis*, perhaps *prostyle*, but without *peristasis*. The blocks of stone are well squared and of excellent workmanship, especially those of the upper courses, but they are perfectly smooth, without *anathyrosis*. The complete

[1] Koldewey, pp. 68–70.

[2] P. Orsi, *Mon. Ant.*, xxv (1919), cols. 370–80, pls. i–ii.

absence of fragments of stone entablature or columns suggests that these members were of wood, a supposition strengthened by the exceedingly rich and abundant fictile revetment. The axis diverges considerably from that of the later temple, which rose, not directly on top of the earlier one, but beside it. All the technical details denote an edifice of a period, certainly early but not of remote archaism, probably the later half of the VI. Century.

The temple was surrounded by a large *temenos* containing other shrines, buildings apparently of an official character, a wide terrace adorned with numerous *stelai* and an altar surrounded by such a deep deposit of ashes and charred remains that they prove an eloquent testimony to a fervid and long-maintained cult.[1] This precinct constituted the heart of the State worship, the most sacred spot in the whole city ; indeed, the primitive sanctity of these monuments was such that when the Deinomenidai wished to erect a larger and more stately shrine for Athena, reverence forbade the ruthless destruction and dispersal of these relics of earlier piety, so the altar was carefully enclosed and the fictile revetments of the buildings removed, broken up and laid down in the area to make the level for the sacred way, a method of disposing of consecrated property which was adopted also at *Marazà*, Locri.

As a rule, it is usual to attribute the material which comes to light during the excavations to the building where it is found, but in this case many reasons militate against this process. The first nucleus of terra-cotta decoration was found at the north-east angle of the substructure D, which, there are reasons to think, was a great altar ; the second within the southern half of the edifice E. Owing to the fact that these buildings were demolished to make way for later constructions, their ground-plan is only vaguely known, and nothing as to their elevation. The latter at least was an *ædicula* of comparatively small dimensions ; yet eight simæ and four geisa were found, all differing in scale and design, a superabundance for one small *ædicula*, even allowing for partial restorations and complete renovations, since even the material reclaimed can only be about half the original quantity, and it is certain that the remainder still lies undisturbed under the old sacristy of the cathedral.

Evidently these revetments belonged to several buildings, one at least, the temple, of considerable size, and their presence on this spot must be accounted for by some drastic change in the history of the sacred area.[2] The terra-cottas were consecrated because they adorned sanctuaries, and when those were demolished, the stones used in their construction may have been employed again in the more splendid edifices which arose upon their site, of ampler proportions and cased with marble, but the fictile revetments could not be cast aside like mere rubbish, so being gathered together they were confided to the hallowed soil of the *temenos* and thus entombed beneath the pavement of the Deinomenid level.

[1] P. Orsi, *Mon. Ant.*, xxv (1919), cols. 391–403.
[2] Orsi, *op. cit.*, cols. 683–6.

This proceeding may be compared with that at the Athenian Acropolis, where all the adornments of the pre-Persian period were piously buried before embarking upon the new scheme of construction.

This systematic destruction and transportation of the terra-cotta decorations renders it a most difficult task to determine accurately to which building the various types belonged and to classify these types, some of which are preserved solely in a couple of minute fragments. Only long and meticulous study on the part of Professor Orsi and his assistants could have produced some order out of the chaos, and their extensive acquaintance with similar material from other sites helped them to reconstruct in an almost miraculous manner whole sections of the geisa and simæ of the once splendid revetments.

The width of the slabs and the quantity of the pieces found furnished some clue as to the approximate length of the various members, even the dimensions of the broken water-spouts afforded indications as to what sized building the revetment must have belonged : the quality of the clay, the colouring, the scale of the designs as well as analogies from other places, all helped to differentiate and to correlate the diverse types. Particularly valuable in this arduous labour were certain angle pieces incorporating sections of the raking cornice and lateral sima, for they were proof positive of the juxtaposition of very unexpected elements. Other precious bits were tiny fragments or the angles of the raking cornice of horizontal geison ; the former give the inclination of the pediment, the latter reveal the birth and gradual increase of the motives and the way in which the geison was crossed by the raking cornice.

The first nucleus was found in an area of a few square metres at the north-east corner of the substructure D, yet it does not seem to have belonged to that building, but to have been brought from other places near by and broken up small to fill in the roadway. Only one fragment of the lateral sima remains, proved to be such by the base of a water-spout which protrudes from it ; the mouth of the spout was also discovered, but the pipe itself had disappeared (lat. simæ 15). Enough of the raking cornice and horizontal geison were preserved to permit of the reconstruction on paper of the whole pediment. Of the former there is the right angle showing the fascia with double guilloche, and a large piece of the upper part of the sima with the cymation and succeeding fascia of lotus flowers. Thus we know that it consisted as a whole of : (*a*) torus with diagonal bands ; (*b*) elongated meander ; (*c*) Doric leaf in red and black with a small three-leaved palmette on the cream ground between each pair of leaves ; (*d*) torus with diagonal bands ; (*e*) fascia with lotus flowers pointing alternately upwards and downwards and united by intertwining stems ; (*f*) torus with vertical bands ; (*g*) fascia with double guilloche ; (*h*) double torus (rak. cor. 17, fig. 26). The horizontal geison exactly repeats the design.

On no other fictile revetment is there a lotus pattern quite like the one here used, for that from Selinus is enframed in the winding stems (rak. cor. 19). The closest comparison is the motives on certain early Corinthian vases. There is a variation of this type which differs only in the lotus pattern, for here the lotus flowers are addorsed and alternate with addorsed flabelliform palmettes, whilst between each pair are two tiny palmettes enframed in the twining stems (rak. cor. 18). This design is close to but rather more complicated than the one from the Hall of Echo, Olympia[1]; it is, however, practically identical with the pattern introduced on a vase found at Ægina, although there the two little palmettes are not inserted between the stems.[2] Given the identical scale of these simæ with almost the same motives employed in the same order, one cannot but imagine that one covered the pediment and the other the lateral sima, although there is no precedent for such a slight change of design, since they are usually identical or entirely different.

The second nucleus came to light within the *ædicula* E and the pieces were far more numerous and complete. These revetments are obviously not all from the same building, but from many constructions of different sizes and periods; therefore it seems best not to discuss them in chronological order, but to adhere to Professor Orsi's classification, which has the merit of presenting first the most complete specimens.

The first type of revetment was very rich and has been preserved in such large quantities that it has been possible with the extant slabs to reconstruct sections of several metres in length. Here again an angle of the raking cornice and lateral sima was discovered, a piece of inestimable value in establishing the juxtaposition of such absolutely diverse motives. The lateral sima had: (*a*) torus with diagonal bands; (*b*) projecting border adorned with a cream cross on a particoloured square alternating with a cream rosette on a black or red square; (*c*) bold Doric leaf, each pair separated by a black dart; (*d*) torus with diagonal bands to left; (*e*) fascia with a metope-like arrangement of cream rosettes on a light square bordered by herringbone pattern: every alternate square is black and contains a water-spout; (*f*) torus with diagonal bands to right; (*g*) geison with double guilloche (lat. simæ 16, fig. 7). The dart between the Doric leaf is found at Croton (lat. simæ 12), but there is no precise parallel in Sicily or Magna Græcia to the arrangement of the rosettes, although they appear within a circle at S. Mauro (simæ 4); at Delphi they are found upon a sima[3]; at the Gorgon Temple, Garitsà, on the other hand, rosettes and herringbone were combined, and on the temple to north of the Gorgon Temple they figure on a lateral sima, for the water-spouts (now destroyed) must have protruded between them.[4] The tubular spouts were set so close together that they were very numerous. They were composed of two tubes which fitted into one another and decreased in

[1] *Olympia*, ii, pl. cxvi, 5.
[2] *A.Z.*, 1882, pl. x; Perrot, *Hist. de l'Art*, x, pp. 75, 79, figs. 66, 69.
[3] Koch, *Röm. Mitt.*, xxx (1915), fig. 47.
[4] Koch, *op. cit.*, p. 96; Doerpfeld, *Athen. Mitt.*, xxxix (1914), p. 167, fig. 4.

circumference as they reached the mouth. The lip was flattened out and painted with groups of three lines ; a few centimetres behind the lip a broad concave disc, decorated with a rosette, was placed (spouts 11). These slabs of the lateral sima were painted at the back with letters in red to indicate their place in the series. A few other examples of this practice have been found, but none so numerous as these with the single exception of S. Mauro, where the letters were scratched and then filled in with colour.[1]

The torus and projecting border of the raking cornice were decorated with the same designs as those of the lateral sima, but the Doric leaf of the cymation was separated by a small reversed two-leaved palmette followed by a fascia with four rows of transverse chequer pattern bordered by a torus ; below this was a border of tongue pattern in red and black and beneath this at frequent intervals hung small flabelliform palmettes which served as a drop and broke the rigid line of the cornice (pen. pal. 1, fig. 25). This raking cornice was moulded with a forked support at the back, of almost the same length as the front slab, and was fastened by metal nails to a wooden beam inserted between the front and back walls of the cornice. This convex support was painted with a simple leaf pattern (rak. cor. 11, fig. 25) ; the same system of strengthening the raking cornice has been found at Rhegium (rak. cor. 2). The two-leaved palmette between the Doric leaf is the precise design found on the raking cornice from the Geloan Treasury, which, like this one, also shows a dissimilarity between the leaf pattern of the cornice and that of the lateral sima.[2] The fascia of chequer pattern is found at the Olympieion, Syracuse (rak. cor. 16) ; on a raking cornice from S. Mauro (rak. cor. 10) ; on a sima from the Athenian Acropolis,[3] and also on one from Mykenai.[4] In Magna Græcia, in the few instances where this motive was employed, for example at Locri (lat. simæ 11) or at Metaurum (lat. simæ 10), it was placed on the projecting border above the Doric leaf ; in Sicily it was invariably black only when on the projecting border ; when, on the contrary, it formed the broad fascia below the leaf pattern, it was in red and black and affords an interesting example of how the scheme of the lateral sima was "split," the guilloche of the geison being carried on round the horizontal geison, and its place on the raking cornice being supplied by the fascia with chequer pattern ; on the pediment of Temple C at Selinus the guilloche of the lateral sima runs along the horizontal geison, and is substituted on the raking cornice by the anthemion pattern. This system has the advantage of harmonising the complete scheme of decoration, and at the same time monotony is avoided by the introduction of these supplementary motives. The pendent palmettes are a feature hitherto unobserved in any other revetment,

[1] Orsi, *op. cit.*, fig. 227.

[2] Doerpfeld, pl. i, 1, 3 ; *Olympia*, ii, pl. cxvii.

[3] Casson, *Cat. Acrop. Mus.*, ii, p. 291, No. 93 ; Wiegand, *Die archaïsche Porosarchitektur* (Cassel, 1904), fig. 192.

[4] Koch, *Röm. Mitt.*, xxx (1915), p. 84.

with the possible exception of S. Mauro (pen. pal. 2) and Selinus (pen. pal. 3), but there can be no doubt as to their exact location. They are painted in red and black on one side only and at the base are clear signs that they have been broken off from some attachment ; there are also small vertical holes which held the ligature by which they were fastened in a pendent position to a base. This base was supplied by the lower surface of the geison casings, where there are marks of attachment at regular intervals and small oblique holes corresponding to the vertical holes of the palmettes, in one of which were the remains of a lead solder. The palmettes fit exactly to these points of cleavage on the slabs. Evidently the craftsmen provided against the danger of breakage by securing the pendent palmettes by a flexible ligature of lead instead of by rigid metal clamps. Thus they served the double purpose of *guttæ* and a hanging frieze which broke the rigid line of the geison. These pendent palmettes recall the hanging friezes from Etruscan temples and especially the little fringe-like border of the early revetment from Satricum[1] : the border of palmettes from Capua somewhat resembles them, for it also hangs down in the same manner.[2] It is noteworthy that the only example of a hanging frieze outside of Italy is from the VII. Century temple to north of the Gorgon Temple, Garitsà,[3] at Corfu, a sister-colony of Syracuse.

The horizontal geison was decorated with the double guilloche, but the under-surface of the casings, visible from below, was painted with a broad single guilloche and a narrow border of chequer pattern, and here again were the pendent palmettes (geisa 15, fig. 25).

There are variants of the lateral sima with very minute differences ; on one the cross on the projecting border has a diamond in the centre instead of a dot within a circle and the rosettes of the lower fascia have a line of dots all round the edge of the petals (lat. simæ 17). With this may be connected a second type of raking cornice, exactly like the first save that a fascia of bold black meander replaces the chequer pattern (rak. cor. 12). This cornice is forked behind and painted like the former one.

To this revetment one is tempted to attribute the large painted kalypter of the ridge-pole found in the early excavations (kal. 10) and also the palmettes in relief which spring from double volutes and were placed in pairs astride the juncture of the vertical kalypteres with those of the ridge-pole (pal. 3, fig. 53). A similar fragment was found in the cortile of the archiepiscopal palace, showing that the palmettes were a not infrequent member of these revetments (pal. 4).

Another extensively preserved revetment belonged to an edifice of small dimensions. Once more a large fragment gives the angle of the raking cornice and lateral sima with the base of a water-spout. This fragment proves that the lateral sima consisted of : (*a*) torus ; (*b*) black meander ; (*c*) Doric leaf separated

[1] Della Seta, *Mus. di Villa Giulia*, p. 273, No. 10145.
[2] Koch, pp. 87, 89, pls. xii, 3, xx.
[3] Doerpfeld, *Athen. Mitt.*, xxxix (1914), p. 166, fig. 4.

by two-leaved palmettes ; (*d*) torus ; (*e*) fascia with black lozenges between which the water-spouts debouched (lat. simæ 5, fig. 22). That this revetment must be considerably earlier than the preceding one is testified by the use of the lozenge pattern, nearly always a sign of early VI. Century work, and apparently never used except upon a lateral sima, as is shown by comparison with the fragments from Gela, *Marazà*, Locri, Megara Hyblæa and Selinus. It is almost certain that the sima was completed by a geison with double guilloche. The water-spouts have certain peculiarities, for the end of the pipe protrudes some way beyond the rosette-painted disc and ends in a broad lip also decorated with a ten-petalled rosette, thus forming a kind of corona within the larger rosette of the mouth. The outside of the lip is ornamented with a zone of half-diamonds (spouts 13).

There are only two pieces of the third type which is similar to the second, but of smaller and squarer dimensions (rak. cor. 9, fig. 23).

The fourth type is represented by a lateral sima only, but its whole character is archaic and especially the fascia of lozenge pattern and the rather stumpy water-spouts. It is composed as follows: (*a*) torus ; (*b*) elongated meander ; (*c*) heart-shaped Doric leaf, each pair separated by a small black heart-shaped leaf ; (*d*) torus ; (*e*) fascia with black lozenges and water-spouts (lat. simæ 4, fig. 2). The heart-shaped leaf pattern is precisely that employed at Caulonia (lat. simæ 14) and on the Geloan Treasury[1] ; the lozenge pattern has been noted on the revetment of the second type.

The fifth type also consists of two pieces which, unfortunately, only give the upper part of the sima. Here one sees a projecting border with four rows of chequer pattern above a Doric leaf diminishing to a sharp point and separated by a black dart (simæ 10, fig. 45). One little peculiarity is here noticeable, each leaf is surrounded by a margin of the contrasting colour, instead of the black outline generally used. The pointed leaf and dart appear on a lateral sima from Croton (lat. simæ 12), although the example from Locri is even closer, for that has the chequer pattern above the pointed leaf (lat. simæ 11).

Type six is reduced to very meagre proportions, only a bit of the cymation upon which the lanciolated leaves contain a superimposed red heart. Below is a torus with chevrons (simæ 17, fig. 46).

The seventh type is perhaps the most archaic of all and is distinguished by some very unusual traits. It is a lateral sima with a leaf pattern which does not diminish towards the base above a red band between two black lines. In this sima the water-spouts debouch from the cymation itself, and not, as usual, from the fascia below (lat. simæ 1, fig. 1). These squarely formed leaves are only met with on a very early cornice from Granmichele (rak. cor. 1), but they must have been the prototype from which derived the square recurved leaf of both the first and second revetments of Temple C, Selinus

[1] *Olympia*, ii, pl. cxvii.

(lat. simæ 20, 21), and the one from Akrai (geisa 35), this latter site a colony of Syracuse.

There are various fragments of geisa which cannot be assigned to any particular revetment. One double guilloche pattern is identical with the horizontal geison of the second type of revetment, save that on this fragment the lower half of the double torus at the bottom is ornamented with vertical bands instead of chequer pattern (geisa 9). Another is a small portion of a double guilloche to left, bordered above by a double torus ; here the triangular spaces are filled by seven-leaved palmettes, the eyes by four-petalled rosettes and a similar rosette covers the sheath of the palmette, a grouping which produces three rows of rosettes placed axially. The geison was finished off by another double torus decorated with vertical bands and half-diamonds (geisa 17). An even more remarkable guilloche has bands in red and black, the eyes filled by concentric circles in red and black, the triangular spaces by five-leaved palmettes, always coloured in the same order, black, cream with a black spot, red, cream and black ; in this case as well, the sheath of the palmette is concealed by an eye with concentric circles. The pattern is bordered by plain red bands, and the whole treatment has a curious " *matte* " effect (geisa 37, fig. 38).

In the course of the excavations one antefix was discovered which seems to have affinities with the unusual guilloche. On a semi-elliptical field enclosed by a projecting border is a palmette painted in red and black in the same " *matte* " technique (ant. 57). The antefix is not unlike one found at Corinth.[1]

Not far from the north-east corner column of the Deinomenid temple and near the substructure D portions of a very important monument were recovered, unfortunately much damaged, but still capable of theoretic reconstruction with the help of analogies from other places. It was the centre akroterion of the temple and embodied a youth on horseback, the same conception which figured on the temples of Camarina, Gela and S. Mauro. The largest fragment is the youth's right thigh with the lower edge of his richly embroidered *chitoniskos* (cent. akr. 8, fig. 72). The work is very fine, of well-mixed clay ; the flesh is painted deep cream, and the indication of the muscles shows that this portion of the leg was in a horizontal position. It is three-quarters in the round, but the back surface, where it pressed against the horse's body, is left rough. There is also part of the left leg between the knee and ankle, showing the top of the high ἐνδρομίς, ornamented with cream rosettes on a red ground, and smaller fragments of the body and red *chitoniskos* with its embroidered border.

To the west of the *ædicula* E large fragments of a left wing came to light, painted on the outer surface with carefully defined feathers. Of the right wing only two small bits exist, but there are two pieces of a tail curled into a large loop. Besides these, the front leg and paw of a feline were unearthed, and a hind leg stretched out almost horizontally, evidently part of a seated quadruped. These

[1] Koch, *Röm. Mitt.*, xxx (1915), p. 83, fig. 38, 1.

legs are rather more than life-size and were modelled freehand out of a greenish tinted clay mixed with lava particles. They are covered with a cream slip, and there is hardly any plastic rendering of the muscles, which are outlined by black lines and rows of little dots to suggest the animal's rough hair. Another strangely shaped fragment is possibly the portion where the right leg joins the body, and here again the muscles are marked in the same way. All these broken bits together composed the figure of a seated sphinx or griffin, the lateral akroterion of some important building (lat. akr. 1, fig. 74). The mutilated fragments of a similar figure were found at Gela (lat. akr. 5) and from Megara Hyblæa comes a wing with long feathers coloured red and black (lat. akr. 4). It is remarkable that in the museum at Corinth is just such a wing as the one described above, the small feathers rendered by scale pattern, the longer ones recurved, for Corinth was the metropolis of Syracuse. Moreover, from the temple at Kardaki, Corfu, the twin colony of Syracuse, comes another similar wing, although in this case it may have belonged to a *Niké*.[1]

Part of a wing belonging to another figure was also found, but in this case the treatment is quite different, because the feathers are plastically rendered and then coloured, and, furthermore, it was unearthed at a spot too distant from the former wing to be connected with it (lat. akr. 2).

Remains of a very problematic group were found, again not far from the north-east corner of the actual temple of the Deinomenidai, problematic because it is hard to determine whether its purpose was architectonic or whether it was one of the ἀγάλματα displayed in the *temenos*. In favour of the latter theory is the consideration that even at a moderate height, far more when raised aloft upon the façade of a temple, most of the effect of the minute workmanship and the elaborate details of polychromy would be lost. On the other hand, the technical detail that the lower half of the figures was set against a background and only the upper half was really in the round, the locality where they were found, mingled with undoubted architectonic remains, and the fact that at Gela, and less certainly at S. Mauro, among the temple *débris* fragments of similar groups were discovered, all suggest that the group served some architectonic function. Against a black background stands out the figure of a Gorgon-Medusa running to left in the ancient scheme with one knee touching the ground (lat. akr. 10, fig. 76). Her broad face, staring eyes and pendent tongue are familiar to us from the great mask from Gela (ped. 1), and so are the spiral curls and the dart up the centre of the forehead, but the Syracusan Gorgon has no beard. She wears a red *chitoniskos* with an elaborate border round the neck, short sleeves and the edge of the skirt. Her girdle probably consisted of two serpents entwined as in the running Gorgon from Gela (cent. akr. 14) and another from Cumæ in the same attitude.[2] Great wings with recurved feathers rise behind her shoulders

[1] Koch, *Röm. Mitt.*, xxx (1915), p. 83, fig. 38, p. 97.

[2] E. Gabrici, *Mon. Ant.*, xxii (1913), pl. lxxi, 1.

and frame her face, and another pair of little wings sprout from the tongues of her high scarlet *endromides*. Under her right arm she carries the small winged Pegasos, and her left arm, bent at the elbow, is turned downwards with the fingers stiffly extended, in the attitude of the archaic runner. The whole group is a magnificent bit of vivid colour and forceful realism ; such a Gorgon-Medusa, in all her malign splendour, is full of an apotropæic quality which, even to-day, makes itself felt in spite of the shattered condition of the figure.

From Gela and S. Mauro (lat. akr. 11, 12) come fragments which must have embodied similar compositions, fragments so battered that it needed the more complete group from Syracuse to reveal their significance.

The Olympieion was situated in the low ground from which Plemmyrion, rising gently, slopes upwards into the steep headland fronting the open sea.[1] The temple faced the island across the intervening stretch of the Great Harbour ; its position was an important one, for it commanded the bridge over the Anapos and all the district to the south called Polichne, a name given to the suburb which gradually sprang up around the sanctuary, consisting of the houses of priests and officials, the many offices connected with the sacred edifice and the booths of sellers of votive offerings. Only two columns now stand, stumpy monoliths without *entasis*, and such fragments of architecture as have been recovered all testify to the extremely archaic character of the building. It was almost certainly a *hexastyle peripteros* with 6–17 columns and must have measured about m. 20·50 × 60·00. All the details of archaism point to the VII. Century as the date when the temple was founded, but curiously enough, the first mention of it is in Diodorus (x, 28), who describes how Hippocrates encamped near by, yet refrained from doing any damage. But his pious wrath was aroused by the discovery of certain miscreants, amongst them the priest of the shrine, carrying off the precious offerings and even the gold-embroidered robe of Zeus himself. Hippocrates angrily drove the robbers back to the city, but history does not relate what befell the treasures, or acquaint us with the priest's version of the incident. This story shows that the shrine was an ancient and long-famous one where a vast store of offerings had accumulated ; we may also gather from it that the image of Zeus was a wooden *xoanon* whose primitive crudity was decorously shrouded under the sumptuous robe.

A further proof of the extreme antiquity of the temple is the fact that at least five quite different types of fictile revetment were found during the excavations, testifying to successive restorations throughout a long period of years, and giving evidence, in spite of a gradual development, of a close adherence to ancient tradition. The close-grained clay is of a peculiarly lovely rosy tint ; it was mixed with particles of lava to give it resilience and was covered with a slip of very pure clay. The fictile slabs were attached to the framework beneath

[1] P. Orsi, *Mon. Ant.*, xiii (1903), cols. 369–92, pls. xvii, xviii ; Serradifalco, *Le Ant. di Sic.*, iv, pp. 153 f., pl. xxix ; Koldewey, pp. 66–8.

by means of metal clamps. Of course some of the pieces may have belonged to buildings in the temple precinct and all one can attempt with such a mass of material is to make a conjectural grouping according to style, analogies or qualities of clay.

What appears to be the earliest revetment is part of a lateral sima : (*a*) torus ; (*b*) projecting border, blurred ; (*c*) cymation with Doric leaf arranged red, cream, black, cream successively ; (*d*) torus with closely set red and black diagonal bands ; (*e*) fascia with black lozenges, apparently seven between each pair of water-spouts (lat. simæ 9). Of the water-spouts themselves there is no trace, but comparison with similar pieces from Gela, *Marazà*, Locri and Megara Hyblæa suggests that this is a lateral sima of the beginning of the VI. Century and, still better, the fragments from the *temenos*, Syracuse and Selinus (lat. simæ 5, 3) show the nature and appearance of the spouts belonging to this type of revetment.

The revetment of the second type is represented by a sima with : (*a*) torus with diagonal bands ; (*b*) projecting border with black meander ; (*c*) cymation with red and black Doric leaf, the space between each pair filled by a reversed two-leaved palmette ; (*d*) torus with diagonal bands (rak. cor. 15). This sima is so exactly the counterpart of the raking cornice of the revetment of the second type from the *temenos*, that we are led to conclude that this also was a raking cornice and, in conformity with the model, to continue with the fascia of five rows of chequer pattern of which sundry small bits exist (rak. cor. 15), and to complete the whole with a fascia of double guilloche. The earliest type found on this site, and the one most in accordance with the archaic character of this revetment, is a double guilloche on a small scale, but of abnormal type as far as one can judge from the scanty remains (geisa 3). It is somewhat more evolved than the specimen of the revetment of the first type from Megara Hyblæa (geisa 2), but has not yet attained to the easy flow of the later motives.

Only shattered pieces of the water-spouts remain, but they were tubular pipes, the disc mouths adorned with rosettes or tongue pattern like those of the Geloan Treasury. The base of one pipe where it entered the sima is decorated with a zone of chequer pattern (spouts 15). A fragment of the triple torus of a kalypter is painted with diagonal bands in red and black (kal. 11) and numerous thick, flat roof-tiles were discovered scattered on the ground both inside and outside the temple (tiles 10).

A small antefix, which, from its archaic character, must be attributed to this revetment, is the head of a Gorgoneion directly capping the master-tile (ant. 4). The left lower half of the face is broken and so is the nose. The eyes are almond shaped, the ears large and very flat and the mouth recessed and furnished with sharp tusks. Up the middle of the forehead runs a deep groove, the modification of the dart employed on still earlier examples, such as the Gorgon-Medusa, Syracuse, to indicate a fierce frown.

The third type is very like the second, but it is on a larger scale. Here again it seems to be the raking cornice which is preserved with: (*a*) torus with diagonal bands; (*b*) projecting border with black meander; (*c*) red and black Doric leaf. A second fragment gives the lower part of the cymation, showing that the leaves tapered to a point and were outlined with a fairly broad black band; below was a torus with diagonal bands (rak. cor. 16). These leaves had no reversed palmette or even a dart between them, and the nearest parallel is the raking cornice of the second type from *Marazà*, Locri (simæ 8). This cornice, like that of the second type, had a fascia of chequer pattern, but on a much larger scale (rak. cor. 16) and was finished off with a double guilloche, the curving bands in red and black, but the three-leaved palmettes wholly black. In these slabs the nail holes are visible, although there is an attempt at concealment by placing them in the eyes of the guilloche (geisa 12).

The angle of a sima constitutes the fourth type of revetment. The profile of the cymation recedes sharply and is decorated by Doric leaf, but here, between each pair of leaves, is a small heart-shaped leaf. The eyes of the double guilloche below are filled alternately with a red or black dot (geisa 36, 45). The lower slab of this casing runs a long way back and is marked by three nail holes and a groove. Some of these slabs are decorated underneath as well, but the motives are much rubbed and hard to discern.

Quite distinct is the early V. Century revetment of the fifth type. Its most marked characteristic is the rosy-red quality of the clay. One large fragment consists of: (*a*) torus; (*b*) fascia with tongue pattern alternately red and black, outlined cream on a black ground; (*c*) torus; (*d*) double meander, black superimposed on red, the spaces filled by four-petalled cream rosettes on a dark square (rak. cor. 29). This double meander in two colours is similar to the geison from the acropolis, Selinus (geisa 63). Another piece is almost identical, only the rosettes are eight-petalled and above the meander is a small astragalos in low relief (rak. cor. 29). Even the cream of this revetment has a rosy tinge, owing to the strong colour of the clay beneath. One little piece showing a small torus above a fascia with bold broken meander may belong to this revetment.

The revetment of the sixth type with black and dead white has a well-marked scheme of design. Part of a sima shows: (*a*) cymation with red and black Doric leaf separated by heart-shaped leaves outlined black on a dead white ground, each containing a five-leaved palmette springing from double volutes; (*b*) torus with black bands; (*c*) fascia with double black meander, the spaces filled by an eight-petalled white rosette on a black square (rak. cor. 30). A slab of the horizontal geison has double black meander between two rows of white astragalos in high relief (geisa 60, fig. 40), whilst another little bit consists of the astragalos above black guilloche (geisa 37). These slabs follow the usual motives noted at Hybla (rak. cor. 25), Caulonia (lat. simæ 23) and elsewhere, but it is surprising not to find any trace of anthemion pattern which generally forms part of the black and dead-white scheme of decoration. A fragment of a palmette in relief springing from double volutes is of the same coarse red clay, and shows that the kalypteres of the ridge-pole were ornamented with palmettes in relief (pal. 8).

The revetment of the seventh type consists of part of a cymation decorated in red and black Doric leaf, each pair separated by a broad white band ending in volutes and enclosing a heart-shaped black space upon which is a seven-leaved flabelliform palmette, the veins marked with red (simæ 16).

Lastly, there is a very fragmentary revetment of the eighth type with the whole design in relief. Curved sprays ending in spirals enclose a reversed five-leaved palmette ; the space between each pair of sprays is filled by a bud (simæ 18). I know of no analogy for this type in Magna Græcia or Sicily, and the nearest fictile parallels are certain IV. Century slabs from Caere and Falerii ; but on some fragments of bronze *repoussé* found in 1903 at Mamariá, Delphi, the identical design is reproduced.[1] Probably to this revetment should be assigned a large and very realistic lion's head (lions' heads 22).

The temple of Apollo on Ortygia was probably one of the first shrines erected by the colonists, as was only natural, for the city was founded in obedience to his oracle and Apollo was looked upon as the ἀρχηγέτης of the settlers. Only two columns still stand, but the construction exhibits all the signs of remote antiquity. The temple was a Doric hexastyle *peripteros* with a double *prostasis* and a *pronaos in antis.*[2] On the highest steps of the basement below the three southern columns of the east front is an inscription in monumental lettering of which only the first words are plain to read : Κλεο ///// ης ἐποίησε τὠπέλλωνι. The arguments concerning this inscription have been endless.[3] The usually accepted restoration Κλεο[μέν]ης has much in its favour, since it is a Doric form ; but the space is more than sufficient for three letters only, and would be more adequately filled by four. For this reason Κλεο[σθέν]ης or Κλεο[κράτ]ης, being possible forms in the Doric dialect, are preferable to the suggested Κλεο[μαχίδ]ης, which is Ionic. There has also been considerable discussion as to whether this inscription referred to some offering set up in the sanctuary or was the dedicatory inscription of the whole temple. The analogy of other similar inscriptions, for instance the Treasuries of the Syracusans and Athenians at Delphi, makes it clear that it can only mean the dedication of the temple as a whole, and Κλεο . . . . ης, according to the Greek usage, cannot have been the architect but the dedicant. At that early period, the very first years of the VI. Century, it is incredible that a private citizen could have put his name on one of the principal shrines of the city. We are therefore forced to conclude that Kleo . . . . es, like Pollis, was one of the earliest tyrants, known to history only by this one act which marks

[1] Perdrizet, *Fouilles de Delphes*, v, p. 127, fig. 473.

[2] P. Orsi, *Mon. Ant.*, xiii (1903), cols. 373–81 ; Koldewey, pp. 62 f. ; O. Puchstein, "Die Tempel auf Ortygia," in *Beiträge zur alten Gesch. u. Geogr.* (*Festschrift für H. Kiepert*) (Berlin, 1898), pp. 199–206 ; H. L. Warren, *The Foundations of Class. Archit.* (New York, 1919), pp. 205 f.

[3] *I.G.*, xiv (1890), No. 1 ; R. Bergmann, *Philol.*, xxvi (1867), pp. 567–71 ; H. Roehl, *Imagines Inscriptionum Græcarum Antiquissimarum*, 3rd ed. (1907), p. 48, section x, No. 34.

him out as the forerunner of the later tyrants, splendid patrons of art and architecture.

Only one fragment of fictile revetment was found here, but that is an important one, the left angle of the horizontal geison where it was crossed by the raking cornice. It shows: (*a*) elongated meander; (*b*) Doric leaf with superimposed heart; (*c*) torus; (*d*) triple guilloche, the cream bands outlined with red; the eyes, filled alternately with red and black knobs, are not placed immediately under one another, but axially (geisa 40, fig. 32). The fragment, with similar angle slabs from the *temenos*, Syracuse (geisa 8), and from Gela (geisa 1), helps to explain the construction of the pediment revetment. On a soffit slab from Cumæ [1] is a guilloche which somewhat resembles the one here used, although there the guilloche is double, not triple. This particular pattern with knobs at the crossing of the braids is more frequently met with on Rhodian vases, for instance, an *oinochoë* in the Louvre, where again the guilloche is triple.[2]

Numerous sporadic finds of antefixes were made in Syracuse and the neighbourhood. These were usually Gorgoneia of the archaic type, which cap the whole face of the kalypter without framing of any kind. One has a broad face, the hair round the forehead is arranged in large spiral curls, the mouth is deeply recessed with pendent tongue (ant. 22). This example belongs to the VI. Century, but another of the early V. Century has only the face preserved with its squat nose, enormous tusks and pendent tongue which here also covers the whole chin (ant. 34). Still another is very broken, but this example has no tusks (ant. 21). A fourth, also without tusks, has the hair arranged in flat curls round the forehead and two thick "pearl-locks" behind either ear (ant. 11). The fifth specimen belongs to another type, for here the hair is in two rows of knobbly curls, the face is broad with puffy cheeks, recessed mouth and pendent tongue; but quite distinctive are the two flanking serpents which rear their heads on a level with the Gorgon's ears (ant. 25). This type recalls similar snake-flanked heads from Camarina (ant. 26), Granmichele (ant. 24) and Ruvo (ant. 27). Lastly, there is an antefix with a Satyr's head; he has a squat nose, beard in rough locks, single straight moustache and widely open eyes (ant. 44), a V. Century work from some small shrine.

The very beautiful female head found in the *Necropolis del Fusco* [3] is not an antefix as commonly stated, but an extremely fine example of the votive heads found in such quantities at Gela, Akragas, Locri and other places. It is worth noting that the clay is of the same excellent quality and rosy tint as that used for the rosy-red revetment of the Olympieion. This rosy clay imparts a living quality to the flesh, enhanced by the delicate features and exquisite care of the

[1] E. Gabrici, *Mon. Ant.*, xxii (1913), col. 552, fig. 200.

[2] E. Pottier, *Vases Ant. du Louvre*, 2me Série, pl. lii, E658.

[3] L. Mauceri, *Ann. d. Inst.*, 1877, p. 43, *Tav. agg.* A, B2; Kekulé, *Terrak. von Sic.*, pl. v; *Bull. Comm. Sic.*, vi (1873), pls. i, 3, iii, 10.

modelling, so that the head has a subtle charm quite unique among figures of this type. A replica was found in the necropolis in 1842 and is now in the possession of Conte Mezio at Syracuse.

The fictile revetments from Syracuse show certain analogies with those from Selinus and the Geloan Treasury, but they are for the most part earlier than those from the other two sites, where long practice has enabled the craftsman to select suitable motives for appropriate members of the entablature, whereas at Syracuse the art was still in the initial stages, designs were tried, altered, rejected or put to another use.

The changes in the Doric leaf well illustrate these experiments. In the extremely archaic sima of the seventh type the squarely shaped leaves without diminution towards the base resemble the design of a sima from the Athenian Acropolis,[1] and the water-spouts which here project from the cymation were soon relegated to a more convenient position on the fascia below. This heavy form of leaf was gradually modified until the pointed leaf and dart of the fifth type was produced; then the dart was softened to the little heart-shaped leaf of the fourth type; this again into the small reversed palmettes of the first type.

It must not be forgotten that these terra-cottas date from a period when Syracuse was independent, before it had fallen under the dominion of the Geloan tyrants. Therefore, although the parallels with specimens found at Gela and with the decoration of the Geloan Treasury are evident, still one notes a distinct independence of treatment, a moulding of foreign influences to suit local needs.

The striking resemblance of many elements found both at Syracuse and at S. Mauro, the rosettes, lozenges and chequer pattern, the rosette-painted discs of the water-spouts, the palmettes of the ridge-pole, would lead one to believe that at one time Syracusan influence predominated at the smaller city.

The closest affinities to the Syracusan revetments are found at Corinth, Corcyra and Delphi, where there seems to have been an earlier Treasury of the Syracusans, later replaced by the one erected in B.C. 413 to commemorate the defeat of the Athenian expedition.[2] At these places, so intimately linked with the Sicilian city, certain distinctive motives recur, rosettes, herringbone and chequer patterns, the "*matte*" technique antefix, as well as the patterns of lotus flowers and entwined stems so common on early Corinthian vases. These analogies with ceramic art illustrate the theory set forth by Koch that the fictile revetments closely followed the technique of vase painting. In Sicily this practice is almost more closely demonstrated than in Greece itself, where the two methods, dark upon light and *vice versa*, are found simultaneously. In Sicily and Magna Græcia designs in colour on a cream ground are universal in the earliest period; only later, with the introduction of the black and dead-white scheme of colouring, do we find a reversal or interchange of the process.

[1] Wiegand, *Die archaïsche Porosarchitektur*, p. 185, No. 193.
[2] Dinsmoor, *B.C.H.*, xxxvi (1912), pp. 460, 462–6.

Yet in these terra-cottas there is another stream of artistic influence which comparison with ceramics again helps to explain. We have seen how closely the peculiar guilloche from the Temple of Apollo resembles the motive used on a Rhodian *oinochoë* ; a fine Rhodian jug, dug up in the very *temenos* of Athena, may have supplied the model for the projecting border of the first type of revetment, for round the lip is a zone of dark squares alternating with rosettes on a square ground. This Rhodian current must have flowed towards Syracuse, not directly, but from its source at Gela, for that city was founded by a united band of Rhodian and Cretan colonists, and must have been strongly influenced by Rhodian art forms and technique.

Nevertheless the Olympieion is witness how swiftly these decorations changed and developed, how short a time each artistic fashion endured before it was replaced by a new style, the earlier revetments yielding to the transitional type and that in turn to the black and dead-white scheme, ending with the last type in high relief, all within the space of two or at most three hundred years.

TARENTUM

THE story ran that the city of Tarentum was founded by a body of Spartan youths who had been born during the first Messenian War. Owing to this circumstance doubts were cast upon the legitimacy of their birth, so the young men, resenting this stigma, determined to seek their fortune in a new land and, sailing away under the leadership of Phalanthos, settled upon a most favourable site on the east coast of Magna Græcia, an island, or what was practically such, commanding an extensive landlocked bay, the only sheltered harbour to be found upon that coast.[1] The early sources agree in stating that the newcomers were received in a friendly spirit by the natives, who, according to Pausanias, already had an important city upon the spot. Whether or no this was the case, it is certainly true that the district had been long inhabited, for the extraordinary abundance of early remains, stretching back to remote prehistoric times, is evidence of a numerous and prosperous population.

The site was well chosen, for the country round was admirably adapted for the cultivation of the olive and also for rearing a breed of sheep celebrated for their fine fleeces. But the city's foremost source of wealth was the excellent harbour, which not only brought much commerce but also furnished an abundant supply of shell-fish, chief amongst them being the *Murex*, from which the renowned purple dye was produced.

Their rapidly growing power brought the Tarentines into antagonism with the Messapians and Peucetians, and it was in thanksgiving for victory over these nations that they dedicated offerings at Delphi. But about the year B.C. 473 they were vanquished with terrible slaughter by these very foes and their subsequent history was a long struggle against the Lucanians, the Messapians and even against

[1] Bunbury, in Smith, *Dict. Geogr.*, ii, pp. 1094–1101 ; Byvanck, pp. 63–71.

Dionysios of Syracuse. They appealed constantly to Sparta for aid, and at last became so enervated by luxury that they were unable to defend themselves, and upon the withdrawal of Pyrrhus from Italy, capitulated to the Romans and henceforth remained subject to them.

The only vestiges of the ancient city are two immense columns of a Doric temple built into an edifice of the present *Città* which occupies the site of the original acropolis.[1] It is remarkable that a place like Tarentum, which did an immense trade in exquisite figurines, *pinakes*, vases and similar terra-cotta objects, should have been almost wholly deficient in fictile revetments in the archaic period. In the IV. Century fictile antefixes and the akroteria of sepulchral monuments abound, even fragments of revetment slabs are found moulded in high relief and painted with a far more extensive range of colour than was ever known in the archaic period (simæ 20).

Nevertheless there is one VI. Century type of great importance, an antefix adorned in relief with a female head of an extremely primitive type (ant. 49, fig. 66). The head covers the whole field without framing of any kind. The hair round the forehead is treated in large, flat spiral curls and hangs over the shoulders in three thick "pearl-locks" on either side. The almond eyes, straight mouth and large flabby ears are all marks of an early date, and the whole contour of the face and treatment of the features recall the female heads of the earliest type from Thermon.[2] The antefix is smooth at the back: it is of pale red clay and there are no traces of colour.

A whole series of Gorgoneia seems to show the evolution of the type from the early V. Century until the middle of the III. Century or even later. The earliest examples are in low relief and cover the whole face of the tile. The Gorgon is usually bearded, with a trefoliate nose, recessed mouth, large tusks and pendent tongue. The long hair is arranged in five "pearl-locks" (ant. 30, fig. 61). In certain cases the face is surrounded by a circle of S-shaped serpents at first rearing themselves against a background, but later standing out free; identical specimens of this last-named type were found at Metapontum, evidently taken from the same mould (ant. 33). This type resembles that from Hipponium (ant. 29), for in both cases the wreath of serpents surmounts rows of tight curls. On another type the little serpents are reduced to two big ones who writhe outward from either side, a motive used for Gorgons found at Granmichele, Syracuse and Camarina in Sicily and also at Ruvo in Magna Græcia (ant. 24–8). One bearded Gorgon is without serpents (ant. 18, fig. 55) and from it derives a rather later type in which the features are somewhat softened, the face more squarely built and the ears embellished with disc earrings (ant. 19, fig. 56).

The variations on the theme can be clearly traced through the succeeding

[1] Viola, *N.S.*, 1881, pp. 379–83, pl. vii; Koldewey, p. 55.

[2] 'Εφημ. 'Αρχ., 1900, p. 191, pl. 10, 1; *Ant. Denkm.*, ii, pl. 53, A2; *Œsterr. Jahresh.*, xiv (1911), p. 26, fig. 26; Koch, *Röm. Mitt.*, xxx (1915), p. 56.

periods, becoming gradually modified and humanised in the process, until in the IV. and III. Centuries we are presented with Gorgons of the beautiful or pathetic type where the serpents are reduced to pleasing arabesques or coil modestly below the ears like pendent earrings.

There is one type of Satyr's head of the second half of the V. Century. The hair is arranged in scalloped waves, the beard marked with herringbone pattern to indicate fine strands (ant. 39, fig. 62). The effect must have depended largely upon the colouring, for the relief is not much accentuated.

There is an antefix decorated with a conventional lotus flower, a work of the early V. Century (ant. 59), and a fine slab of a lateral sima of the end of that century. It has an egg-and-dart moulding and astragalos, also in high relief, above a plain fascia in the middle of which is a very realistic lion's head water-spout (lat. simæ 41, lions' heads 18). Another even more realistic lion's head must be dated V.–IV. Century (lions' heads 21), and even later is the antefix with a palmette in low relief within a pointed arch (ant. 61).

TRINACIA

In the town of Randazzo itself no remains earlier than the mediæval period have come to light, but in the open country and especially near the *Necropolis* of *S. Anastasia*, five miles away, many records of an earlier epoch were discovered. They were, indeed, so numerous as to justify the identification of the place with the Sikel town of Trinacia or Trinacria mentioned by Diodorus and other writers and possibly identical with the Tyracia of Pliny.[1] Its early history is enshrouded in darkness, but it was said to be a small but flourishing township which remained independent until it was attacked by the Syracusans after they had vanquished Ducetius and subdued his vast domain. After fighting bravely in the field, the Trinacians shut themselves up within their city, but were at last overcome, when many of them, especially the aged, preferred death to slavery ; in token of gratitude for the victory the conquerors sent spoils to Delphi.

Diodorus implies that the town was totally destroyed ; perhaps the name was changed to Tyracia when the place was rebuilt after it had lain waste for a certain length of time.

Among the 2,000 objects found in the necropolis there were no architectonic terra-cottas, but evidence that such decoration was used here is afforded by the large antefix of a Gorgoneion, cm. 36 × 21 in height, showing all the marks of VI. Century art (ant. 5). Another rather smaller Gorgoneion from this district is now in the Vagliasindi Collection (ant. 14) ; it is so broken that only the central part of the face is preserved, but the almond eyes and squat nose reveal enough to date it in the first years of the V. Century.

[1] Bunbury, in Smith, *Dict. Geogr.*, ii, pp. 1247 f. ; Freeman, i, pp. 158, 511 f. ; F. di Roberto, "Randazzo e la Valle dell' Alcantara," in *Italia Artistica*, No. 49 (Bergamo, 1909) ; *Röm. Mitt.*, xv (1900), pp. 237 ff.

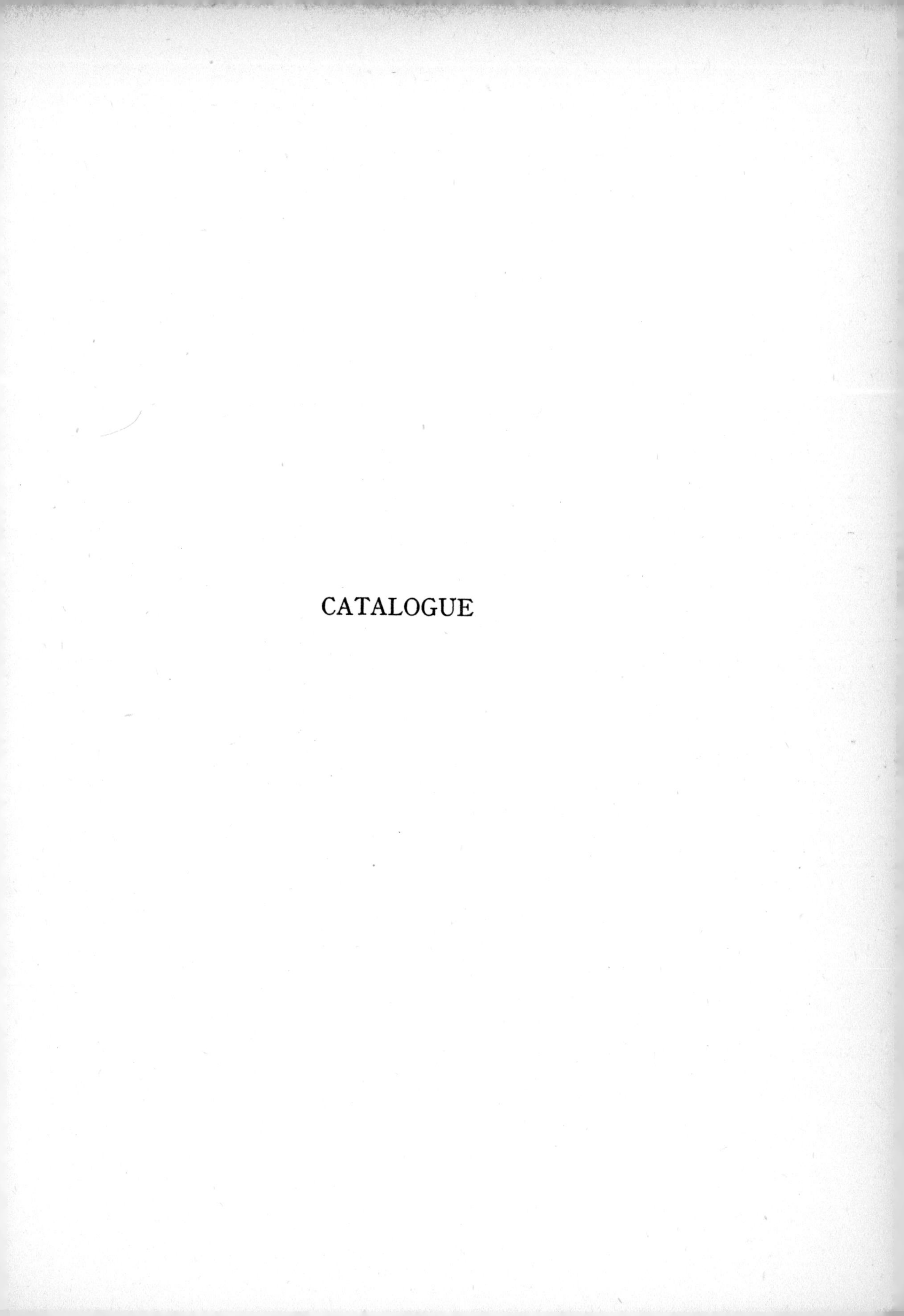

CATALOGUE

CATALOGUE

LATERAL SIMÆ

(1) Syracuse, *temenos*. Mus. Syracuse.

Revetment of the seventh type. A very low sima decorated with squarely shaped Doric leaf, bordered below with a red band between two black lines. A peculiarity of this sima is the fact that the tubular water-spouts debouched from the cymation itself and not, as usual, from the fascia beneath, which here, indeed, is reduced to the meagre proportions of a narrow red band. Early VI. Century.

FIG. 1.

P. Orsi, *Mon. Ant.*, xxv (1919), cols. 668 f., fig. 243.

(2) Locri, earlier temple, *Marazà*. Mus. Naples and Syracuse.

Revetment of the first type. Fragment with tubular spouts (now broken). It consists of: (*a*) traces of Doric leaf; (*b*) torus with diagonal bands in red and black enclosed within two black horizontal bands; (*c*) fascia with seven elongated black lozenges between each pair of water-spouts. The small fragment in the Syracuse Museum, consisting of torus and fascia only, measures cm. 9 × 11·5. First half of VI. Century.

(3) Selinus, to N. of Tower M. Mus. Palermo.

A small fragment of a sima, complete for the total length of the slab, cm. 95, but broken above and below. Still preserved are: (*a*) part of the square Doric leaf in red and black; (*b*) torus with red and black diagonal bands; (*c*) fascia with two black lozenges between every pair of water-spouts. Middle of VI. Century.

N.S., 1894, p. 217, fig. 17; B. Pace, *Arti e Artisti della Sic. Ant.*, p. 133, fig. 81, A; Koldewey, p. 80.

(4) Syracuse, *temenos*. Mus. Syracuse.

Revetment of the fourth type. Part of a sima: (*a*) torus with diagonal bands; (*b*) black meander; (*c*) pointed Doric leaf, each pair separated by a little heart-shaped leaf; (*d*) torus with diagonal bands; (*e*) fascia with a row of three whole and two half black lozenges between each pair of water-spouts which were set in a reserved space coloured black. The only trace of red on this design is the alternate diagonal band upon the torus below the Doric leaf. Middle of the VI. Century.

FIG. 2.

P. Orsi, *Mon. Ant.*, xxv (1919), col. 666, fig. 240.

(5) Syracuse, *temenos*. Mus. Syracuse.

Revetment of the second type. One fine fragment supplied the corner of the raking cornice and lateral sima, and on the two fronts this piece measures cm. 49 × 50 ; ht. cm. 36. The lateral sima is furnished with water-spouts and decorated with : (*a*) torus with diagonal bands ; (*b*) elongated broken meander ; (*c*) cymation with red and black Doric leaf, each pair separated by a reversed two-leaved palmette in red and black ; (*d*) torus with diagonal bands ; (*e*) fascia with black lozenges and with water-spouts projecting at intervals. Second half of VI. Century.

P. Orsi, *Mon. Ant.*, xxv (1919), cols. 660 ff., fig. 234.

(6) Megara Hyblæa, Temple A. Mus. Syracuse.

Revetment of the first type : (*a*) torus with black vertical bands ; (*b*) fascia with elongated black lozenges. There are traces of the openings for the water-spouts ; to left is a metal plug. Ht. of fascia, cm. 10. Early VI. Century.

FIG. 3.

P. Orsi, *Mon. Ant.*, xxvii (1922), col. 163, fig. 7.

(7) Megara Hyblæa, Temple A. Mus. Syracuse.

Revetment of the second type. A fragment of a lateral sima on a larger scale. All that remains is part of the fascia with elongated black lozenge, the spaces below the arms filled by Doric leaf. To right is the opening for a water-spout with part of the torus covering the joint where the pipe was inserted into the sima. Diameter of opening, cm. 10 ; ht. of fascia preserved, cm. 15. Middle of VI. Century.

FIG. 4.

P. Orsi, *Mon. Ant.*, xxvii (1922), fig. 7.

(8) Gela. Mus. Palermo.

Revetment of the first type. A small, much-damaged fragment showing : (*a*) Doric leaf in red and black ; (*b*) very narrow fascia with chevrons in black ; (*c*) torus with diagonal bands ; (*d*) fascia with elongated black lozenges. Middle of VI. Century.

Doerpfeld, pl. ii, 6 ; Koldewey, p. 136.

(9) Syracuse, Olympieion. Mus. Syracuse.

Revetment of the first type. A sima with : (*a*) torus, colour obliterated ;

(*b*) projecting border, blurred; (*c*) cymation with leaf pattern in red, cream and black alternately; (*d*) torus with closely set diagonal bands in red and black; (*e*) fascia (broken) with lozenges. Early VI. Century.

(10) Metaurum. Private collection, Naples.

Fragment of a sima consisting of: (*a*) torus with diagonal bands in red and black; (*b*) projecting border with four rows of small chequer pattern in black; (*c*) bold Doric leaf in red and black. The sima is broken off below. Middle of VI. Century.

N.S., 1902, p. 128, fig. 2, Nos. 3, 5.

(11) Locri, earlier temple, *Marazà*. Mus. Naples.

Revetment of the second type. A splendid piece of the lateral sima: (*a*) projecting border with three rows of chequer pattern in black; (*b*) heart-shaped Doric leaf in red and black; (*c*) band of reversed black triangles, point downwards. Between every five triangles is a semi-elliptical opening to facilitate the dispersal of the water. Second half of VI. Century.

(12) Croton, Temple of Hera.

Revetment of the first type. A fragment of a sima, ht. cm. 35 × 33, consists of: (*a*) torus with diagonal bands; (*b*) projecting border with broken black meander; (*c*) cymation with Doric leaf separated by a dart, alternately red and black; (*d*) torus with broad diagonal bands; (*e*) fascia with water-spouts. These are now destroyed, but from the traces of curving lines the spouts seem to have been masked by lions' heads. Middle of VI. Century.

FIG. 5.

N.S., 1911 Suppl., pp. 105 f., fig. 84.

(13) Megara Hyblæa, Temple A. Mus. Syracuse.

Revetment of the third type; (*a*) torus with diagonal bands; (*b*) Doric leaf in red and black separated by a black dart. The cream of the ground is unusually white. Middle of VI. Century.

(14) Caulonia, *Collina del Faro*; small shrine.

The sima was a very wide one and consisted of: (*a*) cymation with large heart-shaped leaves divided by a similar small leaf; (*b*) torus; (*c*) fascia with reversed palmettes enclosed within broad bands ending in volutes, every pair linked together at the neck. This pattern was interrupted at intervals by tubular spouts, two to each slab. VI.–V. Century.

FIG. 6.

P. Orsi, *Mon. Ant.*, xxiii (1916), cols. 783 f., fig. 48.

(15) Syracuse, *temenos*. Mus. Syracuse.

Revetment of the first nucleus. The lateral sima exactly repeated the design of the raking cornice: (*a*) torus with diagonal bands; (*b*) elongated black meander; (*c*) cymation with enclosed heart-shaped leaves in red and black, separated by cream spaces on which are small enclosed three-leaved palmettes; (*d*) torus with diagonal bands; (*e*) fascia with lotus flowers, one pointing upwards, the next downwards, linked by intertwining stems; (*f*) torus with vertical bands; (*g*) double guilloche with curving bands in black and red, the triangular spaces filled by three-leaved red and black palmettes, the eyes by four-petalled rosettes; (*h*) double torus, the first with diagonal bands to left, the second to right, thus forming a chevron pattern. The water-spouts projected from the lotus fascia. VI. Century.

P. Orsi, *Mon. Ant.*, xxv (1919), fig. 223.

(16) Syracuse, *temenos*. Mus. Syracuse.

Revetment of the first type which was found in large quantities. The slabs of the long sides consist of: (*a*) torus with diagonal bands; (*b*) fascia with squares filled alternately by a cream cross on a dark ground and by a cream rosette surrounded by a cream ring on a dark ground; (*c*) Doric leaf in red and black; (*d*) torus with diagonal bands; (*e*) fascia divided by stripes of herringbone pattern into metopes containing alternately a cream rosette encircled by a cream ring and the pipe of the tubular water-spout; (*f*) double torus with diagonal bands; (*g*) broad fascia with double guilloche, the curving bands in red and black, the triangular spaces filled by three-leaved red and black palmettes, the eyes by four-petalled rosettes. There is no system of "give and take" with these slabs, yet careful observation shows that the edges were flattened over with a tool to make the slabs adhere more closely, and they were fastened with metal nails to the framework beneath. VI. Century.

Fig. 7.

P. Orsi, *Mon. Ant.*, xxv (1919), cols. 642–47, fig. 226, pl. xx.

(17) Syracuse, *temenos*. Mus. Syracuse.

There is a variant of the lateral sima of the revetment of the first type which differs in very slight details. Here the rosette petals are fringed all round their edges by a series of black dots. The cross in the square of the projecting border has in the centre a diamond formed by the intersecting lines of the arms, instead of the circle and dot of the other sima. VI. Century.

P. Orsi, *Mon. Ant.*, xxv (1919), col. 646, fig. 268.

(18) Syracuse, *temenos*. Mus. Syracuse.

A second variant of the revetment of the first type is known by a large piece of the angle of the raking cornice and lateral sima and is therefore of the utmost importance. The lateral sima is broken at the top, but the part preserved shows: (*a*) Doric leaf in red and black separated by a black dart; (*b*) torus with broad diagonal bands to left; (*c*) fascia with "metopes" decorated with eight-petalled cream rosettes on a black circle within a red square; at the sides the "metopes" are not bordered by herringbone pattern, but by a cream line with fine diagonal lines in black. From the intermediate squares the pipes protruded.

A third variant has: (*a*) torus with diagonals in red and black; (*b*) projecting border with a cream cross with a diamond in the centre upon a square black at the top and bottom and red at the sides alternating with a six-petalled cream rosette; (*c*) cymation with Doric leaf alternately black with a red margin and red with a black margin, both outlined black and with a black dart between them; the space at the top of the leaves is filled by a solid black triangle. VI. Century.

(19) S. Mauro, archaic temple. Mus. Syracuse.

Revetment of the second type. The lateral sima of this small temple was exceedingly rich. It consisted of slabs, length cm. 60 × 37, adorned with: (*a*) torus with divisions in red and black separated by a pair of vertical cream rings; (*b*) small cream astragalos in relief; (*c*) projecting border with double black meander, the spaces filled by red squares; (*d*) cymation with lyre-shaped leaf pattern alternated and contrasted, each reversed one being filled by a cream palmette on a red ground; (*e*) small torus with diagonal bands in black; (*f*) fascia with black lozenges, interrupted at intervals by the water-spouts, two to each slab, the space between them corresponding roughly to their diameter; (*g*) torus with vertical bands; (*h*) fascia with double guilloche, the curving bands in red and black, the triangular spaces filled by three-leaved red and black palmettes, the eyes by six-petalled rosettes; (*i*) cream astragalos in relief. The height of this geison was cm. 29, and it was fastened to the framework by bronze nails. VI.–V. Century.

Fig. 8.

P. Orsi, *Mon. Ant.*, xx (1910), cols. 781 f., fig. 43, pl. v.

(20) Selinus, Temple C. Mus. Palermo.

Revetment of the first type: (*a*) square Doric leaf, alternately red and black, the recurved tops of each painted with the contrasting colour; (*b*) torus with vertical bands; (*c*) double guilloche, the curving bands all black, the triangular spaces filled by four-leaved palmettes, the first and third invariably red, the eyes by a simple black dot. VI.–V. Century.

Doerpfeld, pl. iv, 1.

(21) Selinus, Temple C. Mus. Palermo.

Revetment of the second type: (*a*) cymation with square Doric leaf in red and black, the recurved tops coloured in the contrasting tone; (*b*) torus with vertical bands; (*c*) broad fascia with double guilloche, the triangular spaces filled by five-leaved palmettes, the first, third and fifth invariably coloured red, the eyes with a red dot within a circle; (*d*) torus with bands in red and black. Beginning of V. Century.

Doerpfeld, pl. iii, 1; Cavallari, *N.S.*, 1882, pls. xix, xx; Durm, *Baukunst der Griechen*, zweiter Teil, 3rd ed. (1910), pp. 200 f., figs. 174–5; *N.S.*, 1877, pp. 69 f., Nos. 69, 70, 79, 80, 91, 93–5; p. 133, Nos. 10, 17–19, 39–43, 47, 72; Hulot et Fougères, *Sélinonte* (Paris, 1910), pp. 221–3, fig. in text; Perrot, *Hist. de l'Art*, vii, pl. viii, 2; Hittorff, *Recueil* (Paris, 1870), pl. xxiv.

(22) Caulonia, temple, *Monasterace*. Mus. Syracuse.

Revetment of the first type: (*a*) tiny torus; (*b*) anthemia separated and framed by lotus flowers whose outer petals arch over the anthemia which spring from double volutes between each of which is a triangular opening for the water to run away. The design is in relief, painted dead white on a black ground with little touches of red on the middle vein of the leaves and on the calyces of the lotus flowers; (*c*) fascia with double black meander, the spaces filled by a cross within a square. The lower portion of this slab runs far back and was secured by two nails. The lower surface is painted with a narrow band of black meander which gives the exact projection of the slab, for only the part visible was decorated, because that could be seen from below. VI.–V. Century.

FIG. 9.

P. Orsi, *N.S.*, 1922, p. 148, fig. 2.

(23) Caulonia, temple, *Monasterace*. Mus. Syracuse.

The second revetment is remarkable, because the design is painted only in black on a dead-white ground. The lateral sima consisted of: (*a*) black meander on a white ground; (*b*) cymation with a very slight curvature, decorated with reversed tongue pattern in black and red on a white ground; (*c*) astragalos painted only in white on a black ground; (*d*) broad fascia with white anthemia springing from double volutes and separated by lotus flowers whose middle petals are marked by a red line. The band which unites the volutes is also marked with red, the only notes of red in this scheme of a black and dead-white design. In the middle of each slab is a lion's head to mask the water-spout. Early V. Century.

(24) Locri, earlier temple, *Marazà*. Mus. Naples.

Revetment of the fourth type: (*a*) narrow border with very slight projection coloured red; (*b*) small Lesbian cyma, the leaves outlined black with a red dart between them; (*c*) broad fascia with anthemia and lotus flowers in relief upon a black ground. The anthemia spring from broad flat volutes and all the design in relief is picked out in red; (*d*) large ovolo alternately red and black.

Some of the fragments show the hole for the water-spout in the middle of the slab below the central anthemion. Early V. Century.

(25) Locri, earlier temple, *Marazà*. Mus. Naples.
One fragment of a sima exactly similar to that of the fourth type, but thicker and more carelessly worked. No trace of colour. V. Century.

(26) Locri, temple, *Marafioti*. Mus. Syracuse.
The lateral sima was very richly decorated with: (*a*) projecting border, design obliterated; (*b*) reversed palmettes and sprays of lotus flowers with tendrils in relief. Below the palmettes the slab is pierced by triangular openings through which the water escaped from the roof. This pierced design resembled a cresting, although a projecting border ran all along the top. Alternating with the palmettes are lions' heads which project from the face of the revetment like gutter-spouts, but they are not pierced. The height of the slab is cm. 34 × 70. These slabs have no system of "give and take," because the edge was serrated owing to the pierced pattern, but they were held together by metal clamps in the top of the border and occasionally by lead plugs shaped _⊓_. First half of V. Century. FIG. 10.
P. Orsi, *N.S.*, 1911 Suppl., pp. 55 f., fig. 42.

(27) Croton, Temple of Hera.
Revetment of the second type. About a dozen fragments of a sima were discovered decorated with: (*a*) projecting border with double black meander; (*b*) egg-and-dart moulding in high relief, the former painted cream, the latter red; (*c*) tiny torus with vertical red and black bands; (*d*) fascia with large black meander (?). Some of the pieces show the attachments of water-spouts. Upon the greater number of these pieces the egg-and-dart has a very pronounced contour, but there is a variant where the moulding is almost flat and this variant shows an unusual treatment of the egg and dart, for the latter, on the right side, appears to fold over the egg like a leaf. Middle of V. Century.
P. Orsi, *N.S.*, 1911 Suppl., p. 109, figs. 88–9.

(28) Locri, earlier temple, *Marazà*. Mus. Syracuse.
Revetment of the third type. Fragment of a sima with: (*a*) cymation with Doric leaf in red and black; (*b*) torus with broad red and black diagonal bands; (*c*) fascia with black meander pierced by a hole for the water-spout. Diameter of the opening, cm. 4·5. Second half of VI. Century.

(29) Caulonia, temple. Mus. Civico, Reggio.
The lateral sima had: (*a*) projecting border with black meander; (*b*) cymation with reversed tongue pattern in red and black alternately; (*c*) fascia with

anthemia and lotus flowers in relief on a black ground. At intervals were lions' heads to mask the gutter-spouts. V. Century.

P. Orsi, *Mon. Ant.*, xxiii (1916), col. 861, fig. 102.

(30) Caulonia, temple. Mus. Civico, Reggio.

A lateral sima of small dimensions, ht. cm. 19, is adorned with : (*a*) plain (?) projecting border ; (*b*) cymation, design blurred ; (*c*) fascia with anthemia alternating with lotus flowers whose overarching petals meet above the anthemia which spring from the curving stems of the lotus : the design is in relief and is painted white on a dark ground ; (*d*) fascia with double meander in relief. At intervals lions' heads project which cover the lower fascia entirely and the upper partially.

FIG. 11.

P. Orsi, *Mon. Ant.*, xxiii (1916), cols. 861 f., fig. 104.

(31) Caulonia, temple. Mus. Civico, Reggio.

A sima with : (*a*) plain (?) border ; (*b*) moulding with ovolo (?) ; (*c*) cymation with flabelliform palmettes rising from double volutes and separated by lotus flowers whose outer petals overarch. The whole design is in relief on a black ground. The colouring has almost vanished, but seems to have been cream and red ; the design is massive and rather squat with none of the lightness usually associated with these motives ; (*d*) fascia with double meander in relief, the spaces filled by large red squares. In this fascia is a hole for the water-spouts. The height of the slab is cm. 22·5, and there are three variants of the design. V. Century.

FIG. 12.

P. Orsi, *Mon. Ant.*, xxiii (1916), col. 862, fig. 103.

(32) Croton, Temple of Hera.

Revetment of the third type, very richly decorated with : (*a*) projecting border with double black, meander, the spaces filled by red squares ; (*b*) cymation decorated with Lesbian leaf in relief, alternately red and black ; (*c*) astragalos in relief ; (*d*) broad fascia with complicated black meander, the spaces filled by red squares containing eight-rayed cream stars. The immense lions' heads, set one in the middle of each slab, cover the whole sima. The height of each slab is cm. 30. Middle of V. Century.

FIG. 13.

P. Orsi, *N.S.*, 1897, p. 345 ; 1911 Suppl., 107–11, fig. 87.

(33) Hipponium, temple, *Coltura del Castello*. Mus. Civico, Reggio.

Part of a lateral sima, ht. cm. 34 : (*a*) fascia almost obliterated, with traces of anthemia ; (*b*) torus ; (*c*) egg-and-dart in relief ; (*d*) torus ; (*e*) cyma recta ;

(*f*) fascia with complicated meander, painted only: to right is half the opening for the water-spout; (*g*) torus; (*h*) plain (?) border. V. Century.

FIG. 14.

P. Orsi, *N.S.*, 1921, p. 483, fig. 13.

(34) Hipponium, Greek temple, *Belvedere*. Mus. Civico, Reggio.

Fragments which must be assigned to the lateral sima, since they show the remains of the lions' heads emerging from the fascia which is adorned with anthemia and lotus flowers, painted only. VI.–V. Century.

P. Orsi, *N.S.*, 1921, p. 480.

(35) Caulonia, temple, *Monasterace*. Mus. Syracuse.

Revetment of the third type, which was in relief: (*a*) projecting border with broken black meander; (*b*) cymation with reversed tongue pattern alternately red and black; (*c*) astragalos in relief; (*d*) fascia with anthemia separated by lotus flowers painted light on a dark ground. In the middle of each slab is a splendid lion's head to mask the water-spout. The dimensions of the slabs were: cm. 53 × 30. V. Century.

FIG. 15.

P. Orsi, *N.S.*, 1922, p. 147, fig. 1.

(36) Metapontum, Temple of Apollo. Mus. Naples and Potenza.

Revetment of the second type: (*a*) projecting border with double black meander, the spaces filled by red squares; (*b*) pronounced convex moulding with recurved tongue pattern in red and black; the tongues are square in shape and in the centre of each is a line, red in the black tongues and black in the red ones; there are six tongues to each slab; (*c*) fascia with anthemia and lotus flowers in relief; there are five motives on each slab, two half anthemia at the ends and one whole one in the middle, covered by the lion's head, and two whole lotus flowers whose curving sprays form spirals, twice coiled, under the palmettes. There is one lion's head in the middle of each slab. The sides of the slabs are dovetailed for the full height of the sima to make each one fit closely to the next. The slabs measure about cm. 61 × 39. First half of V. Century.

FIG. 16.

Duc de Luynes and Debacq, *Métaponte* (Paris, 1833), pl. vii, 1, 2; Hittorff, *Arch. polychrome*, Atlas, pl. vi, 9; Perrot, *Hist. de l'Art*, pl. ix; Rayet et Collignon, *Hist. de la Céramique*, pl. 86, 2; La Cava, *Topogr. e Storia di Metaponto* (Napoli, 1891), pp. 310–14; *N.S.*, 1889, p. 168.

(37) Metapontum, Temple of Apollo. Mus. Naples, Potenza and Paris, Cabinet des Médailles.

Revetment of the third type: (*a*) projecting border with double meander in red and black, alternately broken and interlocked; (*b*) convex moulding with square tongues in red and black in outline only, pointing upwards, but with no central line; there are nine tongues to each slab; (*c*) fascia with anthemia and lotus; here the spirals form three coils under the anthemia. The lion's head in the middle does not cover so much of the design. The sides of the slabs have an inset and are rabbeted to overlap the next slab. Middle of V. Century.

FIG. 17.

De Petra, *Atti Acc. Napoli*, xvii (1894), pp. 3 f., pl. i, 1, 2; La Cava, *Topogr. e Storia di Metaponto*, pp. 310–14; *N.S.*, 1889, p. 168; Schede, *Ant. Traufleisten Ornament* (Strassbourg, 1909), pl. ii, 10.

(38) Metapontum, Tavole Paladini. Mus. Potenza.

A splendid slab of the lateral sima with: (*a*) projecting border blurred, on the bottom edge is a black meander; (*b*) fascia with chevrons in red and black; then at right angles follows the sima proper with: (*a*) projecting border with double black meander, the spaces filled by a cream star on a red square; (*b*) cymation decorated with hearts alternately red and black, all outlined black, the lower space between each pair filled by reversed three-leaved cream palmettes with a red vein in each leaf; (*c*) torus blurred; (*d*) fascia with lotus flowers and palmettes painted in cream on a black ground, but with details, such as the calyces, in red. The outer petals of the lotus flowers arch over and enframe the palmettes. At the right side of the slab there is a raised curvature, showing that it was the angle-piece where it joined the raking cornice. The projection of the soffit is cm. 14; the projecting border measures cm. 4·5; ht. of sima cm. 19 × 56. As there are no traces of water-spouts, it seems not unlikely that a cresting ran along the top of the sima and that the water escaped through the pierced openings. VI.–V. Century.

FIG. 18.

(39) Metapontum, small shrine. Mus. Naples.

Lateral sima on a very small scale consisting of: (*a*) projecting border with double black meander, the spaces filled by a cream star on a red square; (*b*) fascia of the soffit with complicated black meander painted only, the spaces filled by an eight-rayed cream star on a red square. Then at right angles follows the sima proper with: fascia now blurred, but with a small lion's head projecting from the middle of the slab. The height of the slab was cm. 17 × 28. In the museum at Potenza is the mould used for this sima, showing that the fascia with the lion's head was decorated with lotus flowers in low relief. First half of V. Century.

(40) Hybla. Mus. Syracuse.

Revetment in black and dead white: (*a*) torus; (*b*) black double meander on a white ground; (*c*) cymation with white anthemia in relief springing from double volutes and separated by lotus flowers whose outer petals meet overhead, thus framing the palmettes. At intervals in this cymation are holes for the water-spouts, an unusual feature, because generally the spouts emerge from the fascia below the cymation. Second half of V. Century.

(41) Tarentum. Mus. Taranto.

Fine slab of a lateral sima: (*a*) projecting border; (*b*) egg-and-dart moulding in relief; (*c*) astragalos in relief; (*d*) plain fascia with realistic lion's head in the middle of the slab. Pale cream clay, no traces of colour. Ht. cm. 24 × 55. End of V. Century.

CRESTING

(1) Selinus, Temple C. Mus. Palermo.

Revetment of the first type. A cresting of palmettes and lotus flowers addorsed and alternately reversed, similar in design to that of the later cresting, but thicker and more compact in outline. VI.–V. Century.

N.S., 1876, p. 107, pl. v, A, 4–6; Koldewey, p. 103.

(2) Selinus, Temple C. Mus. Palermo.

Revetment of the second type. A splendid perforated decoration consisting of addorsed palmettes and lotus flowers, alternately reversed and bound together by intertwined bands, all richly painted in red and black. The height of the palmettes is cm. 13 × 15. Beginning of V. Century.

N.S., 1876, p. 107, pl. v, 4; Doerpfeld, pl. iii, 1; Schede, *Ant. Traufleisten Ornament* (Strassbourg, 1909), pl. i, 3; Serradifalco, *Ant. della Sic.*, ii, pl. xvii, B (erroneously stated to be from Temple F); Hittorff, *Arch. polychrome*, Atlas, pl. vi, 16 (upside-down).

(3) Croton, Temple of Hera.

Revetment of the third type. Two important pieces of this cresting were found: the larger, cm. 34, is the right branch of the long curving band which supported the palmettes. The lesser bit is one of the small palmettes which filled the spaces between the branches of the volutes. Besides these, there are pieces from two groups, one an Ionic palmette, of which there are about a dozen large and many smaller bits, and a lotus flower rising from the high spirals of the support. Thus we know that the design consisted of Ionic palmettes alternating with lotus flowers, rising free from a low background masked by the long stems ending in spirals. This cresting rose above the sima with lions' heads. Middle of V. Century.

FIG. 19.

P. Orsi, *N.S.*, 1911 Suppl., pp. 113 f., figs. 96, 97 (reconstruction).

RAKING CORNICE

(1) Granmichele, temple, *Pojo dell' Aquja.* Mus. Syracuse.

Only the left side of the raking cornice is complete, for it is broken to right and below. It measures cm. 21 × 29 and is of reddish clay mixed with lava particles and covered with a cream slip upon which a Doric leaf is painted in rusty black and purplish red, and a rudimentary meander upon the projecting border. The very simple form, without torus above or below, and the unskilful drawing show extreme archaism. Early VI. Century.

FIG. 20.

P. Orsi, *Mon. Ant.*, vii (1897), col. 261, fig. 44.

(2) Rhegium, temple. Mus. Civico, Reggio.

A magnificent example of a very archaic cymation. It has a forked support at the back painted with bold, simple Doric leaf. The front face has: (*a*) projecting border with double black meander; (*b*) cymation with Doric leaf in red and black diminishing to a point and separated by a dart. Ht. about cm. 75. There are other smaller fragments of this cornice. Early VI. Century.

P. Orsi, *Mon. Ant.*, xxv (1919), col. 649; Putortì, *Bull. Soc. Calabrese St. Patria*, ii (1918 Aprile), fasc. 1–2, p. 24, fig. in text.

(3) Megara Hyblæa, Temple A. Mus. Syracuse.

Revetment of the first type: (*a*) torus with vertical bands in black; (*b*) fascia with single meander, half red, half black in an unusual combination. Length, cm. 16. Early VI. Century.

FIG. 21.

(4) Megara Hyblæa, Temple A. Mus. Syracuse.

Revetment of the second type. A fragment, similar to the raking cornice of the first type, but with meander wholly black. One fragment of this same black meander is painted behind with simple lines in red and black alternately on a cream ground. The slab is cm. 4·5 thick. Middle of VI. Century.

(5) Megara Hyblæa, Temple A. Mus. Syracuse.

Revetment of the third type. A fine fragment of a sima has: (*a*) torus with black diagonal bands; (*b*) projecting border with black double meander, the spaces filled by an eight-petalled cream rosette on a black square; (*c*) cymation with very large black Doric leaf framed in a black outline. Second half of VI. Century.

P. Orsi, *Mon. Ant.*, xxvii (1922), col. 162.

(6) Metaurum, "*contrada Monacelli.*" Private Collection, Naples.

The whole slab of a cornice, about cm. 60 in length, decorated with: (*a*) projecting border with narrow and very numerous recurved flutings, alternately red and black; (*b*) torus with narrow, closely set diagonal bands in black; (*c*) fascia with double guilloche, the curving bands in red and black. Each slab is pierced by two round holes, apparently to allow the water to escape, for it is grooved behind. There are no traces of the attachment of pipes to this slab, and the pattern is in no way covered or blurred; the form, too, is that of a raking cornice rather than a lateral sima. Second half of VI. Century.

N.S., 1902, p. 128, fig. 2, No. 1.

(7) Caulonia, private houses, *Collina del Faro*. Mus. Civico, Reggio.

A fragment with: (*a*) narrow recurved concave flutings, alternately red and black; (*b*) small torus with diagonal lines; (*c*) double meander in relief; (*d*) convex moulding with lateral scale pattern. VI.–V. Century.

N.S., 1891, p. 67.

(8) Syracuse, *temenos*. Mus. Syracuse.

Revetment of the second type: (*a*) torus with diagonal bands; (*b*) projecting border with black meander; (*c*) cymation with Doric leaf, each pair separated by a reversed two-leaved palmette in red and black; (*d*) torus with diagonal bands; (*e*) fascia with chequer pattern; (*f*) torus with elongated lozenge; (*g*) double guilloche with curving bands in red and black, the triangular spaces filled by three-leaved palmettes, the eyes by four-petalled rosettes; (*h*) torus with diagonal bands; (*j*) torus with chequer pattern. The lower surface of the casing is painted with a narrow border of black triangles. Second half of VI. Century.

FIG. 22.

P. Orsi, *Mon. Ant.*, xxv (1919), col. 659, fig. 234, pl. xxii; Doerpfeld, pl. ii, 5.

(9) Syracuse, *temenos*. Mus. Syracuse.

Revetment of the third type, of which only two pieces exist: (*a*) meander; (*b*) cymation with Doric leaf, the red leaves with a black margin, the black ones with a red margin and all outlined black; each pair were separated by a reversed two-leaved palmette; (*c*) torus; (*d*) fascia with five rows of chequer pattern. It is similar to the second type, but of smaller and squarer dimensions. Second half of VI. Century.

FIG. 23.

P. Orsi, *Mon. Ant.*, xxv (1919), col. 666, fig. 239.

(10) S. Mauro, archaic temple. Mus. Syracuse.

Revetment of the first type: slabs of a small cornice, ht. cm. 24; (*a*) torus; (*b*) projecting border with broken black meander; (*c*) Doric leaf in red and black;

(*d*) convex moulding with chevrons ; (*e*) chequer pattern in red, black and cream. Second half of VI. Century.

FIG. 24.

P. Orsi, *Mon. Ant.*, xx (1910), col. 782, fig. 44.

(11) Syracuse, *temenos*. Mus. Syracuse.

Revetment of the first type of the second nucleus : (*a*) torus with diagonal bands ; (*b*) projecting border with squares filled alternately by a cream cross on a parti-coloured ground and a six-petalled rosette enclosed in a cream circle ; (*c*) Doric leaf in red and black, the spaces between each pair of leaves filled by a reversed two-leaved palmette ; (*d*) double torus with diagonal bands ; (*e*) fascia with four rows of chequer pattern placed transversely ; (*f*) torus with diagonal bands ; (*g*) small fascia inset with tongue pattern in red and black. These casings are painted on the under-surface with torus with diagonal bands and a pattern of large single guilloche, the curving bands in red and black and the eyes filled by six-petalled rosettes. At intervals from the lower surface of these casings hung small palmettes in relief. Small oblique holes are visible in the under-surface of the casings, and into these a lead solder was poured ; these holes fit exactly to corresponding holes in the bases of the palmettes and demonstrate that they could not have been fastened in any other position, but hung free, thus forming a drop or curtain, comparable to the hanging frieze of an Etruscan temple. This raking cornice was moulded with a forked support behind, which was almost as long as the front wall of the sima. Thus it was possible to secure the sima in position by setting it astride a rounded beam to which it was fastened by metal nails. The convex support in the rear was painted with broad, simple Doric leaf. VI. Century.

FIG. 25.

P. Orsi, *Mon. Ant.*, xxv (1919), cols. 647–60, figs. 227, 230, 233, pls. xix C, xxi.

(12) Syracuse, *temenos*. Mus. Syracuse.

A variant of this cornice of the first type of revetment is preserved in a fine fragment of the angle of the raking cornice and lateral sima. It is broken at the top, but shows : (*a*) Doric leaf in red and black separated by a small double palmette reversed ; (*b*) torus with chevrons in red and black ; (*c*) fascia with five rows of red and black chequer pattern arranged diagonally.

A second variant is represented by one fragment consisting of : (*a*) torus with red and black diagonal bands ; (*b*) projecting border with a cream cross on a square divided into sections coloured red at the top and bottom, black at the sides. The centre of the cross is marked by a black spot within a black ring. The cross alternates with a black square upon which is an eight-petalled cream rosette enclosed within a cream circle ; (*c*) cymation with Doric leaf alternately red with a black margin and black with a red margin, outlined black. The space above the Doric leaves is filled by a two-leaved palmette outlined only in black: (*d*) torus with red and black diagonals to left, margined in the contrasting colour; (*e*) fascia with bold black single meander. At the back the forked support of this cornice is painted with large simple Doric leaf in red and black. The lower surface of the casing is painted cream, but there is no design. VI. Century.

P. Orsi, *Mon. Ant.*, xxv (1919), col. 648, fig. 229.

(13) Syracuse, *temenos*. Mus. Syracuse.

A third variant of the raking cornice of the revetment of the first type has: (*a*) torus with diagonal bands in red and black; (*b*) projecting border with an eight-petalled cream rosette enclosed in a cream ring upon a black square followed by a square with a cream cross, the centre marked by a black dot within a black circle, the ground of the square black at the top and bottom and red at the sides: this is succeeded by a four-petalled cream rosette enclosed within a cream ring upon a black square; (*c*) cymation with Doric leaf in red with a black margin and black with a red margin, all outlined black, the spaces above left void; broken below. The forked support at the back is painted with immense Doric leaf in black only. VI. Century.

(14) Medma. Mus. Civico, Reggio.

Revetment of the first type. Two pieces belong to one slab consisting of the following elements: (*a*) projecting border with reversed tongue pattern, alternately red and black; (*b*) broad fascia with broken black meander; (*c*) torus with diagonal bands. Second half of VI. Century.

FIG. 27.

P. Orsi, *N.S.*, 1913 Suppl., p. 65, fig. 70.

(15) Syracuse, Olympieion. Mus. Syracuse.

Revetment of the second type. A sima of small dimensions and much broken: (*a*) torus with red and black diagonal bands; (*b*) projecting border with black meander; (*c*) cymation with red and black Doric leaf outlined black and the space between each pair of leaves filled by a reversed two-leaved palmette; (*d*) torus with diagonal bands. It seems probable that this cornice was completed by a fascia with five rows of chequer pattern in red and black on a small scale; of this fascia certain little pieces exist. Second half of VI. Century.

P. Orsi, *Mon. Ant.*, xiii (1903), col. 383, fig. 2; Doerpfeld, pl. ii, 5.

(16) Syracuse, Olympieion. Mus. Syracuse.

Revetment of the third type. A sima of large dimensions with: (*a*) torus with diagonal bands in red and black; (*b*) projecting border with bold black meander; (*c*) cymation with red and black Doric leaf outlined black. The lower part of this sima is shown on another fragment which proves that the leaf diminished almost to a point, and below was another torus, also with red and black diagonal bands. A third fragment supplies the lower fascia decorated with chequer pattern in red and black on a large scale. Second half of VI. Century.

P. Orsi, *Mon. Ant.*, xiii (1903), col. 382, pl. xix, 1, 2, 5, and fig. 1 in text.

(17) Syracuse, *temenos*. Mus. Syracuse.

Revetment of the first nucleus: (*a*) torus with diagonal bands; (*b*) projecting border with black meander; (*c*) cymation with pointed heart-shaped leaves in red and black separated by small enclosed three-leaved palmettes on the cream spaces between each pair of leaves; (*d*) torus with diagonal bands; (*e*) fascia with lotus flowers, pointing alternately upwards and downwards and linked by intricately intertwined stems; (*f*) torus with vertical bands; (*g*) double guilloche, the curving bands in red and black, the triangular spaces filled by three-leaved red and black palmettes, the eyes by four-petalled rosettes; (*h*) double torus with diagonal bands, the first to left, the second to right. There are numerous pieces of this cornice: one gives the angle of the geison; another the angle of the lotus fascia and the lateral sima, including the cymation and its border. This fragment measures cm. 24·5 in height. The colours used are brownish black and purplish red. VI. Century.

FIG. 26.

P. Orsi, *Mon. Ant.*, xxv (1919), cols. 637–42, figs. 223–5, pls. xviii, xix.

(18) Syracuse, *temenos*. Mus. Syracuse.

The revetment of the first nucleus has a variant showing slight changes: (*a*) torus; (*b*) meander; (*c*) Doric leaf as above; (*d*) torus; (*e*) palmettes addorsed and connected by intertwining stems; between each pair the stems curve outwards and enclose two tiny flabelliform palmettes, both pointing inwards. Colouring as before. VI. Century.

P. Orsi, *Mon. Ant.*, xxv (1919), col. 641, fig. 224 *bis*.

(19) Selinus, archaic Temple C. Mus. Palermo.

A little fragment with: (*a*) recurved leaf pattern; (*b*) torus; (*c*) fascia with lotus flowers addorsed and united by intertwined stems. Middle of VI. Century.

Doerpfeld, pl. ii, 4.

(20) Selinus, Temple C. Mus. Palermo.

Revetment of the first type: (*a*) square recurved Doric leaf in red and black; (*b*) torus with vertical bands; (*c*) anthemia and lotus flowers addorsed and alternately reversed, enclosed by entwined stems; the design is painted in red and black on a cream ground. The back of the sima is painted with a large, simple Doric leaf. VI.–V. Century.

Doerpfeld, p. 26, pl. ii, 2; Koldewey, p. 103; Hulot et Fougères, *Sélinonte*, p. 223, fig. in text.

(21) Selinus, Temple C. Mus. Palermo.

Revetment of the second type: (*a*) square recurved Doric leaf in red and black; (*b*) astragalos in relief; (*c*) anthemia springing from double spirals and separated by lotus flowers whose inner petals overarch; this design is painted in red and black; (*d*) astragalos; (*e*) black meander. This cornice is painted behind with a large, simple Doric leaf pattern. Beginning of V. Century.

Doerpfeld, p. 26, pl. ii, 3; Koldewey, p. 103; Serradifalco, *Ant. della Sic.*, ii, pl. xvii, E (erroneously stated to be from Temple F).

(22) Caulonia, temple, *Monasterace*. Mus. Syracuse.

Revetment of the second type: (*a*) black meander; (*b*) reversed tongue pattern in red and black; (*c*) white astragalos painted only on a black ground; (*d*) fascia with white anthemia and lotus flowers painted only on a black ground. VI.–V. Century.

(23) Metapontum, Temple of Apollo. Mus. Naples and Potenza.

Revetment of the second type: (*a*) projecting border with double black meander, the spaces filled by a red square; (*b*) convex moulding with reversed tongue pattern in red and black; (*c*) fascia with anthemia and lotus flowers in low relief; each slab has a whole anthemion in relief flanked by two lotus buds, and the design terminates at each end in a half anthemion. Middle of V. Century.

Duc de Luynes et Debacq, *Métaponte*, pl. viii, 4, 5; De Petra, *Atti Acc. Napoli*, xvii (1894), p. 5; *N.S.*, 1889, p. 168.

(24) Locri, Doric temple, *Marafioti*. Mus. Syracuse.

The raking cornice consisted of slabs measuring cm. 34 × 76: (*a*) projecting border with complicated broken meander, black on a white ground, the spaces filled by crosses in red; (*b*) cymation with leaf and dart; (*c*) anthemia in relief springing from double volutes and separated by lotus flowers. Each slab contains three whole and two half motives. These slabs well illustrate the method of "give and take" employed to secure them in place, for the side of each one is dovetailed so that it interlocks with its neighbour. They were further secured by metal clamps, mostly of bronze, although one specimen was of iron coated with bronze. V. Century.

FIG. 28.

P. Orsi, *N.S.*, 1911 Suppl., pp. 39 f., fig. 31.

(25) Hybla. Mus. Syracuse.

The design is in relief, painted dead white on a black ground: (*a*) very small torus with diagonal bands; (*b*) astragalos in relief; (*c*) projecting border with meander; (*d*) cymation with anthemia springing from double volutes and separated by lotus flowers whose overarching petals meet and thus enclose the anthemia. End of V. Century.

(26) Caulonia, temple, *Monasterace.* Mus. Syracuse.

Revetment of the third type: (*a*) projecting border with broken black meander; (*b*) reversed tongue pattern in relief, the centres marked alternately red and black; (*c*) astragalos in relief; (*d*) fascia with anthemia in relief between lotus flowers. Middle of V. Century.

P. Orsi, *N.S.*, 1922, p. 147.

(27) Caulonia, temple. Mus. Civico, Reggio.

The raking cornice had: (*a*) border with meander; (*b*) broad fascia with anthemia and lotus flowers in relief. The anthemia rise above double volutes; the outer petals of the lotus flowers almost enframe the anthemia. The design in relief is coloured red and cream on a black ground. The dimensions of the slabs are cm. 55 × 29·2. The slabs were joined by a system of "give and take" and also by metal clamps, shaped _⊓_, which were inserted into the top corners to knit the slabs firmly together. V. Century.

FIG. 29.

P. Orsi, *Mon. Ant.*, xxiii (1916), cols. 857–61, fig. 101.

(28) Locri, earlier temple, *Marazà.* Mus. Syracuse.

Revetment of the third type. The fragment of a sima with: (*a*) cymation with Doric leaf in red and black; (*b*) torus with broad red and black diagonal bands; (*c*) fascia with black meander. Second half of VI. Century.

(29) Syracuse, Olympieion. Mus. Syracuse.

Revetment of the fifth type. The slabs are of small dimensions and the clay is mixed with volcanic particles. Little fragment: (*a*) small astragalos in very low relief; (*b*) fascia with double meander, black superimposed on red, the spaces filled by eight-petalled rosettes, cream on a black square. These pieces are slightly curved. A large fragment has: (*a*) torus (broken); (*b*) cymation with Doric leaf in red and black, outlined with cream on a black ground; (*c*) torus with black bands (?); (*d*) fascia with double meander in red and black, but here the spaces are filled by four-petalled rosettes, cream on a dark square and further framed by a square black border. First half of V. Century.

(30) Syracuse, Olympieion. Mus. Syracuse.

Revetment of the sixth type. Fragment with: (*a*) cymation with heart-shaped leaves outlined black on a dead-white ground; in the centre of each is a five-leaved palmette, the middle of the leaves defined always in the same order; the first, third and fifth are black, the second and fourth red. The heart-shaped leaves are separated by a Doric leaf alternately red and black; (*b*) torus with black bands; (*c*) fascia with double black meander on a white ground, the spaces filled by eight-petalled white rosettes on a black square. Another fragment has: (*a*) cymation with heart-shaped leaves outlined black on a white ground and containing a six-leaved palmette springing from double volutes, the veins marked with red. First half of V. Century.

(31) Metapontum, *Tavole Paladini*. Mus. Potenza.

This cornice is on a large scale, for the slab measures cm. 24 × 71: (*a*) projecting border, broken; (*b*) cymation with hearts alternately red and black outlined black, the lower space between each pair filled by a reversed three-leaved cream palmette with a red vein in each leaf; (*c*) fascia with black meander; (*d*) small torus; (*e*) very large convex moulding. The lower surface of the casing, which is undecorated, runs back to a length of cm. 36. VI.–V. Century.

(32) Selinus, Acropolis. Mus. Palermo.

Splendid fragment of a cornice, broken on one side. The whole front surface of the sima measures cm. 21 × 27; the cymation alone, ht. cm. 7·5: the lower surface of the casing cm. 11 × 26. The cymation is decorated with a beautiful design in relief of red Doric leaf outlined by a broad black band which passes behind the horizontal band which runs along the bottom of the design and reappears on either side to form volutes from which rise seven-leaved red and black palmettes. From the top of the black middle leaf of each palmette rises a large red bud sheathed in a black calyx, and this bud and the top of the black outline band are both detached from the background and appear to stand out in very high relief, giving an extremely rich effect. The lower surface of the casing is ornamented with: (*a*) cream astragalos in relief; (*b*) fascia with broken meander in black and red; (*c*) astragalos. VI.–V. Century.

FIG. 30.

GEISA

(1) Gela, archaic temple. Mus. Syracuse.

There is a little bit which gives the right upper angle of the geison where it was crossed by the raking cornice: (*a*) torus with diagonal bands; (*b*) black meander; (*c*) bold squarely formed Doric leaf in red and black. First half of VI. Century.

FIG. 31.

P. Orsi, *Mon. Ant.*, xxv (1919), col. 663, fig. 237.

(2) Megara Hyblæa, Temple A. Mus. Syracuse.

There are numerous fragments of a geison of the first type of revetment decorated with: (*a*) double torus with vertical bands; (*b*) fascia with guilloche of an abnormal type: the curving bands are all black, the eyes are filled by four-petalled cream rosettes on a black ground and by red and black circles. These slabs are cm. 3 thick. Middle of VI. Century.

FIG. 33.

(3) Syracuse, Olympieion. Mus. Syracuse.

Revetment of the second type: (*a*) torus with black diagonal bands; (*b*) double guilloche of an abnormal type. The curving bands seem to be black; the eyes are filled by four-petalled cream rosettes on a red circle. Second half of VI. Century.

P. Orsi, *Mon. Ant.*, xiii (1903), col. 382, pl. xix, 4.

(4) Unknown provenance. Paris, Mus. du Louvre. Salle B, No. 364.

A small fragment of guilloche. The curving bands are in red and black; the eyes are filled by a red spot within a black circle. The design is abnormal and there are no traces of palmettes. The greyish-cream clay is fine in texture and is covered with an almost white slip. VI. Century.

Fig. 35.

(5) Locri, earlier temple, *Marazà*. Mus. Naples.

Revetment of the second type. Four fragments of a guilloche of abnormal type with red and black bands on a cream ground. The eye is filled by a black dot within a red circle. Second half of VI. Century.

Fig. 36.

E. Petersen, *Röm. Mitt.*, v (1890), p. 175, fig. 2.

(6) Rhegium, found in the Odeon. Mus. Civico, Reggio.

A very fine piece of the left angle of the frontal geison. The left corner of the slab is broken, all the lower part and the upper part of the right side. The upper edge, cut on the slant, fitted under the slope of the raking cornice. The design consisted of: (*a*) projecting border with large single guilloche in red and black, the central eyes filled by four-petalled rosettes; (*b*) Doric leaf in red and black alternately, separated by reversed three-leaved palmettes, the central leaf always red; (*c*) torus with red and black diagonal bands; (*c*) fascia, broken with obliterated design, but with traces of two water-spouts. These must have been dummy pipes, for in such a position they can have had no functional purpose. The fragment measures cm. 47 in length; its present maximum height is cm. 29, but when complete it must have measured cm. 45–50. VI. Century.

Fig. 37.

P. Orsi, *N.S.*, 1922, p. 171, fig. 21.

(7) Caulonia, temple, *Monasterace*. Mus. Syracuse.

Revetment of the first type: (*a*) torus; (*b*) elongated meander; (*c*) cymation with Doric leaf enclosed, black on a white ground; (*d*) torus; (*e*) guilloche with rosettes in the eyes. VI.-V. Century.

P. Orsi, *N.S.*, 1922, p. 148.

(8) Syracuse, *temenos*. Mus. Syracuse.

Revetment of the second type: (*a*) torus with diagonal bands; (*b*) black elongated meander; (*c*) chequer pattern in red and black arranged transversely; (*d*) torus with elongated lozenge; (*e*) double guilloche, the curving bands in red and black, the triangular spaces filled by three-leaved palmettes, the eyes by four-petalled rosettes; (*f*) torus with diagonal bands; (*g*) torus with chequer pattern. One fragment of this geison is of immense importance despite its minute dimensions, because it formed the right upper angle of the horizontal geison where it was crossed by the raking cornice. It shows: (*a*) tiny projecting border with black meander which starts at zero and increases in scale; (*b*) moulding with leaf pattern increasing in the same way; (*c*) torus with diagonal bands; (*d*) chequer pattern. Another tiny bit has great value, because it forms the extreme right lower angle of the geison where it diminishes to nothing below the raking cornice. The slab was cut sharply to give the correct angle and there is a hole for a metal pin which confirms the exact position of the piece in the cornice, because the holes are usually made in the guilloche where they merge into the design and also occupy an almost central position in the slab, whereas here, owing to want of space, before firing the hole was pierced between the two contiguous toroi. These casings are decorated on the lower surface with a narrow band of black triangles. Second half of VI. Century.

FIG. 22.

P. Orsi, *Mon. Ant.*, xxv (1919), cols. 662–6, figs. 236, 238, pl. xxii.

(9) Syracuse, *temenos*. Mus. Syracuse.

One slab of a geison, measuring cm. 37 × 60, is identical with that of the second type of revetment save that the lowest torus has vertical bands instead of chequer pattern. It has: (*a*) torus with elongated lozenge; (*b*) double guilloche; (*c*) double torus, the first with diagonal bands, the second with vertical bands. Second half of VI. Century.

P. Orsi, *Mon. Ant.*, xxv (1919), cols. 671 f., fig. 244.

(10) Catana (?). Mus. Biscari.

(*a*) Tiny double torus; (*b*) double guilloche to left, the curving bands in red and black, the triangular spaces filled by three-leaved black palmettes, the eyes by four-petalled rosettes; (*c*) double torus. VI.–V. Century.

Hittorff, *Arch. polychrome*, Atlas, pl. x, 6.

(11) Megara Hyblæa, Temple A. Mus. Syracuse.

Revetment of the second type. Fragment of a fascia with double guilloche. The curving bands are in red and black, the triangular spaces are filled by three-leaved black palmettes, the eyes by four-petalled cream rosettes. Height of fascia when complete about cm. 33. Second half of VI. Century.

P. Orsi, *Mon. Ant.*, i (1890), cols. 762 f., pl. vi, 2, 3.

(12) Syracuse, Olympieion. Mus. Syracuse.

Revetment of the third type: (*a*) torus with black diagonal bands; (*b*) double guilloche to left, the triangular spaces filled by three-leaved black palmettes, the eyes by four-petalled rosettes. Second half of VI. Century.

P. Orsi, *Mon. Ant.*, xiii (1903), pl. xix, 6; Doerpfeld, pl. iv, 7; Koldewey, p. 67.

(13) Syracuse. Mus. Syracuse.

(*a*) Double guilloche to left, the curving bands in red and black. The triangular spaces are filled by three-leaved red and black palmettes, the eyes by four-petalled rosettes; (*b*) torus with red and black diagonal bands. The lower surface of the slab is painted with a band of cream meander, the spaces above filled with black, those below with red. VI.–V. Century.

Doerpfeld, pl. iv, 8.

(14) Syracuse, *temenos*. Mus. Syracuse.

In the revetment of the first nucleus the geison exactly repeats the design of the lateral sima and raking cornice: (*a*) torus with diagonal bands; (*b*) elongated black meander; (*c*) cymation with heart-shaped leaves in red and black, separated by cream spaces on which are small enclosed three-leaved palmettes; (*d*) torus with diagonal bands; (*e*) fascia with lotus flowers, one pointing upwards, the next downwards and linked by intertwining stems; (*f*) torus with vertical bands; (*g*) double guilloche with curving bands in red and black, the triangular spaces filled by three-leaved palmettes, the eyes by four-petalled rosettes; (*h*) double torus with diagonal bands. VI. Century.

FIG. 27.

Mon. Ant., xxv (1919), pl. xviii.

(15) Syracuse, *temenos*. Mus. Syracuse.

Revetment of the first type: (*a*) double torus with diagonal bands; (*b*) broad fascia with double guilloche, the curving bands in red and black, the triangular spaces filled by three-leaved palmettes, the eyes by four-petalled rosettes. The under-surface of these casings is decorated by a band of single guilloche, the curving bands in red and black, the eyes filled by four-petalled rosettes and bordered by three rows of chequer pattern. Pendent palmettes hung from the lower surface of the geison as well as from the raking cornice and served the double purpose of *guttæ* and a hanging frieze which broke the rigid line of the horizontal geison. VI. Century.

FIG. 25.

P. Orsi, *N.S.*, 1910, p. 527, fig. 7; *Mon. Ant.*, xxv (1919), cols. 647–60, figs. 231, 232, pls. xix, B, xxi (reconstruction in colour).

(16) Caulonia, temple, *Monasterace.* Mus. Syracuse.

Revetment of the second type: (*a*) torus; (*b*) double guilloche; (*c*) torus. VI.–V. Century.

(17) Syracuse, *temenos.* Mus. Syracuse.

Fragment of a geison of small dimensions, ht. cm. 31: (*a*) double torus, the first decorated with red and black chevrons, the second with vertical bands in red and black; (*b*) double guilloche to left, the curving bands in red and black, the triangular spaces filled by seven-leaved palmettes, the eyes by four-petalled rosettes; the sheaths of the palmettes are covered by rosettes like the eyes and thus there are three rows of rosettes placed axially; (*c*) double torus, the first ornamented with hammer pattern, the second with black triangles. VI.–V. Century.

There are two fragments with identical design, but the colouring is entirely black; the slip and paint are very poor and the pieces were most likely inferior restorations.

P. Orsi, *Mon. Ant.*, xxv (1919), col. 672, fig. 245.

(18) Megara Hyblæa, Temple A. Mus. Syracuse.

Revetment of the third type. Fragments of a fascia with guilloche on a very large scale. The curving bands are red and black, the triangular spaces are filled by immense cream three-leaved palmettes on a red ground, the eyes by four-petalled cream rosettes on a black circle. The sheath of the palmettes is also red. The slab seems to have been finished off with a torus and the lower surface of the casing was painted with bold black meander. Middle of VI. Century.

FIG. 34.

P. Orsi, *Mon. Ant.*, xxvii (1922), col. 162, fig. 6.

(19) Metapontum, small shrine. Mus. Naples.

Fragment of a narrow slab, possibly the lower surface of a geison casing: (*a*) torus with diagonal bands; (*b*) double guilloche to left, the curving bands in red and black, the triangular spaces filled by three-leaved palmettes in cream on a reserved fan-shaped space coloured alternately red and black; the eyes are filled by four-petalled rosettes; (*c*) torus with red and black diagonal bands. VI. Century.

(20) Metapontum. Paris, Cabinet des Médailles.

Small fragment with guilloche, much blurred. VI.–V. Century.

(21) Rhegium, temple. Mus. Civico, Reggio.

Numerous fragments of a geison decorated with double guilloche, the eyes filled by four-petalled rosettes. At the edge of the slab is a triple torus. First half of VI. Century.

Koldewey, p. 50.

(22) Selinus, Acropolis. Mus. Palermo.

Part of a great slab, ht. cm. 61, decorated with double guilloche, the curving bands in red and black, the triangular spaces filled by five-leaved palmettes, the first, third and fifth coloured red, the second and fourth black, the eyes with five-petalled rosettes ; (*b*) torus with chequer pattern in red and black. VI.–V. Century.

(23) S. Mauro, temple. Mus. Syracuse.

Revetment of the second type : (*a*) torus with vertical bands in red and black ; (*b*) fascia with double guilloche, the curving bands in red and black, the triangular spaces filled by three-leaved palmettes in red and black, the eyes by six-petalled rosettes ; (*c*) astragalos in relief. VI.–V. Century.

P. Orsi, *Mon. Ant.*, xx (1910), cols. 781 f.

(24) Locri, earlier temple, *Marazà*. Mus. Naples and Syracuse.

Revetment of the third type. Fragments of a geison : (*a*) double torus with black hammer pattern ; (*b*) double guilloche, the curving bands in red and black, the triangular spaces filled by five-leaved palmettes, the first, third and fifth always red, the second and fourth black ; the eyes are filled by six-petalled cream rosettes, outlined black on a cream ground and with a black dot in each petal. There are at least nine fragments of this geison, which is on a different scale from the other revetments. Second half of VI. Century.

(25) Selinus, to N. of Tower M. Mus. Palermo.

Slabs of geisa which vary in details of decoration. One has : (*a*) torus with vertical bands in red and black ; (*b*) fascia with double guilloche to left, the triangular spaces filled by five-leaved black palmettes, the eyes by six-petalled rosettes. Middle of VI. Century.

N.S., 1894, p. 217, fig. 16 ; B. Pace, *Arte e Artisti della Sic. Ant.*, fig. 81, *c* ; Koldewey, p. 80.

(26) Selinus, Acropolis. Mus. Palermo.

Colossal slab of a geison measuring cm. 65 in height by cm. 92 in length. The fascia is adorned with double guilloche, the curving bands in red and black, the triangular spaces filled by five-leaved palmettes, the eyes by seven-petalled rosettes ; (*b*) torus with hammer (?) pattern. On the lower surface is : (*a*) band of narrow black broken meander ; (*b*) torus with red and black diagonal bands. The width of the ornamentation on the lower surface is cm. 16. VI.–V. Century.

(27) Selinus, Acropolis. Mus. Palermo.

There are only little bits of a geison on an enormous scale, but they are enough to show that the design consisted of a double guilloche with curving bands in red and black, the triangular spaces filled by five-leaved black palmettes, the eyes by eight-petalled rosettes which alone measured cm. 8·5 in diameter. V. Century.

Doerpfeld, p. 9, pl. iv, 2.

(28) Selinus, Temple C. Mus. Palermo.

Revetment of the first type: (*a*) cymation with square recurved Doric leaf in red and black; (*b*) torus with vertical bands in black and red; (*c*) fascia with double guilloche, the curving bands in black only, the triangular spaces filled by four-leaved palmettes, the eyes by a black dot within a circle; (*d*) torus with red and black vertical bands. These slabs measure cm. 62 in length. VI.–V. Century.

Doerpfeld, pl. iv, 1.

(29) Selinus, Acropolis. Mus. Palermo.

Small fragment of the angle of a geison: (*a*) tiny torus; (*b*) double guilloche with curving bands in red and black, the triangular spaces filled by four-leaved palmettes, the eyes by a black dot within a circle; (*c*) torus with black vertical bands. Ht. of fragment cm. 9·5 × 9. VI.–V. Century.

(30) Selinus, to N. of Tower M. Mus. Palermo.

(*a*) Torus with red and black vertical bands; (*b*) double guilloche to left, the curving bands in red and black, the triangular spaces filled by five-leaved palmettes, the eyes by a black dot within a circle; (*c*) torus with hammer pattern. Middle of VI. Century.

N.S., 1894, p. 217, fig. 15; B. Pace, *Arte e Artisti della Sic. Ant.*, fig. 81, *b*; Koldewey, p. 80.

(31) Selinus, Acropolis. Mus. Palermo.

Tiny fragment of a geison with: (*a*) double guilloche to right, the curving bands in red and black, the triangular spaces filled by four-leaved red and black palmettes, the eyes by a black dot within a circle; (*b*) astragalos in relief. The fascia measures ht. cm. 11 × 16. VI.–V. Century.

(32) Selinus, Acropolis. Mus. Palermo.

(*a*) Recurved red and black square Doric leaf; (*b*) astragalos in relief; (*c*) double guilloche, the curving bands in red and black, the triangular spaces filled by four-leaved palmettes, the eyes by a black dot within a circle; (*d*) astragalos in relief. VI.–V. Century.

(33) Hybla. Mus. Syracuse.

(*a*) Bold white astragalos in high relief ; (*b*) black double guilloche to left on a white ground, the triangular spaces filled by three-leaved palmettes, the eyes by a black dot within a circle ; (*c*) bold astragalos. End of VI. Century.

(34) Selinus, Temple C. Mus. Palermo.

Revetment of the second type : (*a*) square recurved Doric leaf ; (*b*) torus with vertical bands ; (*c*) double black guilloche, the triangular spaces filled by five-leaved red and black palmettes, the eyes by a red dot within a circle ; (*d*) torus with vertical bands. These slabs measure cm. 70·5 in length. There is a corner-piece from the right angle of the pediment. It is the portion of the horizontal geison where it was crossed by the raking cornice and is left rough above. Another right angle-piece is fully preserved (cm. 36·5) with a nail hole pierced cm. 32 from the front border. Beginning of V. Century.

Hulot et Fougères, *Sélinonte*, p. 223, fig. in text ; Koldewey, p. 104.

(35) Akrai. Mus. Palermo.

In the museum at Palermo are several examples which must have come from Akrai. One may be identified as a geison from its likeness to the specimen from Selinus. It shows : (*a*) cymation with square recurved Doric leaf ; (*b*) astragalos in relief ; (*c*) double guilloche, the triangular spaces filled by three-leaved palmettes, the eyes by a dot alternately red and black ; (*d*) astragalos. The peculiarity of this example is that the ground of the design is black. VI.–V. Century.

Doerpfeld, pp. 9, 24, pl. iv, 4 ; Koldewey, p. 75.

(36) Syracuse, Olympieion. Mus. Syracuse.

Revetment of the fourth type. The angle of a geison with : (*a*) projecting border with elongated meander ; (*b*) cymation with sharply receding profile decorated with Doric leaf with a heart-shaped leaf enclosed between each pair of large leaves ; (*c*) thick torus with diagonal bands ; (*d*) double guilloche, the eyes filled with a red and black dot alternately, not placed directly under one another, but axially. VI.–V. Century.

(37) Syracuse, *temenos*. Mus. Syracuse.

Part of a geison, ht. cm. 30, length approximately cm. 50. Double guilloche to left, the curving bands in red and black. The eyes are filled by concentric circles in red and black, the triangular spaces by five-leaved palmettes always coloured in the same order, black, cream with a black spot in the upper end of the petal, red, cream and black : the sheath of the palmette is covered like the eyes by a dot within concentric circles. There are no toroi either above or below the fascia, but the guilloche is bordered by two plain bands in red. The whole appearance of the slab is peculiar, for the colour is laid on in a thin wash giving to the design a " matte " effect. Second half of VI. Century.

FIG. 38.

P. Orsi, *Mon. Ant.*, xxv (1919), cols. 672 f., fig. 246.

(38) Croton, Temple of Hera. Coll. Marchese Albani.

Revetment of the first type. A fragment of a geison with: (*a*) fascia with painted rosettes; (*b*) torus with diagonal bands; (*c*) double guilloche, the eye filled by a plain dot. Middle of VI. Century.

P. Orsi, *N.S.*, 1897, p. 345.

(39) Syracuse, Olympieion. Mus. Syracuse.

Revetment of the sixth type. Fragment of a geison: (*a*) astragalos in high relief; (*b*) black guilloche on a white ground, too damaged to discern details. The lower surface of the casings is painted with simple guilloche on a large scale. First half of V. Century.

(40) Syracuse, Temple of Apollo. Mus. Syracuse.

The left upper angle of the horizontal geison where it was crossed by the line of the raking cornice: (*a*) elongated meander; (*b*) Doric leaf with superimposed heart; (*c*) torus with diagonal bands; (*d*) triple guilloche with cream curving bands outlined red; the eyes are filled by alternate red and black spots placed axially. As the eyes are placed axially and not immediately below one another, the arrangement produces a horizontal row of eyes alternately red and black and a diagonal row, first red, then black. The slab is broken below. Middle of VI. Century.

FIG. 32.

P. Orsi, *Mon. Ant.*, xxv (1919), col. 663, fig. 237.

(41) Selinus, Acropolis. Mus. Palermo.

Part of a slab with: (*a*) double torus with vertical bands in black arranged to form a hammer pattern on the two toroi; (*b*) single guilloche, the curving bands in red and black, the eyes filled by four-petalled rosettes; (*c*) torus with black vertical bands. The casing is painted on the lower surface with a border of black triangles. The height of the slab, which is complete, measures cm. 23·5, but it is broken at one end so that the present length is also cm. 23·5. VI.–V. Century.

Doerpfeld, pl. iv, 5.

(42) Selinus, Acropolis. Mus. Palermo.

A portion of a geison slab: (*a*) torus; (*b*) fascia with single guilloche consisting of closely set bands outlined only in black, the eyes filled by four-petalled rosettes. Ht. cm. 12 × 14·5. VI.–V. Century.

(43) Selinus, Acropolis. Mus. Palermo.

Design on a very large scale with : (*a*) torus blurred ; (*b*) single guilloche, the curving bands in red and black, the eyes filled by multi-petalled rosettes. V. Century.

Doerpfeld, pl. iv, 3.

(44) Croton, Temple of Hera. Mus. Metaponto.

(*a*) Triple torus, the first and third painted with vertical bands, the middle one with diagonal bands in red and black ; (*b*) single guilloche, the eyes filled by multi-petalled rosettes. The piece may be the lower surface of a geison casing. Middle of VI. Century.

N.S., 1897, p. 345 ; Doerpfeld, pl. iv, 10.

(45) Syracuse, Olympieion. Mus. Syracuse.

Revetment of the fourth type : (*a*) torus with chequer pattern ; (*b*) large single guilloche, the eyes filled by a black spot ; in the centre of one is a nail hole ; (*c*) torus with bands of red and black. The casing runs far back and the upper surface of the top slab is marked by a groove where the other member overlapped and by three nail holes. Some of the slabs are decorated on the lower surface also, but owing to the minute size of the bits preserved it is difficult to ascertain the motives : on certain examples there are parallel lines in red and black on a cream ground. Others are left rough underneath and were evidently not visible from below. VI.–V. Century.

(46) Catana. Mus. Biscari.

A fragment of revetment consisting of : (*a*) thick convex moulding decorated with three rows of horizontal scale pattern in red and black ; (*b*) extraordinarily large single guilloche, the curving bands in red and black, the eyes black ; (*c*) small torus with hammer pattern in red and black. The slab is unusual because it has nail holes above and also in the middle of the guilloche. VI. Century.

Hittorff, *Arch. polychrome*, p. 768, Atlas, pl. x, 7 ; Doerpfeld, p. 10.

(47) Syracuse. Mus. Syracuse.

Casing of a geison : (*a*) torus with vertical bands ; (*b*) single guilloche, the curving bands in red and black, the eyes filled by a black spot ; (*c*) convex moulding with single horizontal scale-pattern bordered by a little row of vertical bands. The top slab of this casing runs far back and is marked by a ledge upon which the member above rested. The casing was fastened to the framework beneath by metal nails placed in the middle of the eyes. VI.–V. Century.

Durm, *Die Baustile* (Darmstadt, 1881), i, 2, p. 162, fig. 133 ; Avolio, *Ant. Fatture in Argilla*, pl. viii, 1.

(48) Locri, earlier temple, *Marazà*. Mus. Naples.

Revetment of the second type. A large fragment of a slab with immense black meander painted on a cream ground. Possibly the under-side of a horizontal geison. Middle of VI. Century.

E. Petersen, *Röm. Mitt.*, v (1890), p. 175 (*a*).

(49) Gela.

Narrow revetment slab with : (*a*) single guilloche, the curving bands in red and black, the eyes filled by a red spot ; (*b*) torus with hammer pattern. Probably the lower slab of the geison casing. Middle of VI. Century.

Cf. Doerpfeld, p. 11, pl. iv, 11.

(50) Metapontum. Mus. Naples and Metaponto.

Single guilloche, the eyes filled by a red dot within a circle ; (*b*) double torus with black hammer pattern. VI.–V. Century.

Doerpfeld, pl. iv, 11 ; Koldewey, p. 40.

(51) Rhegium, temple. Mus. Civico, Reggio.

The slabs of the lower surface of the geison casings had a small border on the front face painted with double black meander alternating with cream rosettes on a black square. The lower surface of the slab has a bold double black meander. VI. Century.

N.S., 1884, p. 284 ; 1886, p. 242 ; Koldewey, p. 50.

(52) Locri, earlier temple, *Marazà*. Mus. Naples and Syracuse.

Revetment of the fourth type. In the Naples Museum are ten pieces of the lower slabs of the geison casing. The largest bit in the museum at Syracuse measures cm. 14 × 10·5. Here and there are round or square nail holes. (*a*) Torus with black diagonal lines ; (*b*) fascia with a black ground upon which are white palmettes addorsed and rising between broad white circular bands or volutes united by a triple band. The eyes of these circles are filled by large eight-petalled rosettes with a reddish purple dot in the middle. The pieces are too fragmentary to permit one to reconstruct the whole design. On the front edge of the slab is a border (cm. 2·5) of roughly drawn black meander, the spaces filled by black hammer pattern. Early V. Century.

FIG. 39.

(53) Locri, earlier temple, *Marazà*. Mus. Naples and Syracuse.

Revetment of the fifth type. There are several small pieces of the lower surface of the geison casing, roughly painted with a floral design in black and white. The pieces are too broken to permit one to make out the whole design. The narrow front border of the slab was painted with a hastily drawn black single meander, the spaces filled by hammer pattern. As this design closely resembles that employed on the slabs with palmettes and rosettes in cream on a black ground, it is probable that these rough pieces were part of a late restoration. The largest fragment measures cm. 11·5 × 8 and the slabs were cm. 2·5 thick. V. Century.

(54) Croton, Temple of Hera.

Revetment of the second type. There are two fragments which seem to have formed one slab. The design is almost obliterated, but appears to consist of the following elements: (*a*) plain (?) projecting border; (*b*) fascia with meander; (*c*) egg-and-dart moulding in relief; (*d*) small torus; (*e*) broad fascia with meander (?); (*f*) double torus with chevrons in red and black; (*g*) narrow plain fascia. In the upper part of the geison is a nail hole. Beginning of V. Century.

P. Orsi, *N.S.*, 1911 Suppl., p. 109, fig. 90.

(55) Metapontum, Temple of Apollo. Mus. Naples and Potenza.

Revetment of the first type: (*a*) egg-and-dart in high relief; (*b*) small astragalos in relief painted cream; (*c*) complicated meander, painted black in a broad, simple fashion and with the spaces unfilled; (*d*) Lesbian sima in low relief picked out in red and black; (*e*) torus with broad diagonal bands in red and black. Beginning of V. Century.

Koldewey, p. 40.

(56) Locri, earlier temple, *Marazà*. Mus. Naples and Potenza.

Revetment of the fourth type. A fragment: (*a*) double torus with black diagonal bands to right on the upper torus, to left on the lower one, so that the design forms a chevron pattern; (*b*) broad fascia with complicated meander painted white on a black ground. Here and there are round nail holes to fasten the slabs. Early V. Century.

(57) Metapontum, Temple of Apollo. Mus. Naples and Potenza.

Revetment of the second type: (*a*) egg-and-dart in relief, the egg painted cream, the dart red; (*b*) red astragalos in relief; (*c*) broad fascia with complicated double meander, painted only in cream on a black ground, the spaces filled by a cream star on a red square. There are holes at irregular intervals for the square copper nails; (*d*) convex moulding with leaf and dart, painted only, the leaf cream with a red line in the middle, the dart black; (*e*) torus with diagonal bands in red and black. The torus of the front slab of the casing is moulded three-quarters in the round and thus borders the under-surface of the casing which therefore shows: (*a*) torus (of the front slab); (*b*) double guilloche, the curving bands in red and black, the triangular spaces filled by fan-shaped palmettes, one red, the next black; the eyes are filled by cream spots; (*c*) torus with diagonal bands. Middle of V. Century.

De Petra, *Atti Acc. Napoli*, xvii (1894), p. 6, pl. iii ; Koldewey, p. 4 ; *N.S.*, 1889, p. 168.

(58) Metapontum, Temple of Apollo. Mus. Naples, Potenza and Paris, Cabinet des Médailles.

Revetment of the third type : (*a*) egg-and-dart in relief, the egg painted white, the dart red ; (*b*) red astragalos in relief ; (*c*) complicated double meander in relief painted white on a black ground ; the squares are filled alternately by a white star on a red field and by a red cross on a white field ; (*d*) convex moulding with Lesbian leaf in white, outlined black on a red ground ; the moulding here has a more pronounced curvature, so that it hides the torus which belongs entirely to the lower surface of the casing which consists of : (*a*) torus with red and black diagonal bands to right ; (*b*) black double guilloche on a white ground, the triangular spaces filled by three-leaved palmettes, the first and third invariably coloured red, the middle one black ; the sheaths of the palmettes are always red and the eyes are a black dot upon a white circle ; (*c*) torus with diagonal bands. Middle of V. Century.

De Petra, *Atti Acc. Napoli*, xvii (1894), p. 5, pl. ii ; Duc de Luynes et Debacq, *Métaponte* (Paris, 1833), pl. viii, 1–3 ; Hittorff, *Arch. polychrome*, Atlas, pl. x, 5 ; La Cava, *Topogr. e Storia di Metaponto* (Napoli, 1891), pls. v, vi ; Perrot, *Hist. de l'Art*, vii, pl. ix ; Durm, *Die Baustile* (Darmstadt, 1881), i, 2, p. 162, fig. 133 ; Koldewey, p. 40.

(59) Metapontum, *Tavole Paladini*. Paris, Cabinet des Médailles.

Fragments of geison slabs with meander, portions of the egg-and-dart moulding, very similar to those from the Temple of Apollo, but of smaller dimensions. Middle of V. Century.

Duc de Luynes, *Métaponte*, p. 45, *cf*. pl. viii, 2 ; Koldewey, p. 37 ; La Cava, *Topogr. e Storia di Metaponto*, p. 87.

(60) Syracuse, Olympieion. Mus. Syracuse.

Revetment of the sixth type. Broad slab of geison with : (*a*) white astragalos in relief ; (*b*) wide fascia with double black meander in relief ; (*c*) white astragalos in relief. First half of V. Century.

FIG. 40.

E. Mauceri, " Siracusa," *Italia Artistica*, No. 47, p. 102, fig. in text.

(61) Locri, Doric temple, *Marafioti*. Mus. Civico, Reggio and Syracuse.

The geison ran round all four sides of the temple and consisted of : (*a*) plain (?) fascia ; (*b*) complicated double meander in high relief, painted white on a black ground, the spaces filled by four square dots ; (*c*) plain (?) fascia ; (*d*) torus with horizontal scale pattern. V. Century.

FIG. 41.

P. Orsi, *N.S.*, 1911 Suppl., pp. 39 f., fig. 32.

(62) Rhegium, temple. Mus. Civico, Reggio.

The design is carried out entirely in black and cream: (*a*) palmettes enclosed within bands which form pointed arches above and end below in spirals, the eyes filled by four-petalled rosettes; (*b*) torus with black diagonal bands; (*c*) fascia with double black meander, the spaces filled by a cream star on a black square. VI. Century.

(63) Selinus, Acropolis. Mus. Palermo.

Small fragments of a geison: (*a*) astragalos in relief, coloured black with a red reel; (*b*) double meander, black superimposed on red. First half of V. Century.

Serradifalco, *Ant. della Sic.*, ii, pl. xvii, D; Hittorff, *Arch. polychrome*, Atlas, pl. x, 4; Koldewey, p. 130.

(64) Selinus, Acropolis. Mus. Palermo.

Fragment of a sima: (*a*) projecting border with three rows of small black chequer pattern; (*b*) Doric leaf in red and black, diminishing to a point, outlined black and separated by a black dart. The fragment measures cm. 11 × 13; ht. of projecting border only, cm. 3·5. Another small piece possibly gives the lower part of this sima: (*a*) red and black Doric leaf as above; below the Doric leaf a band of broken meander is painted, the upper red, the lower black; (*b*) torus with red and black vertical bands. VI.–V. Century.

(65) Catana (?). Mus. Biscari.

A fragment with: (*a*) egg-and-dart in relief between two small toroi; (*b*) double meander, the spaces filled by a small square within a square bordered field. First half of V. Century.

Serradifalco, *Ant. della Sic.*, v, pl. xviii, 5.

(66) Selinus, Acropolis. Mus. Palermo.

Tiny fragment of a slab which, by analogy with the revetments from Metapontum and Croton, must have been part of a geison. It has: (*a*) astragalos in relief; (*b*) black meander which must have been of the complicated quadruple design. V. Century.

(67) Caulonia, temple, *Monasterace*. Mus. Syracuse.

Revetment of the third type. Geison with astragalos and meander both in relief. V. Century.

P. Orsi, *N.S.*, 1922, p. 147.

(68) Metaurum. Naples, private collection.

A very small fragment of a geison slab with complicated meander in relief. Much rubbed, no colour. Poor work of the second half of the V. Century.

(69) Locri, earlier temple, *Marazà*. Mus. Naples and Syracuse.

Revetment of the fifth type. Numerous pieces of a geison with: (*a*) double torus with black chevrons; (*b*) very complicated quadruple black meander coarsely painted on a cream ground. The largest fragment measures cm. 13 × 10·5 and the one in Naples has a nail hole in the middle of the meander. Most likely this is a restoration of the earlier meander of the fourth type. V. Century.

(70) Caulonia, private houses, *Collina del Faro*. Mus. Civico, Reggio.

Fragment of a geison, measuring about cm. 10 in length. The design consists of anthemia alternating with lotus in relief, the anthemia springing from the curving stems of the lotus; below is a border of complicated meander in relief. End of V. Century.

P. Orsi, *Mon. Ant.*, xxiii (1916), col. 820, fig. 81.

(71) Medma. Mus. Civico, Reggio.

Revetment of the second type. A geison slab, ht. cm. 19 × 31, with: (*a*) projecting border with broken meander in red and black; (*b*) Lesbian cyma; (*c*) design in relief, painted white on a black ground, of nine-leaved anthemia springing from double spirals between which are small reversed palmettes; the anthemia are separated by lotus flowers which overarch and meet, thus framing the anthemia. The design is delicately wrought in fairly high relief and details here and there, such as the middle petals and calyx of the lotus and the sheath of the anthemia, are picked out in red. Beginning of V. Century.

FIG. 42.

P. Orsi, *N.S.*, 1913 Suppl., p. 65, fig. 71.

(72) Croton, Temple of Hera. Mus. Civico, Reggio.

Revetment of the third type. A quantity of small geison slabs were discovered, ht. cm. 22·5, decorated with anthemia in relief alternating with lotus flowers, both springing from broad spiral bands which are bound together by a single band under each motive. The ground is deep cream, the relief being picked out in red and black. There are at least three variations of this pattern, due to the greater fullness or slenderness of the leaves, the different spacing of the lotus or spirals and other little details. The length of each slab may be calculated as cm. 42·5, because each one comprised an anthemion flanked by two lotus flowers and two half anthemia or *vice versa*. A little lead clamp is noticeable in many of the slabs; some were employed to mend ancient breakages, and these are visible towards the middle of the back side and pass obliquely through the thickness of the slab; the upper ones, on the other hand, shaped _⊓_, served to unite contiguous pieces. Middle of V. Century.

FIG. 43.

P. Orsi, *N.S.*, 1911 Suppl., p. 111, fig. 95.

SIMÆ OF UNCERTAIN ATTRIBUTION

(1) Croton, Temple of Hera.

Tiny pieces of revetment slabs ornamented with a cursive meander which almost develops into a scroll pattern. VI.-V. Century.

P. Orsi, *N.S.*, 1911 Suppl., p. 106.

(2) Catana (?). Mus. Biscari.

Very small pieces of revetment slabs with: (*a*) goose-beck moulding; (*b*) fascia with scroll pattern. VI.–V. Century.

Serradifalco, *Ant. della Sic.*, v, pl. xviii, 5.

(3) Croton, Temple of Hera.

One little fragment is decorated with imbrications; it was probably part of a convex moulding. VI. Century.

P. Orsi, *N.S.*, 1911 Suppl., p. 106, fig. 85.

(4) S. Mauro, archaic temple. Mus. Syracuse.

There are two types of designs consisting of painted rosettes. In the first the red multi-petalled rosette is enclosed in a double black circle; below is an astragalos in relief. The rosette of the second type is not enclosed in any way. Second half of VI. Century.

P. Orsi, *Mon. Ant.*, xx (1910), col. 782, fig. 45.

(5) Croton, Temple of Hera.

There are two large pieces of a sima with pronounced bird's beck moulding. They are decorated with narrow stripes in red and black which resemble flutings, but are painted only; below is a design of Doric leaf. VI. Century.

FIG. 44.

P. Orsi, *N.S.*, 1911 Suppl., p. 106, fig. 86.

(6) Croton, Temple of Hera.

Revetment of the first type. There are two large fragments of a revetment with: (*a*) fascia with meander; (*b*) torus; (*c*) plain fascia which served as a base. As the frontal plane of these slabs is perfectly vertical, one may attribute them to a geison, in which case they may complete the sima with narrow stripes. Middle of VI. Century.

P. Orsi, *N.S.*, 1911 Suppl., p. 108.

(7) Selinus, Temple D. Mus. Palermo.

Fragments of a sima painted with palmettes and meander. Beginning of V. Century.

Cavallari, *Bull. Comm. Sic.*, ii (1874), p. 19; Koldewey, p. 109.

(8) Locri, earlier temple, *Marazà*. Mus. Naples and Syracuse.

Revetment of the second type. A sima with: (*a*) torus with closely set diagonal bands in red and black to right; (*b*) projecting border with four rows of black chequer pattern; (*c*) cymation with Doric leaf diminishing to a point, the red leaves with a black outline and the black leaves with a red one; the space between the leaves at the top is filled by a small black bud; (*d*) torus with closely set red and black diagonal bands to left. Second half of VI. Century.

(9) Selinus, Acropolis. Mus. Palermo.

Small fragment: (*a*) torus blurred; (*b*) projecting border with three rows of black chequer pattern; (*c*) cymation with Doric leaf. VI. Century.

(10) Syracuse, *temenos*. Mus. Syracuse.

Revetment of the fifth type, of which only two pieces remain: (*a*) projecting border with five rows of black chequer pattern; (*b*) cymation with Doric leaf in red and black, the red leaves with a black outline and the black leaves with a red one; each pair of leaves is separated by a black dart; (*c*) torus with diagonal bands. It is remarkable that here the red Doric leaf and also the red band outlining the black leaf have no black margin as is almost always the case; but the black margin to the red diagonal bands is well marked. The spaces above the leaves is filled in solidly with black. The dimensions of the sima are very small. Middle of VI. Century.

FIG. 45.

P. Orsi, *Mon. Ant.*, xxv (1919), cols. 666 f., fig. 241.

(11) Selinus, Acropolis. Mus. Palermo.

One small fragment, ht. cm. 5·7, has: (*a*) torus blurred; (*b*) projecting border with elongated black meander alternately broken and interlocked; (*c*) traces of Doric leaf. The projecting border only measures cm. 3·5 in height. VI. Century.

(12) Metapontum. Paris, Cabinet des Médailles.

Small fragment with: (*a*) torus much broken with traces of tongue (?) pattern; (*b*) projecting border with broken meander painted yellow; (*c*) cymation with Doric leaf in red and yellow alternately, outlined black. Ht. cm. 7 × 9. V. Century.

FIG. 47.

Duc de Luynes et Debacq, *Métaponte*, p. 45, pl. viii, 5.

(13) Selinus, Acropolis. Mus. Palermo.

(*a*) Torus with black vertical bands; (*b*) projecting border with black broken meander; (*c*) cymation with red and black Doric leaf diminishing to a point, outlined black and separated by a black dart. Below the Doric leaf a band of chevrons is outlined only in black ; (*d*) torus with very closely set diagonal lines in black. The height of this sima is cm. 22 × 36. VI. Century.

(14) Locri, earlier temple, *Marazà*. Mus. Naples.

Revetment of the first type. Fragment of a cymation with very large Doric leaf, alternately cream with a red outline and black with a red outline. First half of VI. Century.

(15) Locri, earlier temple, *Marazà*. Mus. Naples.

Revetment of the fourth type. Fragment of cymation with Doric leaf in black only. Beginning of V. Century.

E. Petersen, *Röm. Mitt.*, v (1890), p. 175 (*c*), fig. 3.

(16) Syracuse, Olympieion. Mus. Syracuse.

Revetment of the seventh type. Fragment of a cymation with red and black Doric leaf ; between each pair is a heart-shaped space enclosed within a broad white band ending in volutes ; within this space is a white seven-leaved flabelliform palmette on a black ground, the veins marked red. First half of V. Century.

(17) Syracuse, *temenos*. Mus. Syracuse.

The revetment of the sixth type appears to be a variant of type four, but the lanceolated leaves contain a superimposed red heart. VI.–V. Century.

FIG. 46.

P. Orsi, *Mon. Ant.*, xxv (1919), col. 667, fig. 242.

(18) Syracuse, Olympieion. Mus. Syracuse.

Revetment of the eighth type. Very fragmentary. Curved sprays in high relief enclose a bud and end in spirals between which spring reversed five-leaved palmettes. Middle of V. Century.

(19) Rhegium, *Collina del Salvatore*. Mus. Civico, Reggio.

Designs in high relief, curving bands enclosing palmettes, etc., all much broken. No colour. V. Century.

N.S., 1890, p. 196.

(20) Tarentum. British Museum.

(*a*) Projecting border with meander in red and black ; (*b*) egg-and-dart moulding in high relief ; the eggs are outlined black and striped vertically with red, the darts are green (blue ?) ; (*c*) cream astragalos in relief. Ht. cm. 18·5.

Another moulding has : (*a*) projecting border with broken meander in red and black ; (*b*) egg-and-dart in high relief, the eggs very large, outlined black and with a red line up the middle, the dart with traces of blue. Ht. cm. 11 × 26·5. End of V. Century.

Brit. Mus. Cat. Terrac., D 704, D 705.

(21) Locri, Temple of Athena Mannella.

Various small architectonic pieces, painted only, without relief. Second half of VI. Century.

P. Orsi, *N.S.*, 1911 Suppl., p. 67.

WATER-SPOUTS

(1) Syracuse, *temenos*. Mus. Syracuse.

Revetment of the seventh type. The water-spouts debouched from the cymation itself, and not as usual from the fascia below. To this revetment may possibly belong a very large disc from the mouth of a tubular pipe, almost flat and decorated with a rosette in red and black, outlined black on a cream ground. Early VI. Century.

P. Orsi, *Mon. Ant.*, xxv (1919), cols. 666 f.

(2) Metaurum. Private Collection, Naples.

Twelve pieces of tubular spouts were found in the excavations. They are very simply fashioned and seem to belong to the earlier type of spouts, without elaborately painted disc mouths. Middle of VI. Century.

N.S., 1902, p. 128, fig. 2, No. 12.

(3) Syracuse, *temenos*. Mus. Syracuse.

Revetment of the first nucleus. There exists only one fragment with the base of a water-spout, but the pipe has disappeared. It is too fragmentary to reconstruct. VI. Century.

P. Orsi, *Mon. Ant.*, xxv (1919), col. 639.

(4) Locri, earlier temple, *Marazà*. Mus. Syracuse.

Revetment of the third type. The water-spouts consisted of two tubes which fitted into each other and diminished in circumference as they approached the mouth, which had no disc, but at the end the pipe widened out slightly and the lip was rolled over almost like a torus, so that the diameter of the mouth was cm. 7. A small torus covered the joint where the pipe issued from the sima and a scotia-like moulding concealed the juncture of the two tubes, and was decorated with black bands. Second half of VI. Century.

(5) Caulonia, *Collina del Faro*. Mus. Civico, Reggio.

The water-spouts did not project very far from the sima. They are tubular in form and end in a broad, flat lip painted with tongue pattern alternately red and black, outlined with cream. VI.–V. Century.

P. Orsi, *Mon. Ant.*, xxiii (1916), cols. 783–4, fig. 49.

(6) Hybla. Mus. Syracuse.

This revetment was remarkable, because the tubular spouts debouched from the cymation itself, not from the plain fascia beneath. End of V. Century.

(7) Locri, earlier temple, *Marazà*. Mus. Naples.

Revetment of the first type. The lateral sima shows traces of the circular openings and torus painted black from which the tubular spouts projected, but there are no pieces of the pipes themselves. First half of VI. Century.

(8) Selinus, to N. of Tower M. Mus. Palermo.

Only a small piece of a sima was discovered, but sufficient to show there were two tubular spouts to each slab. Of the pipes themselves nothing remains save the circular opening surrounded by a torus where the pipes debouched from the sima. Middle of VI. Century.

N.S., 1894, p. 217, fig. 17 ; B. Pace, *Arte e Artisti della Sic. Ant.*, fig. 81, A.

(9) Megara Hyblæa, Temple A. Mus. Syracuse.

Revetment of the first type. There are traces of the openings for the tubular spouts in the fascia with lozenge pattern, but the pipes no longer exist. Early VI. Century.

The revetment of the second type also reveals a lateral sima with the openings for the spouts, and here the openings were concealed by a torus painted cream and decorated with black diagonal bands. The end of the pipe was finished off by a flat lip adorned with hammer pattern in red and black. The disc mouth had a pattern of tongue in red and black framed in a black outline and surrounded by a raised border with red and black triangles on a cream ground. Middle of VI. Century.

The revetment of the third type had pipes with very similar disc mouths, decorated in this case with a cream rosette on a black ground surrounded by a raised border with broad diagonal bands in red and black. Second half of VI. Century.

Fig. 48.

P. Orsi, *Mon. Ant.*, xxvii (1922), col. 163, fig. 8.

(10) Medma, small sanctuary. Mus. Civico, Reggio.

Revetment of the first type. Only one fragment of a water-spout, tubular in form and with a simple disc mouth, was found. Second half of VI. Century.

P. Orsi, *N.S.*, 1913 Suppl., p. 67.

(11) Syracuse, *temenos*. Mus. Syracuse.

Revetment of the first type. The tubular spouts were very numerous, for they were set close together, two to each slab. They measured cm. 23 in length and were formed of two separate pipes which diminish in diameter towards the mouth and thus fit into one another, the joint being covered by a torus, black where the pipe protrudes from the sima, red where the smaller pipe fits into the larger. A concave disc is set a few centimetres back from the end of the pipe, and is decorated with eight-petalled rosettes in red and black, outlined cream on a black ground. The end of the pipe forms a flat lip decorated with tongue pattern. The pipes were set at an angle of fifteen degrees to the revetment slabs, and therefore give the slope of the roof, which must have been identical. VI. Century.

FIG. 7.

P. Orsi, *Mon. Ant.*, xxv (1919), cols. 642–7, figs. 226, 268, pl. xx.

(12) Syracuse, *temenos*. Mus. Syracuse.

The water-spouts of the first variant of this revetment of the first type were identical; those of the second variant were almost the same, but here the first torus was wholly black, the second wholly red. The disc mouths are slightly larger in diameter.

(13) Syracuse, *temenos*. Mus. Syracuse.

Revetment of the second type. The water-spouts are much shorter than those of the first type and consist of one tube only. The torus which covers the point of egress from the sima is coloured cream with black diagonal lines; the second torus, which held the disc mouth in place, is either wholly red or else cream with black diagonal lines. The concave disc of the mouth was decorated with ten-petalled rosettes, the petals alternately red and black, outlined black on a cream ground. The pipe ended in a broad lip flattened out and decorated with a ten-petalled red and black rosette. Second half of VI. Century.

P. Orsi, *Mon. Ant.*, xxv (1919), cols. 660 f., figs. 234, 235.

(14) Syracuse, *temenos*. Mus. Syracuse.

To the revetment of the fourth type seem to belong certain unusually large spouts. The tube was short but thick, and was surrounded at the point where it projected from the sima by an extremely thick torus, coloured cream like the pipe, but decorated with narrow black diagonal lines. A second torus, set a little behind the disc mouth, was painted with a broad black circular band bordered by two narrow red lines. The disc is pronouncedly concave, with a flat border like the rim of a plate. It was ornamented with a rosette in red and black, the border with black triangles. The lip at the end of the pipe is narrow and adorned with groups of lines only. Middle of VI. Century.

(15) Syracuse, Olympieion. Mus. Syracuse.

Revetment of the second type. Only a few bits of the water-spouts now remain, but they were of the tubular type and show a remarkable variety of treatment. One disc was ornamented with a rosette, another with tongue pattern, whilst the base of the pipe where it entered the sima was surrounded by a zone of chequer pattern. Second half of VI. Century.

P. Orsi, *Mon. Ant.*, xiii (1903), col. 385, pl. xix, 7.

(16) Selinus, archaic Temple C. Mus. Palermo.

During the excavations in 1876 a water-spout was found with a wide mouth painted with a rosette; the external diameter was cm. 12·5 and the interior diameter cm. 4. VI.–V. Century.

N.S., 1882, p. 329, fig. in text, pl. xix; Perrot, *Hist. de l'Art*, vii, p. 502, fig. 238.

(17) Gela, archaic temple. Mus. Syracuse.

The lip and mouth of a tubular water-spout. The disc is slightly concave and is decorated with a multi-petalled rosette. The dimensions are unusually large, nearly as big again as those of the revetment of the first type from the *temenos*, Syracuse. Middle of VI. Century.

(18) Caulonia, temple. Mus. Civico, Reggio.

Part of the pipe of a water-spout has been preserved with a piece of the disc mouth painted with a rosette. As the spouts on the lateral sima were masked by lions' heads, this pipe was probably the gutter behind the angle of the raking cornice. V. Century.

P. Orsi, *Mon. Ant.*, xxiii (1916), col. 892.

(19) Rhegium, found in the Odeon. Mus. Civico, Reggio.

Four fragments of the disc mouths of tubular pipes, all of the same type. The concave surface is painted with a many-petalled rosette in red and black, the flat border with a circle of black triangles. Diameter cm. 22·7. VI. Century.

P. Orsi, *N.S.* 1922, p. 173, fig. 22.

(20) S. Mauro, archaic temple. Mus. Syracuse.

Revetment of the second type. The spouts were rich and varied, for no less than six different designs have been found. The mouth of the pipe was finished off by a flat disc upon which the designs were painted. These consist of rosettes, some with a few large, others with numerous small petals; square red meander; cream lotus buds outlined black on a red ground; red-pointed rays on a cream ground; whirligigs in red, black and cream alternately. The tubular pipe measured cm. 22 in length and the mouth was finished off by a disc cm. 20·7 in diameter. VI.–V. Century.

FIG. 49.

P. Orsi, *Mon. Ant.*, xx (1910), cols. 781 f., fig. 43, pls. v, vi.

(21) Metapontum, *Tavole Paladini*. Mus. Potenza.

Beautiful gutter in the shape of a rectangular trough which widens out towards the base. It is painted on the lower surface with a graceful palmette and spiral motive, and on the right side only with a complicated black meander, the spaces filled by a cream star on a red square. The considerable projection of this gutter and the fact that it was painted on one side only prove that it was the gutter behind the right angle of the raking cornice with which it ran parallel, thus concealing the left side. Length cm. 24; ht. cm. 7; width at mouth cm. 10·5, at base cm. 11·7; depth of trough cm. 4. VI.–V. Century.

Doerpfeld, p. 20.

LIONS' HEADS SPOUTS

(1) Medma, small edifice. Mus. Civico, Reggio.

The lateral sima was decorated at intervals with lions' heads which masked the spouts for the discharge of the water collected on the roof. The heads projected for a length of cm. 15, but there are three examples, not uniform in measurement and probably from different very small buildings, not from the temple. The heads only faintly resemble lions, and their long, pointed muzzles, smooth faces and prick ears seem rather those of dogs. The whiskers are rendered by little holes. Judging by the modelling these heads appear to be among the earliest known in Magna Græcia and Sicily, and to be contemporaneous with the tubular spouts. Middle of VI. Century.

FIG. 50.

P. Orsi, *N.S.*, 1913 Suppl., p. 67, fig. 72.

(2) Metaurum, temple. Naples, private collection.

There is a small lion's head which once masked a water-spout. It is very archaic in character, with pointed muzzle conventionally decorated with incised lines forming a Rhodian rosette to indicate folds of flesh. The jowl is open and the throat pierced. The clay is very finely worked and has a beautifully polished cream slip. Since there are no signs of more than one revetment on this temple and since the head seems absolutely contemporaneous with the tubular spouts, it is evident that this must be one of the four lions' heads which carried off the water from the angle of the raking cornices. Middle of VI. Century.

N.S., 1902, p. 128, fig. 3, No. 9.

(3) Megara Hyblæa, Temple A. Mus. Syracuse.

Revetment of the second type. Jaw of the lion's head which formed the gutter behind the angle of the raking cornice. Only the lower jaw remains with the skin of the gums curling back. The chin and throat are the natural colour of the clay, the gums dark red, the teeth white. Length cm. 11. There is also part of the lion's mane standing out in long straight rays. The back of this piece shows a smooth convex surface covered with a cream slip, thus showing that it could not have been placed flat against the sima, but had a considerable projection and stood free from any background, features characteristic of the angle gutter, which had a greater projection to carry off the water from the pediment. Middle of VI. Century.

FIG. 51.

P. Orsi, *Mon. Ant.*, xxvii (1922), col. 163, fig. 8.

(4) Croton, Temple of Hera.

Revetment of the first type. The lateral sima is much broken, but one fragment remains with traces of a large opening for the dispersal of the water. This was originally covered by a large head in relief, most likely a lion's head; yet the filaments still visible on the fascia suggest serpents rather than a lion's mane. In that case the head would be that of a Gorgon; if this is correct, it is a new and unparalleled form which must have succeeded the tubular spouts and preceded the lions' heads. Middle of VI. Century.

FIG. 5.

P. Orsi, *N.S.*, 1911 Suppl., pp. 105–8, fig. 84.

(5) Croton, Temple of Hera.

Revetment of the third type. The lions' heads which mask the gutter-spouts are immense and cover the whole cymation. They are most realistic and beautifully modelled, for out of the ten almost complete examples preserved, no two are identical, but all vary in details: some have a rougher mane, others a more pointed muzzle; in some the eyes are deep-set, others have deeply furrowed brows. Each one must have been carefully worked up by hand. Only one specimen still retains its colouring—a yellow jowl, black brows, lashes and iris, red lips and tongue and a tawny mane. The medial height of these heads is cm. 25, and the prominence of the muzzle varies from cm. 8·5 to cm. 18. Middle of V. Century.

FIG. 13.

P. Orsi, *N.S.*, 1911 Suppl., pp. 107–11, figs. 87, 91–4.

(6) Caulonia, temple. Mus. Civico, Reggio.

The lion's head was set in the middle of the fascia with anthemia and lotus flowers. It was very well modelled and painted in a lifelike manner. The rough mane was in flamelike strands, the eyes were deeply set. V. Century.

P. Orsi, *Mon. Ant.*, xxiii (1916), col. 861, fig. 102.

(7) Caulonia, temple. Mus. Civico, Reggio.

On the sima of small dimensions the lion's head was set between the two lower fasciæ and partially covered both. The mane was conventionally rendered by small thick locks, the leaf-shaped ears stood out from the head. V. Century.

P. Orsi, *Mon. Ant.*, xxiii (1916), col. 862, fig. 104.

(8) Caulonia, temple, *Monasterace*. Mus. Syracuse.

Revetment of the second type. The middle of each slab of the lateral sima was pierced by an opening to carry off the water. This gutter was masked by an extraordinarily realistic lion's head with a double mane, the outer ruff longer and more flamelike than the inner one. The beast's mane, jowl and iris are dark red, the tongue bright red, the pupils of the eyes black with a black circle round the iris and lids. Early V. Century.

(9) Caulonia, temple, *Monasterace*. Mus. Syracuse.

Revetment of the third type. There was a lion's head in the centre of each slab. The mane stood out from the back of the head in a double ruff of short, erect locks. The face in comparison appears smooth, but a ferocious expression is imparted to it by the widely opened eyes, gaping mouth and large leaf-shaped ears. V. Century.

FIG. 15.

P. Orsi, *N.S.*, 1922, p. 148, fig. 1.

(10) Metapontum, Temple of Apollo. Mus. Naples, Potenza and Paris, Cabinet des Médailles.

The central space, where the whole palmette should stand on the fascia, is filled by a lion's head in high relief, rendered with great realism, through whose open mouth the water ran away. There are two varieties of these lions' heads, belonging respectively to the second and third revetments. On the first the ruff is in minute parallel locks round the head, but grows in more natural tufts under the chin. The brow forms a strong angle with the nose ; the mane covers the two flanking lotus buds.

The second variety has a tufted ruff round both the head and throat ; the brow and nose form an almost straight line. The lotus buds at the sides are in no way hidden. In both types the mane is tawny, the teeth painted white, the gums and the inside of the mouth dark red, the tongue and lachrymal glands bright red. There are a few roughly modelled heads which seem to belong to late restorations. Twenty-eight heads were found, some almost perfectly preserved. V. Century.

FIG. 16.

Duc de Luynes et Debacq, *Métaponte* (Paris, 1833), pl. vii, 1, 2 ; De Petra, *Atti Acc. Napoli*, xvii (1894), pp. 3 f., pl. i, 1, 2 ; La Cava, *Topogr. e Storia di*

Metaponto (Napoli, 1891), p. 80, pl. iv; Hittorff, *Arch. polychrome*, Atlas, pl. vi, 9; *N.S.*, 1889, p. 168; Rayet et Collignon, *Hist. de la Céramique*, pl. 16, 2; Perrot, *Hist. de l'Art*, vii, pl. ix.

(11) Metapontum, *Tavole Paladini*. Mus. Potenza.

Fragments of lions' heads. V. Century.

La Cava, *Topogr. e Storia di Metaponto*, p. 87; Koldewey, p. 37.

(12) Selinus, Temple C. Mus. Palermo.

Revetment of the second type. Small and much-broken pieces were found which indicate that the temple was embellished by water-spouts masked by lions' heads. The heads are spiritedly executed and the manes rayed out in detached locks. There was no need of water-spouts on the lateral sima of this revetment, because the water escaped through the holes pierced in the cresting. As parts of three heads only were found, it is obvious that they must have masked the gutters behind the angles of the raking cornice, for there can be no doubt from the place where they were found that they belonged to the revetment of the temple. V. Century.

N.S., 1876, p. 15; 1877, p. 133, No. 45.

(13) Locri, earlier temple, *Marazà*. Mus. Naples.

Part of one of the lions' heads which decorated the lateral sima. The fragment shows the left cheek with the edge of the mouth with curled-back lip, and the mane in sharply defined strands coloured reddish brown. The clay is cream. Very fine work.

(14) Locri, Doric temple, *Marafioti*. Mus. Syracuse.

On the rich lateral sima of this temple the water ran away through the triangular openings in the sima, and the lions' heads were merely decorative. They project from the sima like gutter-spouts, yet they are not pierced. The heads are moulded with splendid realism: the open mouth, from which the lips are drawn back in a thick, fleshy roll, shows the pointed teeth. The wrinkled muzzle and forehead slope up to the bristling dark red mane which, by its astonishing vivacity, gives a ferocious expression to the whole head. First half of V. Century.

P. Orsi, *N.S.*, 1911 Suppl., p. 55 f., figs. 42, 44.

(15) Hipponium. Mus. Civico, Reggio.

A lion's head, half life-size, which masked a water-spout. The mane is conventionally treated in thick separate strands raying out from the head. The jowl is open. Strong traces of colour. V. Century.

(16) Hipponium. Mus. Civico, Reggio.

A lion's head, three-quarters life-size. The muzzle is pointed like that of a dog, the mane falls back in crinkly strands. The eyes were vividly painted with white eyeballs and black iris. The lower jaw, which formed the spout, protrudes considerably. Very fine work. Beginning of V. Century.

(17) Hipponium, Greek temple, *Belvedere*.

Badly broken lions' heads which masked the water-spouts. VI.–V. Century.

P. Orsi, *N.S.*, 1921, p. 480.

(18) Tarentum. Mus. Taranto.

The lion's head has a mane in rippling, flamelike strands. The eyes are small, the mouth open. Lively, realistic treatment. Pale cream clay. End of V. Century.

(19) Metaurum. Private collection, Naples.

There is one small lion's head, roughly worked and quite realistic in style. The open mouth is pierced to allow the water to disperse. This head is of rather coarse, greyish clay and, together with a fragment of meander in relief, probably decorated some small building near the temple. V. Century.

N.S., 1902, p. 128, fig. 3, No. 2.

(20) Gela. Mus. Palermo.

A very realistic lion's head with shaggy mane and well-modelled face. One eye is slightly higher than the other. Only the upper part of the head remains, for it is broken off at the lower jaw. The width is cm. 23. The clay is red, but the face has been covered by a thick cream slip. Only in the ears does the red clay of the core glint through. On the gums and nose are traces of red paint; the mane is tawny yellow. Late V. Century.

Kekulé, *Terrac. von Sic.*, p. 45, fig. 97.

(21) Tarentum. Mus. Taranto.

A lion's head with mane in fine strands, pointed muzzle and open mouth. The treatment is quite realistic. Cream clay. Ht. cm. 9·5; projection of head cm. 10. V.–IV. Century.

(22) Syracuse, Olympieion. Mus. Syracuse.

Revetment of the eighth type. A large and very realistic lion's head. The lower jaw is broken off. Length from the tip of nose to behind ears where the head breaks off cm. 16. Middle of V. Century.

(23) Metapontum, small shrine. Mus. Naples and Potenza.

The little lateral sima was adorned with tiny conventional lions' heads with pointed muzzles and open jaws. The mane is in stylised flamelike rays, the ears are leaf-shaped. In the example at Naples the lower jaw is broken, but it projected considerably. The mould in the museum at Potenza shows that the heads were moulded hollow, in one with the sima. First half of V. Century.

La Cava, *Topogr. e Storia di Metaponto*, p. 115, *g*.

(24) "Sicily." Formerly Rome, Coll. Kopf.

The exact provenance of this head is uncertain, but it is thought to be from Sicily. The lion's mane radiates out in thick locks. The large eyes and brows are painted black, the mane red. The clay is cream. Ht. cm. 24, width cm. 17. As the head does not project straight out, but is turned sharply on the neck, it is probable that this was the spout behind the right angle of the raking cornice. End of VI. Century.

L. Pollak, *Joseph von Kopf als Sammler* (Rom. 1905), No. iii, pl. vi.

(25) Rhegium, sporadic. Mus. Civico, Reggio.

Gutter in the shape of a marine monster with pointed snout, prick ears, small round eyes and rough hair or crest which resembles the dorsal fin of a fish. The work is extremely fine, the clay is red, but all traces of colour have disappeared. Length about cm. 30. This splendid head must have masked the gutter behind the angle of the raking cornice. VI.–V. Century.

PALMETTES OF THE RIDGE-POLE

(1) Gela, archaic temple. Mus. Syracuse.

A very few fragments of rather small palmettes were discovered which must have decorated the ridge-pole of the temple. One example was larger than the others and probably marked the centre of the roof. Middle of VI. Century.

P. Orsi, *Mon. Ant.*, xxv (1919), col. 680.

(2) S. Mauro, archaic temple. Mus. Syracuse.

Revetment of the second type. More than thirty pieces of small palmettes were found, apparently not all from the same mould, for there are slight divergences of dimensions and treatment. A double volute supports the calyx of the palmette, and the thirteen leaves, alternately red and black, rise tall and slender with slightly concave surfaces to a height of cm. 35 × 30·5. These palmettes were attached to a small base which was fixed astride the rounded kalypter covering the ridge-pole, from which they rose along the whole length of the roof. They are consequently painted alike on both sides, as both sides were equally visible. One Ionic palmette, approximate height cm. 50, probably adorned the middle of the ridge-pole ; it was coloured alike on both sides with leaves alternately red and black. VI.–V. Century.

FIG. 52.

P. Orsi, *Mon. Ant.*, xx (1910), cols. 782–7, figs. 46, 47, pl. vii, 1 ; xxv (1919), col. 680.

(3) Syracuse, *temenos*. Mus. Syracuse.

Revetment of the first type. Very fragmentary is the large palmette, ht. cm. 31 × 47·5, but enough is preserved to show that it rose from a support of two volutes bound at the neck and having the eyes of the volutes decorated with rosettes. A secondary spiral sprang from the main stem, and in the fork nestled a little palmette. This large palmette was not applied to the end of the beam like an akroterion, but was placed astride the kalypter which covered the ridge-pole. The palmettes were therefore placed in pairs at intervals along the roof, and were designed to be seen from either side. VI. Century.

FIG. 53.

P. Orsi, *Mon. Ant.*, xxv (1919), col. 673, fig. 248 ; *N.S.*, 1910, p. 527, fig. 7.

(4) Syracuse, Cortile of the archiepiscopal palace. Mus. Syracuse.

Part of a large palmette, cm. 23 × 18, analogous to that found in the *temenos*. VI. Century.

P. Orsi, *Mon. Ant.*, xxv (1919), col. 496, fig. 88.

(5) Selinus, Temple C. Mus. Palermo.

Revetment of the first type. Fragments of the palmettes which decorated the ridge-pole, painted on both sides. VI.–V. Century.

N.S., 1877, p. 67, Nos. 21–5 ; p. 133, Nos. 2, 3, 9 ; *Mon. Ant.*, xx (1910), col. 784 ; Perrot, *Hist. de l'Art*, vii, p. 536, pl. vii, 1.

(6) Selinus, Temple D. Mus. Palermo.

Two fragments of palmettes decorated on both sides and fastened with long nails were found on the west side of the temple. First half of V. Century.

N.S., 1877, p. 133, No. 44.

(7) Caulonia, temple, *Monasterace*. Mus. Civico, Reggio.

Revetment of the first type. Palmettes in relief, painted on both sides and springing from double volutes. VI.-V. Century.

(8) Syracuse, Olympieion. Mus. Syracuse.

Revetment of the sixth type. A fragment of a palmette in slight relief. It seems to spring from double volutes painted cream with a central knob marked black. The palmette has seven leaves, the middle of each defined by a line alternately red and black, and each leaf is outlined black. The clay is rather coarse and red. First half of V. Century.

(9) Locri, Doric temple, *Marafioti*. Mus. Naples.

A small palmette springing from broad double volutes; no trace of colour. Ht. about cm. 15. There is a second example, not identical, but with more pointed leaves. First half of V. Century.

(10) Akragas. Mus. Girgenti.

Near the two columns which decorated the *opisthodomos* of the Temple of Herakles a fictile palmette was found, adorned on both sides. Well preserved, but the lower part missing. A similar palmette was found in 1833 and is now in the Palermo Museum. V. Century.

N.S., 1883, p. 189; Serradifalco, *Ant. della Sic.*, iii, pl. xvii, 10, 11; Koldewey, p. 149.

PENDENT PALMETTES

(1) Syracuse, *temenos*. Mus. Syracuse.

Revetment of the first type. A large number of small palmettes, ht. cm. 14, were found. They are painted on one side only in red and black. The base of these palmettes shows that they have been broken off from some support to which they were attached by a lead solder. Little vertical holes are still visible at the base of the palmettes, and these holes correspond to small oblique holes in the lower surface of the casings of the raking cornice and horizontal geison where traces of cleavage are very evident. The palmettes fit exactly to these points of attachment and prove that they were placed precisely in this position, hanging down like a frieze and secured in place by a flexible ligature applied by fusion. Thus they served the purpose of a " drop " or *guttæ* and at the same time formed an ornamental hanging border. VI. Century.

P. Orsi, *Mon. Ant.*, xxv (1919), cols. 654–6, fig. 233, pls. xix, C, xxi.

(2) S. Mauro, archaic temple. Mus. Syracuse.

Revetment of the second type. One very small palmette with a diameter of only cm. 8 is extremely thick, cm. 7·4. It is not certain what function it fulfilled, but a comparison with the more recently discovered palmettes of the revetment of the first type from the *temenos*, Syracuse, may show that here also this little palmette was used in like manner. VI.–V. Century.

P. Orsi, *Mon. Ant.*, xx (1910), col. 786.

(3) Selinus, Temple C. Mus. Palermo.

Revetment of the first type. There are certain small palmettes, decorated in relief on one side only, which may have hung from the lower surface of the geison, because they have a curved base which seems to show traces of attachment. VI.–V. Century.

ROOF-TILES

(1) Granmichele, Acropolis. Mus. Syracuse.

On the summit of the hill masses of roof-tiles and kalypteres were lying around, all injured by fire. V. Century.

P. Orsi, *Mon. Ant.*, vii (1897), col. 203.

(2) Locri, Temple of Athena, Mannella.

A very few fictile tiles were found ; on the border of one of them the sign Φ was incised and repeated four times. Second half of VI. Century.

P. Orsi, *N.S.*, 1911 Suppl., p. 64.

(3) Megara Hyblæa, Temple B. Mus. Syracuse.

The tiles were curved and at one side had a raised border to fit into the inset in the neighbouring tile which consequently fitted tightly over and interlocked. These tiles are cm. 3·5 thick. Middle of VI. Century.

P. Orsi, *Mon. Ant.*, xxvii (1922), col. 171.

(4) S. Mauro, archaic temple. Mus. Syracuse.

Among the material from the temple were curved roof-tiles and kalypteres, painted black and reduced to a few little bits. VI. Century.

P. Orsi, *Mon. Ant.*, xx (1910), cols. 779, 790.

(5) Selinus, Acropolis. Mus. Palermo.

A certain number of roof-tiles were discovered. They are flat, but with an upturned edge at each side, so that they might adhere compactly one to another at the edges where they were covered by the vertical kalypteres. At the third side the tile had a concave moulding which lapped over the tile of the upper row. Some of these tiles retain traces of red or black colour, showing that the whole roof was painted in order to render the tiles impervious to weather. A fine example, found in the necropolis of *Manicalunga,* where it was used as the cover of a burial, is now in the museum at Castelvetrano. The tiles measure cm. 57 × 79. VI.–V. Century.

Salinas, *N.S.*, 1884, p. 336, pl. vi, *a* ; Doerpfeld, p. 17, fig. in text ; Hittorff, *Recueil* (Paris, 1870), pl. xlvi, 7–8 (erroneously stated to be from Temple F).

(6) Caulonia, temple, *Monasterace.* Mus. Syracuse.

Revetment of the third type. These tiles have an interesting system of interlocking. Two off-sets are cut on the left side of a tile and two corresponding projections on the right side of the next tile, which consequently fitted over it and interlocked so securely that it could not possibly slip. The tiles overlapped for one-fourth of their total breadth ; that is, one tile was covered by its neighbour on the right side and overlapped its fellow on the left. With this system there was no need of kalypteres, because there was no exposed juncture. Middle of V. Century.

(7) Locri, Doric temple, *Marafioti*.

During the excavations a large number of flat roof-tiles and also kalypteres were found. These latter were of considerable length, cm. 78, and in certain cases were moulded in one with the tiles, so that each tile was covered by the convex edge of its fellow on the right. V. Century.

P. Orsi, *N.S.*, 1911 Suppl., p. 36, fig. 27.

(8) Gela, Heroön of Antiphemos. Mus. Comunale, Terranova.

Several pieces of roof-tiles and kalypteres were found in the excavations. VI. Century.

P. Orsi, *Mon. Ant.*, xvii (1906), col. 558.

(9) Croton, Temple of Hera.

Many fictile tiles of the usual types, but differing in size and shape, were found, thus showing that although the larger ones may have come from the temple, the others must have belonged to adjacent buildings. VI.–V. Century.

P. Orsi, *N.S.*, 1911 Suppl., p. 115.

(10) Syracuse, Olympieion. Mus. Syracuse.

Revetment of the second type. Numerous pieces of thick, flat roof-tiles. VI. Century.

P. Orsi, *Mon. Ant.*, xiii (1903), col. 383.

(11) Caulonia, temple, *Monasterace*.

" Besides the tiles of Parian marble, a great quantity of fictile tiles, kalypteres and bricks were discovered : perhaps some of the tiles were a late restoration when it was no longer possible to procure the splendid marble tiles." Late V. Century.

P. Orsi, *Mon. Ant.*, xxiii (1916), col. 866.

(12) Rhegium, below the new Prefecture. Mus. Civico, Reggio.

Two pieces of tiles were discovered, moulded on each side where the tiles joined with a raised margin which was covered by the vertical kalypteres. These tiles measure cm. 64 × 62 and are mm. 8 thick. On the lower surface they are painted with an anthemion design in red and white on a dark ground for a length of cm. 23·5, that being the distance which they projected beyond the wall.

The front edge is decorated with black meander on a light ground, the spaces filled by stars.

P. Orsi, *N.S.*, 1922, p. 158, fig. 8.

KALYPTERES OF THE RIDGE-POLE

(1) S. Mauro, *Anaktoron.* Mus. Syracuse.

Two kalypteres were found, painted reddish brown, among the other small broken bits of architectonic terra-cottas. VII.–VI. Century.

P. Orsi, *N.S.*, 1903, p. 432 ; 1904, p. 373 ; *Mon. Ant.*, xx (1910), col. 740.

(2) Monte Bubbonía, area of Acropolis, *Anaktoron.* Mus. Syracuse.

A kalypter painted with a coarse, bold meander in black on a cream ground. Early VI. Century.

(3) Megara Hyblæa, Temple A. Mus. Syracuse.

Revetment of the second type. Fragment of a large kalypter painted with a simple tongue pattern in red and black. Middle of VI. Century.

P. Orsi, *Mon. Ant.*, xxvii (1922), col. 164, fig. 9.

(4) Gela, archaic temple. Mus. Syracuse.

A splendid kalypter, length cm. 70, richly patterned with designs on a cream ground. On the saddle of the kalypter is a bold meander in black ; below it comes a row of red and black tongue pattern, outlined with cream on a black ground ; next, triangles in red and black. The double toroi which edge the mouth of the kalypter have contrasting diagonal bands in red and black. On each side in the wall of the kalypter is a semicircular space which fitted over the line of vertical kalypteres covering the tiles. Middle of VI. Century.

FIG. 54.

P. Orsi, *Mon. Ant.*, xvii (1906), col. 284, fig. 211, pl. xxiv, 2 (in colour).

(5) Rhegium, archaic temple. Mus. Civico, Reggio.

Several kalypteres were found, both the larger kalypteres of the ridge-pole and also the small vertical kalypteres, but they were all the same shape, rounded with a torus at one end. The kalypteres of the ridge-pole had a triple torus, the first and third painted with diagonal bands in red and black, the second with vertical bands. The rounded body of the kalypter was adorned with bold double black meander, the sides with red and black tongue pattern. Early VI. Century.

Koldewey, p. 50.

(6) Caulonia, temple, *Monasterace.* Mus. Civico, Reggio.

Revetment of the first type. Numerous large kalypteres, richly painted on the top of the rounded body with black meander and at the sides with tongue pattern, chevrons, etc. Length cm. 68. VI.–V. Century.

(7) Caulonia, *Collina del Faro.* Mus. Civico, Reggio.

Among the ruins of the house in the eastern part of the city were found numerous kalypteres with triple toroi round the edges, and one with a semi-cylindrical opening in the side which proves it to have been one of the kalypteres of the ridge-pole. VI.–V. Century.

P. Orsi, *Mon. Ant.*, xxiii (1916), col. 822, fig. 83.

(8) Caulonia, temple. Mus. Civico, Reggio.

One large fragment of a kalypter, decorated with double toroi at the edge, measured cm. 32 across the mouth. Fragments of other kalypteres. V. Century.

P. Orsi, *Mon. Ant.*, xxiii (1916), col. 667, fig. 107.

(9) Locri, earlier temple, *Marazà.* Mus. Syracuse.

Revetment of the second type. There are a great number of rounded kalypteres coloured solidly either red or black. Second half of VI. Century.

(10) Syracuse, *temenos.* Mus. Syracuse.

Revetment of the first type. A fragment of the border of an enormous kalypter, painted with diagonal bands in red and black. VI. Century.

N.S., 1910, p. 532, fig. 11.

(11) Syracuse, Olympieion. Mus. Syracuse.

Revetment of the second type. A fragment of the triple torus of a kalypter, painted with diagonal bands in red and black on a cream ground ; there are also several bits of kalypteres painted reddish brown. VI. Century.

P. Orsi, *Mon. Ant.*, xiii (1903), col. 383.

(12) Selinus, Acropolis. Mus. Palermo.

Many fragments were discovered of certain colossal kalypteres of the ridge-pole of a large temple. They were of the usual form, rounded and finished off at one end with triple toroi, and they have semicircular openings in the sides for the insertion of the vertical kalypteres. The scale is so enormous that these kalypteres have a diameter of at least m. 2·00. The first and third toroi were painted with vertical bands, the middle one with red and black chevrons. The saddle of the kalypter was ornamented with black double meander, the body with meander, tongue pattern and various designs. VI. Century.

N.S., 1882, p. 331, pl. xx, 2 (Cavallari) ; 1884, pp. 334–6, pl. vi, *v*.457, *v*.62, *v*.63, *v*.110, vi, 276 (Salinas).

(13) Selinus, Temple C. Coll. Calcara, Castelvetrano and Mus. Palermo.

Revetment of the first type. In the west portico of Temple C were found a quantity of kalypteres and roof-tiles. Amongst the former were a number of large dimensions which covered the ridge-pole. They were rounded and finished off at one end with triple toroi painted with vertical bands and chevrons. The body of the kalypter was adorned with various designs, meander and triangles in red and black. The openings in the sides for the insertion of the vertical kalypteres are not perfectly semicircular, but slightly lop-sided. The fragments are too shattered to allow of a complete reconstruction. The kalypteres had a diameter of cm. 75. VI.–V. Century.

Salinas, *N.S.*, 1884, pp. 334–6, pl. vi, A, *s*, *n*, *v*.26, 2 (the reconstruction is purely conjectural and therefore the designs reproduced give a false impression ; *cf*. Salinas, *op. cit.*, pl. vi, A, B) ; Perrot, *Hist. de l'Art*, vii, pl. xliv, 5, 6 ; Durm, *Bauk. der Griechen* (1910), p. 203, fig. 176 ; Hulot et Fougères, *Sélinonte*, p. 227, fig. in text ; Doerpfeld, p. 17, fig. in text.

ANTEFIXES

(1) Granmichele, *Predio Ventura*. Mus. Syracuse.

The fragment of a large semi-elliptical slab which, when complete, must have measured cm. 21·5, as one can judge from the semi-cylindrical attachment behind. On the front face a rudimentary meander is painted in black outlined with brownish red ; between the two rows of meander are red wriggling lines. Although artistically this piece is crude and negligible, yet it is important as being the only specimen of the kind hitherto known. VII. Century.

P. Orsi, *N.S.*, 1903, p. 434 ; *Mon. Ant.*, xviii (1907), col. 146, fig. 7.

(2) Hipponium. Mus. Civico, Reggio.

Antefixes with the face capping the master-tile. The field is shaped like a pointed arch, and on it is depicted a lion's head in relief so low that the whole effect was produced by colour. Against a black background the cream face of the beast stands out ; the eyes are black circles in almond lids outlined black. There are two sizes ; the larger measures about cm. 15 in height, but the lower half is broken. The smaller size is about cm. 12 in height. Middle of VI. Century.

(3) Monte Bubbonía, area of Acropolis. Mus. Syracuse.

Half the forehead of a Gorgon with the hair in a thick roll or fringe. In the lower *Anaktoron* a fragment of another Gorgoneion was found ; here again only the forehead and hair remain ; the fragment shows traces of fire, as if the building to which it belonged had been burnt down. Early VI. Century.

(4) Syracuse, Olympieion. Mus. Syracuse.

Revetment of the second type. A small antefix, ht. about cm. 10 × 9·5, decorated with a Gorgoneion applied directly to the face of the tile. The hair is combed forward over the forehead in crinkly lines ending in a knoblike curl, five on each side set slightly apart. Arched brows, staring almond eyes, large, very flat ears just indicated; nose broken and all the left lower side of the face. The right corner of the mouth shows that it was recessed, with sharply pointed tusks also set a little apart. Up the middle of the forehead is a groove; there are three "pearl-locks" on either side. Second half of VI. Century.

(5) Trinacia, *S. Anastasia.* Mus. Palermo.

The slab is broken on the right side, but is sufficiently preserved to enable one to ascertain its dimensions: ht. cm. 36. The Gorgoneion is in low relief, but here the mask does not occupy the whole space, for the neck also is given almost to the shoulders. The face is triangular, with wrinkled forehead, squat nose and gaping mouth encircled by a thick roll of flesh. Sharp tusks protrude from the outer corners of the mouth and the pendent tongue covers half the chin. The eyes are rendered by an almond-shaped swelling upon which the iris was painted; the eyebrows overarch like a heavy roll, and the cheeks are puffy owing to the deeply recessed mouth. The hair grows in two layers of tight spiral curls round the forehead, and hangs down on to the shoulders in six "pearl-locks" on either side. VI. Century.

E. Gabrici, *Atti R. Acc. di Palermo*, serie 3, xi, p. 10, pl. ii, 4.

(6) S. Mauro, Acropolis. Mus. Syracuse.

Gorgoneion, greatest breadth, cm. 14. The slab, which was in the shape of a blunt triangle, has been entirely broken away above and on the left side, leaving only the widespreading nostrils and the mouth with its tusks and pendent tongue intact. The mouth is encircled by a roll of flesh; the teeth are absolutely even and the tongue only covers half the chin. Three "pearl-locks" on the right side hang down to the lower edge of the slab, which has no border in relief to finish it off. The clay is red. End of VI. Century.

P. Orsi, *Mon. Ant.*, xx (1910), col. 751, fig. 11.

(7) Gela. Mus. Syracuse.

The lower part of a large triangular slab with a Gorgoneion in relief. The cheeks are puffy, the nose well formed, the gaping mouth has a narrow band of relief to indicate the lips; the teeth are even, but there are no tusks or beard. The pendent tongue half covers the chin. In each corner of the mouth is a round hole, perhaps for the insertion of the tusks, which would in that case have been made separately and stuck in, but have now fallen out. The hair is in six narrow waves. The clay is red. Ht. from root of nose, cm. 10 × 20·5. Late VI. Century.

(8) Syracuse. Mus. Syracuse.

The face of the antefix is almost triangular in form and the Gorgoneion covers the whole surface. The brows are arched, the eyes are an almond-shaped swelling, the nose pointed rather than squat, the mouth recessed, but almost closed with pendent tongue which only covers half the chin, and no tusks. The hair behind the large, flat ears is in crinkly strands, but round the forehead it is in big, flat spiral curls and is surmounted by a diadem. First half of V. Century.

Kekulé, *Terrac. von Sic.*, p. 42, fig. 87.

(9) Caulonia, dwelling-houses, *Collina del Faro*. Mus. Civico, Reggio.

Fragments of at least three Gorgoneia were found, all varying slightly in details. The largest piece measures cm. 15·5 × 12·5 and has the hair combed straight forward and ending in spirals. The eyes are an almond-shaped swelling between thick lids. Large tusks protrude from the corners of the thick-rimmed mouth. The second type has the hair in wide convex waves which end in flat spirals. The eye is an almond-shaped swelling surrounded by a narrow rim. The third example has small tight knobs for curls, almond-shaped eyes below highly arched thick brows. The ear is small and very flat. VI. Century.

P. Orsi, *Mon. Ant.*, xxiii (1916), col. 795, fig. 64.

(10) Croton. Cotrone, Coll. Lucifero.

A life-sized Gorgoneion covers the whole field without any border around it. The hair is in spiral curls round the forehead. The eyes are large and staring, the ears enormous; the mouth is surrounded by a thick roll of flesh and at the corners are great tusks. The pendent tongue covers the whole chin. The mask is very effective, but it is more conventional than really archaic. VI.–V. Century.

N.S., 1897, pp. 352 f., fig. 10.

(11) Syracuse. Mus. Syracuse, No. 16491.

A small antefix directly capping the face of the tile and depicting a Gorgoneion with a very broad face, hair in four closely set bossy spirals on each side of the forehead and in two "pearl-locks" hanging down on to either shoulder. She has enormous flat ears, arched brows, small almond-shaped eyes between thick rims, a pointed nose, a deeply recessed mouth and pendent tongue which covers the whole chin. Only the upper row of teeth are indicated and there are no tusks. Ht. cm. 5 × 7. VI. Century.

(12) Syracuse. Mus. Syracuse.

A small antefix of a Gorgoneion with brows in relief, almond eyes, pointed nose, mouth with a thick rim, even teeth, tusks in the extreme corners and pendent tongue which covers the whole chin. The ears and hair are broken and the whole antefix is much rubbed. Red clay. Early V. Century.

(13) Syracuse. Mus. Syracuse.

The top of the Gorgon's head is broken, but there are traces on the left temple of spiral curls. The cheeks are puffy, the mouth recessed with tusks and a pendent tongue which covers the whole chin. Late V. Century.

Hittorff, *Recueil* (Paris, 1870), p. 119, pl. xxviii, 3; Kekulé, *Terrac. von Sic.*, p. 42.

(14) Trinacia, *S. Anastasia*. Coll. Vagliasindi, Randazzo.

A much battered antefix with the head of a Gorgon. The top part is broken, and all the lower part from the upper lip downwards. The face is round with puffy cheeks, arched plastic brows, almond-shaped eyes obliquely set, squat nose and large, flat ears. Beginning of V. Century.

F. di Roberto, "Randazzo e la Valle dell' Alcantara" in *Italia Artistica*, No. 49 (Bergamo, 1909), p. 41, fig. in text.

(15) Catana. Mus. Biscari.

A Gorgoneion with hair parted and waved to either side round the forehead, but hanging in loose locks over the shoulders. The arched brows almost meet over the squat nose. The eyes are an almond-shaped swelling, the cheeks very puffy, the mouth recessed and surrounded by a thick fleshy rim. A pair of sharp tusks sticks out on either side of the pendent tongue which covers the whole chin. End of V. Century.

Serradifalco, *Ant. della Sic.*, v, pl. xviii, 6; Kekulé, *Terrac. von Sic.*, p. 43.

(16) Rhegium. Mus. Civico, Reggio.

An immense Gorgoneion; only the right half of the forehead with the brow and eye are preserved. The hair was waved in scallops. VI.–V. Century.

(17) Selinus, Acropolis. Mus. Palermo.

The perfectly round mask of a Gorgoneion; ht. cm. 18. The hair is in scalloped waves, the forehead wrinkled, the eyes almond-shaped between arched brows in relief, the nose broken, but with spreading nostrils; the mouth is surrounded by a thick roll of flesh and the pendent tongue half covers the chin. The ears are placed rather high and are very crudely rendered. Middle of V. Century.

N.S., 1876, pp. 46, 108, pl. v, 1; 1877, p. 133; Kekulé, *Terrac. von Sic.*, p. 42, fig. 83.

(18) Tarentum. New York, Metrop. Mus., No. 44; The Hague, Mr. C. W. Lunsingh Scheurleer, No. 1105; Munich, Antiquarium; Mannheim, Antiquarium.

A semi-elliptical antefix representing a Gorgoneion in relief, the face rather broad with a chin ending in double lobes. The brows are rendered by sharp ridges, the eyes are almond-shaped, the nose trefoliate and the mouth slightly recessed and outlined by a narrow rim. The teeth are small and regular, but at each side of the mouth is a pair of long and very pointed tusks. The pendent tongue covers half the chin, round which there is a short beard in flamelike strands. The ears are extremely conventionally rendered and are placed on a level with the brows. The hair round the forehead is in scalloped waves, but hangs down on either side in four fine " pearl-locks." There is a narrow framing round the head consisting of a three-grooved border. First half of V. Century.

FIG. 55.

Photograph, Deutsches Archäol. Inst., Rome, No. 74.5.

(19) Tarentum. Marseilles, Coll. Vlasto, No. 1.

Gorgoneion with an unusually square type of countenance. The hair is arranged in large spiral curls over the forehead and in numerous fine " pearl-locks " below the ears. The brows are almost straight, the eyes small and round between almond-shaped lids. The straight nose has spreading nostrils and the recessed mouth is bordered by a narrow rim ; the tongue is pendent and there are tusks at each corner of the gaping mouth. The Gorgon is bearded and wears disc earrings in her small, highly placed ears. The head is surrounded by a narrow frame and is set directly against the face of the tile which ran back for some distance. Ht. cm. 17·5 ; width, cm. 24·5. Middle of V. Century.

FIG. 56.

(20) Tarentum. Trieste, Mus. Civico, 1389.

Gorgoneion with corkscrew curls round the forehead ending in tight spirals. The face is plump and almost round. The eyes are almond-shaped, the mouth deeply recessed, with even teeth, tusks and pendent tongue. The chin ends in double lobes. This example is broken at the sides and top, so that it is impossible to say if it was bearded or if there were serpents at the sides. Late V. Century.

FIG. 57.

Photograph, Alinari, No. 21163.

(21) Syracuse. Mus. Syracuse.

A very broken antefix of a Gorgon with trefoliate nose, a pendent tongue covering the whole chin, but no tusks. V. Century.

(22) Syracuse. Mus. Syracuse.

An antefix with a Gorgoneion which covers the whole field. The hair over the forehead is in flat curls, but hangs down on to the shoulders in thick " pearl-locks." The large flat ears follow the contour of the skull. The eyes are almond-shaped, the nose squat, the mouth recessed with square teeth but no tusks. The pendent tongue covers the whole chin. End of VI. Century.

Hittorff, *Recueil* (Paris, 1870), p. 119, pl. xxviii, 3.

(23) Selinus, Propylaia, Gaggera. Mus. Palermo.

" Found, two archaic masks with holes for suspension. The first with a kind of cap and especially noteworthy for its dimensions, ht. cm. 19, and for the accurate work and hitherto unknown type."

N.S., 1894, p. 206.

(24) Granmichele, *Predio Ventura.* Mus. Syracuse.

During the excavations two semi-elliptical antefixes were found. They are decorated in relief, both apparently from the same mould, with the head of a Gorgon. Her hair is parted and waved back in spiral curls ; she has almond eyes, a squat nose, gaping mouth with pointed tusks, a pendent tongue and highly placed ears from behind which on either side writhes a great bearded, red-spotted serpent. The hair, beard and eyes of the Gorgon are black. Second half of the VI. Century.

P. Orsi, *N.S.*, 1903, p. 434 ; *Mon. Ant.*, xviii (1907), col. 146, fig. 6.

(25) Syracuse. Mus. Syracuse, No. 8959.

A large Gorgoneion : the face is very flat, the hair in a double row of curls, the triangular forehead wrinkled, the brows in low relief, the eyes almond-shaped between thick rims, the nose pointed, the mouth recessed. She has even teeth, tusks at the corners of the mouth and a pendent tongue which covers half the chin, from below which two bearded serpents rear themselves upwards to a level with her ears. The clay is grey with many black particles. V. Century.

(26) Camarina. Mus. Syracuse.

A Gorgoneion in very low relief : the hair is in spiral curls round the forehead, the brows are arched ; she has round eyes, a pointed nose, gaping mouth, tusks and pendent tongue which covers the whole chin. The beard is indicated by three spirals on each side of the tongue. A bearded serpent rears his head on either side of the cheeks. Red clay. Ht. about cm. 8 × 8. V. Century.

(27) Ruvo. London, British Museum.

A semi-elliptical antefix with a Gorgoneion in low relief. The face is broad with elongated almond eyes, a pointed nose and recessed mouth with small sharp tusks. The pendent tongue covers the whole chin, which is surrounded by a conventional beard. The small ears are placed very high and the hair is in scalloped waves. Two bearded serpents, one on each side, rear their heads level with the Gorgon's ears. The clay is pale red with a cream slip ; there is no trace of colour. Late V. Century.

Brit. Mus. Cat. Terrac., B. 581.

(28) Tarentum. New York, Metrop. Mus.

Gorgoneion with hair round forehead in scalloped waves. The eyebrows are a sharp ridge ; the eyes are almond-shaped in very low relief, the nose is trefoliate, the gaping mouth recessed, with even teeth, very sharp tusks and pendent tongue.

The chin ends in a double lobe and is surrounded by a beard of large flamelike strands. The ears are highly placed and extremely conventionalised. From behind either cheek a large bearded serpent rears outward. The head is framed by a narrow raised border with a double groove. Early V. Century.

FIG. 58.

Bull. Metrop. Mus., xvii (1922), p. 115; photograph, Deutsches Archäol. Inst., Rome, No. 74.5, left.

(29) Hipponium. Mus. Civico, Reggio.

The Gorgoneion has hair in tight curls, small tusks and a pendent tongue which covers half the chin. Above her head rise a number of little serpents forming *S*. Ht. about cm. 30. The clay is reddish with a cream slip; there is no trace of colour. Early V. Century.

(30) Tarentum. The Hague, Mr. C. W. Lunsingh Scheurleer, 1103; New York, Metrop. Mus., No. 46; Munich, Antiquarium.

A Gorgoneion with a double row of spiral curls round the forehead and hair hanging down below the ears in very numerous "pearled" strands on each side. The brows are a sharp ridge, the eyes almond-shaped and slightly oblique, the nose trefoliate, the gaping mouth recessed, with tusks and pendent tongue, and the chin ending in a double lobe. Round the head is a circle of *S*-shaped serpents which stand out against the background, which is finished off by a narrow flat raised border. In this type the face is small in comparison to the wide border of serpents surrounding it. Early V. Century.

FIG. 61.

Photograph, Deutsches Archäol. Inst., Rome, No. 74.4.

(31) Tarentum. The Hague, Mr. C. W. Lunsingh Scheurleer, 1106; Trieste, Mus. Civico, No. 1388; Marseilles, Coll. Vlasto, No. 2a.

Gorgoneion with hair in two rows of tight curls, small round eyes obliquely set, straight nose with spreading nostrils, deeply recessed mouth with narrow rim, pendent tongue and very sharp tusks. The head is entirely framed in a ring of small *S*-shaped serpents set against a solid background which extends beyond the serpents' heads. Ht. cm. 21, width cm. 24. White slip. V. Century.

FIG. 59.

Photograph, Alinari, No. 21163.

(32) Tarentum. Trieste, Mus. Civico, No. 5; Marseilles, Coll. Vlasto, No. 2.

Gorgoneion with hair in two rows of tight curls. The eyes are small and obliquely set, the nostrils spreading and the gaping mouth recessed with pendent tongue and sharp tusks. The face is broad and is entirely encircled by a ring of *S*-shaped serpents who stand out free from any background. The face was covered with a creamy slip; the hair, lips and tongue were red, the eyes, eyebrows and serpents black, but the serpents' tongues were red. At the back the head protruded beyond the triangular support. Ht. cm. 19; width cm. 20. V. Century.

FIG. 60.

Photograph, Alinari, No. 21163.

(33) Metapontum. Mus. Provinciale, Potenza.

A Gorgoneion absolutely identical with the above specimen from Tarentum.

La Cava, *Topogr. e St. di Metaponto*, pl. iv, 3.

(34) Syracuse. Mus. Syracuse.

A Gorgoneion covering the whole face of the antefix. The forehead is wrinkled, the nose squat, the eyes almond-shaped. The mouth is recessed with sharp tusks and a pendent tongue which covers the whole chin. The hair is piled up on the head and is elaborately waved. On top of the head are traces of serpents (?). Ht. cm. 22. One example was found on Ortygia, another in the *Necropolis del Fusco*. Late V. Century.

Kekulé, *Terrac. von Sic.*, p. 42, fig. 84.

(35) Inessa. Mus. Syracuse.

An antefix with a large round Gorgoneion in low relief. She has two rows of tight curls and round eyes between almond lids so large that they meet across the root of the nose. She wears a high diadem with painted bosses in high relief at intervals. All the lower part of the face is broken. Pale red clay. V. Century.

(36) Gela. London, British Mus.

Gorgoneion, quite circular in form. The hair is parted and waved back in two rows of curls over the forehead and looped-up tresses on either side. The teeth are indicated in the gaping mouth, and the tongue is pendent. The Gorgon wears a *stephané* and circular earrings. The antefix, which is injured at the sides, is cut off flat below; at the back is a curved projection. V. Century.

Brit. Mus. Cat. Terrac., B. 580.

(37) Leontini. Mus. Syracuse.

The small head of a Satyr. He has a wrinkled forehead, arched brows, almond eyes set wide apart between thick lids, a small nose, a mouth with lips slightly parted to show the teeth, a long beard indicated by wavy lines, a " mouche " and a very long straight moustache. His equine ears curve round his skull and from below them hang four spiral curls on either side, although the rest of his head is bald, but is encircled by a fillet. The work is very fine and the head directly caps the face of the tile. There are traces of red on the hair, beard and inside the ears. Ht. about cm. 12·5 × 11. Middle of V. Century.

(38) Gela. Mus. Syracuse.

The small head of a Satyr, bald with a wrinkled forehead, frowning brows, widely opened eyes, squat nose and animal's ears curving round the skull. He has an open mouth with thick lips and small even teeth, a straight moustache, a " mouche " and beard in narrow strands radiating outwards. A background of crinkly lines rises straight out behind his head like a diadem. The lower part of his beard is broken and the whole face is much rubbed. Red clay with a cream slip. Ht. cm. 18·7 × 17. V. Century.

(39) Tarentum. Trieste, Mus. Civico, No. 15.

Head of a Satyr. The hair is in scalloped waves which run back in grooves over the crown. Below the ears, which are very long and pointed, the hair hangs in fine " pearled " locks, whilst the beard is carefully trimmed and pointed and marked with herringbone pattern. The forehead is very narrow, the widely opened eyes slightly oblique, the nose squat and the lips thick. The head is surrounded by a small rolled border. Second half of V. Century.

FIG. 62.

Photograph, Alinari, No. 21162.

(40) Camarina. Mus. Syracuse.

Heads of Satyrs, three types. In the first the hair is in a solid mass over the crown and ends in scallops round the forehead ; he has very pointed equine ears, a wrinkled forehead and small almond eyes below frowning brows ; his beard seems to have been in rayed strands, but all the lower part of the face is broken. Cream clay. Early V. Century.

The second type has hair in a thick mass on the head but scalloped over the forehead ; the ears are large and placed lower than on the preceding example. He has a wrinkled forehead, widely opened eyes set in thick-rimmed lids, arched brows in relief and a squat nose. The lower part of the face is broken. Cream clay. Early V. Century.

In the third type the Satyr's head is shown in relief against a small semi-elliptical background ; the hair is in tight curls ; he has round eyes, a squat nose, a straight moustache and a long pointed beard indicated by fine wavy lines. Early V. Century.

(41) Akragas. The Hague, Mr. C. W. Lunsingh Scheurleer ; Munich, Sammlung Loeb.

A Satyr's head with thick hair over the head, strongly arched brows in high relief, round eyes, a squat nose and long, straight moustache. The strands of hair on the head and on the full beard are indicated by rippling lines. Ht. cm. 22. Greenish-yellow clay. The clay and the whole character of the work suggest that this head comes from Sicily or Magna Græcia, although the exact provenance of the Munich example is unknown. Early V. Century.

FIG. 63.

Sammlung Loeb Terrakotten, ii (J. Sieveking, München, 1916), p. 60.

(42) Naxos. Mus. Palermo.

A Satyr's head directly capping the face of the antefix without any frame. The features are refined, the nose normal, the eyes almond-shaped, the mouth closed. Only the long pointed ears are bestial. The thick hair is arranged in orderly locks round the forehead and the long beard has rippling strands in low relief. The straight moustache is rather long. Ht. cm. 19. There are two examples, one consisting of the upper part of the face only, the other of the lower part. The two have been united in the sketch. The clay is reddish yellow and was covered on the surface with a layer of finer clay of a cream tint. End of V. Century.

Kekulé, *Terrac. von Sic.*, p. 43, fig. 90.

(43) Gela. Mus. Syracuse.

A small Satyr's head with hair standing straight upon end and marked by wavy lines, a small triangular wrinkled forehead, arched brows in relief, oblique almond eyes, pointed nose and straight moustache. His equine ears stand straight up and on his head is a high diadem or headdress. Ht. about cm. 11 × 13. Late V. Century.

(44) Syracuse. Mus. Syracuse.

Satyr's head with rough hair, round eyes, a squat nose, open mouth, straight moustache and a beard in rough locks. The top and left side of the head are broken. V. Century.

(45) Naxos. Mus. Palermo.

A Satyr's head which covers the whole face of the antefix. The forehead is wrinkled, the eyes round and staring, the nose squat and the ears equine. The hair rises in thick rough locks above the forehead and flows out behind the ears. The moustache is straight. The lower part of the face and beard are broken. Ht. from mouth to roots of hair, cm. 8. V. Century.

Kekulé, *Terrac. von Sic.*, p. 43, fig. 91.

(46) Tarentum. Copenhagen, Ny Carlsberg.

The three antefixes in the Ny Carlsberg Glyptothek are all late. Nos. 1 and 2 are Satyrs' heads, the second a development of the savage type as illustrated at Naxos. No. 3 is a head of Acheloös, the fine, pathetic type of the IV. Century.

Ny Carlsberg Glypt., pl. 179, 1–3.

(47) Medma. Mus. Civico, Reggio.

A Satyr with bald head and thick pointed beard runs to left. He has a great domed forehead and the usual squat features of his race. He wears a little loin-cloth and his flesh is marked with thickly strewn brown dots to represent tufts of hair. He runs in the usual archaic attitude, and carries a *rhyton* in his raised right hand. His flesh is light, his beard brown, whilst the loin-cloth is red. The ground of the antefix is black, and is surrounded by a raised horseshoe border which gives the effect of a niche or cave from which the Satyr issues. Ht. cm. 15·5. There are two examples. VI. Century.

FIG. 64.

P. Orsi, *N.S.*, 1913 Suppl., p. 68, fig. 73.

(48) Catana. Mus. Palermo.

A small elliptical field enclosed by a projecting frame is decorated in relief with a bearded Satyr running to left. His right hand rests on his right knee, and with his left hand he holds his own tail. His face, much blurred, is fully frontal, but one can make out a full round beard and thick rough hair over the forehead. The clay is coarse and red in tone ; there is no trace of colour. Ht. cm. 17 × 17. VI. Century.

(49) Tarentum. Mus. Taranto; Trieste, No. 14.

An antefix with a female head, the hair arranged in flat spirals round the forehead and in two thick "pearl-locks" on either side. The brows are plastically rendered by a sharp ridge, the eyes are almond-shaped *à fleur de tête :* the nose was pointed, but the nostrils are now broken. The bow-shaped mouth is deeply recessed and the ears large, leathery and very flat. Pale red clay with no trace of colour. Ht. cm. 19·5 × 16·5. VI. Century.

FIG. 66.

Photograph, Alinari, No. 21162.

(50) Caulonia, temple, *Monasterace*. Mus. Syracuse.

A female head of a very archaic type. The features are merely blocked out, the eyes being indicated by a slight swelling. The hair is parted and waved back. Reddish clay. Much battered. Early VI. Century.

(51) Medma. Mus. Civico, Reggio.

A female head, ht. cm. 19. It is unusual, because the gaze is not lowered, but directed upward and outward, which gives it a very alert expression. The features are plump, the nose and ears large but correctly placed. The full lips are closed. The eyes consist of brown circles painted upon a very slight swelling from the plane of the cheeks, and the brows also are painted only. The hair is in twisted masses over the forehead and is surmounted by a diadem adorned with hammer pattern above and below alternately. The hair over the shoulders hangs in a solid mass. The flesh is deep cream. Second half of VI. Century.

FIG. 65.

P. Orsi, *N.S.*, 1913 Suppl., p. 68, fig. 74.

(52) Rhegium. Mus. Civico, Reggio.

A small female head with very slight relief. The reddish brown hair is in crinkly waves round the forehead and there were evidently side-locks, now broken. The brows are plastically rendered by a sharp ridge painted black; the eyes are a black circle between almond lids outlined black. The nose is broken, the mouth straight; the red lips are in relief. She wears a diadem decorated with a red line. The pale red clay is covered by a cream slip. Ht. about cm. 18. The sides, the background, ears and locks are broken. VI. Century.

N.S., 1886, p. 242; Koldewey, p. 50.

(53) Metaurum, archaic temple. Private collection, Naples.

A small antefix with a female head very finely modelled. The head must have been set against a semi-elliptical background, now destroyed. The small oval face has almond-shaped eyes *à fleur de tête*, with sharply carved lids and a bow-shaped mouth which appears deeply recessed owing to the high cheekbones. The hair is very unusual; over the crown it is quite smooth, which gives it a caplike effect; it is tied on each side on a level with the ears by a triple fillet, and below this band it is braided and the braids coiled round and round like a serpent, so that they form a kind of "layer-wig." Each braid is carefully incised with herringbone pattern to give the effect of plaited hair and the lowest coil finishes off below with a rounded edge, just as in nature. Ht. about cm. 15. The work is very fine, but no trace of colour remains. Early VI. Century.

(54) "Metapontum." Paris, Cabinet des Médailles.

A female head entirely in the round rises above a small base decorated on the upper part with red hammer pattern, and in the middle with a rudimentary black meander. Her hair is parted and waved back; it is in fine crinkled strands and falls loosely over her shoulders. Her brows are painted only, but the eyelids are in strong relief outlined black, whilst the eyes are a circle painted black. She has a well-shaped nose, rounded chin and full red lips firmly closed. She wears a *stephané* with rosettes and lotus buds in relief, and a thick twisted necklace with a large ornament in the front. The work is very fine, but the head is broken at the back. The pale cream clay is covered by a cream slip. Ht. about cm. 17. Middle of V. Century. The antefix was presented by Lenormant in 1845.

FIG. 67.

(55) Caulonia, *Collina del Faro*. Mus. Civico, Reggio.

A narrow projecting border encloses a triangular field adorned in low relief with a young man riding upon a dolphin who swims to left. He is nude and sits at ease upon his plunging steed, playfully holding on to the dolphin's right fin to steady himself. In his left hand he holds a small round shield. The upper part of the relief is damaged, so that his head is missing. Ht. cm. 10 × 20. V. Century.

FIG. 68.

P. Orsi, *N.S.*, 1891, pp. 64 f., fig. in text; *Mon. Ant.*, xxiii (1916), col. 779, fig. 45.

(56) Selinus, archaic Temple C. Mus. Palermo.

A semi-elliptical antefix directly capping the face of the tile, decorated in low relief with a palmette. VI. Century.

Hittorff, *Recueil* (Paris, 1870), pl. xxv, 4 (reproduced upside-down); Koldewey, p. 104.

(57) Syracuse, *temenos*. Mus. Syracuse.

A small antefix, ht. cm. 13·5 × 18, the semi-elliptical field enclosed by a projecting border. It is decorated with a seven-leaved palmette, painted only and rising from a reversed lotus bud and two long bands which end in spirals. Each leaf is outlined with black and is coloured inside with red and black alternately. The technique is uncommon, for the colour is laid on in thin flat washes. Second half of VI. Century.

P. Orsi, *Mon. Ant.*, xxv (1919), col. 673, fig. 247.

(58) Megara Hyblæa. Mus. Syracuse.

Fragment of an antefix incised only with a design which seems to have depicted palmettes rising from spirals. A design of palmette leaves is also scratched on the back. VI. Century.

(59) Tarentum. Mus. Taranto.

An antefix with a lotus flower surmounted by a palmette, all in very low relief. Spiral bands seem to have curved outward on each side. Ht. cm. 26; width preserved, cm. 17. Cream clay. Early V. Century.

(60) Croton, Temple of Hera.

"Numerous terra-cotta palmettes."

N.S., 1897, p. 345.

(61) Tarentum. Mus. Taranto.

An antefix with the field in the shape of a pointed arch. On the field is a palmette in relief, the space below filled by spirals and smaller three-leaved palmettes. Only the right half is preserved. Ht. cm. 22·5 × 9. Cream clay. V.–IV. Century.

(62) S. Mauro, temple. Mus. Syracuse.

A small fragment decorated with broken meander in red and black, which seems to have been the base of an antefix. VI. Century.

P. Orsi, *Mon. Ant.*, xx (1910), col. 789, fig. 49.

(63) Selinus, Temple C. Mus. Palermo.

Various broken pieces of antefixes were found at different times scattered round the temple. VI. Century.

N.S., 1877, p. 133, Nos. 1–8, p. 327.

(64) Gela, *Bitelmi*. Mus. Syracuse.

The amorphous fragment of an antefix.

P. Orsi, *Mon. Ant.*, xvii (1906), col. 718, fig. 550.

AKROTERION BASES

(1) Caulonia, *Collina del Faro*. Mus. Civico, Reggio.

An architectonic piece of unusual form. Its height is cm. 19·5 × 28·7, and it consists of a projecting border with a round hole in the centre. Below is a small cornice of dentils, once painted dark red like the upper border. Below the dentils comes a fascia of ten flutings, dark brown alternating with the natural colour of the clay. Almost in the middle of the top surface of the block is a square hole, cm. 1 deep by cm. 10 wide. This piece must have served as the block to support the akroterion, the base of which was sunk into the recessed square, whilst it was further secured by a metal nail whose head protruded from the small hole in the sima and was probably hidden by a metal rosette or other ornament. Middle of V. Century.

P. Orsi, *N.S.*, 1891, p. 66, fig. in text ; *Mon. Ant.*, xxiii (1916), col. 782, fig. 46.

(2) Caulonia, *Collina del Faro*. Cotrone, Coll. Lucifero.

A fragment almost identical with the preceding and differing only in so far as the uppermost member is concerned, for here that is pointed like a pediment, and would thus screen more completely the inserted base of the akroterion. Middle of V. Century.

FIG. 69.

Von Duhn, *N.S.*, 1897, p. 359, fig. 17 ; P. Orsi, *Mon. Ant.*, xxiii (1916), col. 784, fig. 50.

(3) Caulonia, *Collina del Faro.* Mus. Civico, Reggio.

One large fragment, cm. 47 in length, shows the triangular pediment, and behind it the recessed square for the insertion of the akroterion base is very evident. There is also the front part of another large slab, length cm. 29, with a pediment supported by dentils. Middle of V. Century.

N.S., 1891, p. 67.

CENTRAL AKROTERIA

(1) S. Mauro, archaic temple. Mus. Syracuse.

Fragment of a large circular disc, slightly concave, diameter cm. 55·5. It was decorated with a zone of tongue pattern in red and black with a little dart between each pair. Beyond this was a further border of which only a trace now remains. This fragment was part of the smaller inner disc placed inside the larger outer one. The piece is important, because it shows how the larger disc radiated out behind the smaller one and thus it supplies just that link left without definite proof by the fragment from Gela. Early VI. Century.

P. Orsi, *Mon. Ant.*, xx (1910), col. 789, fig. 48.

(2) Gela, archaic temple. Mus. Syracuse.

A large disc with numerous zones of decoration consisting of: (*a*) torus with bands alternately cream and black; (*b*) fascia with six-petalled cream rosettes, outlined black on a red ground; (*c*) a border, convex in form, with cream tongues on a black ground; (*d*) the concave curve of the disc adorned with whirligigs alternately red and black on a cream ground. Here the piece breaks off, but a second fragment seems to have formed the centre of the disc, like a smaller concave plate within the larger outer one. This smaller disc has a convex border painted with circular bands, red, cream and black. Then follows the concave plate with: (*a*) flabelliform tongue pattern in red outlined black on a cream ground; (*b*) double black circle; (*c*) red fascia with five-petalled cream rosettes outlined black; (*d*) a single red circle between two black lines. Here the disc is again broken.

A fragment of a second disc shows rays alternately red, black and cream, and it is fluted like the petals of a marguerite. It is painted at the back in the same way and must therefore have been visible from front and back. Early VI. Century.

(3) Rhegium, archaic temple. Mus. Civico, Reggio.

There are at least three discs like concave platters with a raised border; they are painted with tongue pattern, stripes and similar designs, and measure about cm. 50 in diameter. Early VI. Century.

N.S., 1886, p. 242.

(4) Rhegium, *Collina del Salvatore.* Mus. Civico, Reggio.

Large discs like concave platters with raised borders. One has a plain border, but the interior of the disc has a scale pattern in relief. The second example has two holes pierced in the only half of the concave platter preserved, and a third hole in the middle, showing that it was fastened to a background. The body of this disc is adorned with zones of tongue and other patterns, the raised border with guilloche in relief. If these discs were really those of the akroteria, one does not see the purpose of the nail holes, unless the discs were maintained in position by a solid support at the back to which they were fastened by nails. Second half of VI. Century.

(5) Metapontum. Paris, Cabinet des Médailles.

Part of a disc with a flat raised border incised with a double tongue pattern addorsed. The red clay is covered with a cream slip, but there is no trace of colour. Length cm. 16 ; thickness cm. 5 × 11. V. Century.

FIG. 70.

(6) Camarina. Mus. Syracuse.

In the mud of the River Hipparis a damaged group was discovered which must have once occupied the position of central akroterion of the temple. It represented a youth mounted on a powerful horse. Only the trunk and one leg of the youth are preserved ; but he was of notably smaller proportions than his steed and seems to have worn a tight-fitting chiton. The horse's head and flowing mane are finely modelled, but the chest and withers are merely blocked out. The present height of the group is cm. 96 × 98. Early VI. Century.

FIG. 71.

P. Orsi, *Boll. d'Arte*, i (1907), fasc. iii, p. 7, fig. 1 ; *N.S.*, 1911 Suppl., p. 49 ; *Mon. Ant.*, xxv (1919), col. 627 ; A. Della Seta, *Italia Antica* (Bergamo, 1922), fig. 104 ; B. Pace, *Mem. R. Acc. Lincei*, cccxiv (1917), p. 526, note 5.

(7) Gela, archaic temple. Mus. Syracuse.

Among the terra-cottas found at the archaic temple was the forepart of a horse entirely in the round. The animal's back is covered with a richly decorated saddle-cloth finished at the corners with a small tassel and edged all round with a double border of tongue pattern, and at intervals along the sides are rosettes in a square field. Only a fragment of the horse's forehead and eyes remains, but many parts of the rider's figure exist, although badly mutilated. These pieces are : the rider's left thigh ; the left foot shod with a soft boot ; the under part of the left knee ; the right shin with the top of the ἐνδρομίς ; fragment of an arm (?) ; part of the shoulders or back with drapery (?) ; a small piece of the red chiton with meander border ; the right side of his head covered with black hair ending in spiral curls round the forehead and bound with a fillet ; the ear is rendered purely conventionally, a mere cornucopia-shaped twist of clay. The ἐνδρομίς is decorated with a rich tongue pattern, and has carefully marked lacings. This group was analogous to those found at Camarina and at the *temenos*, Syracuse, but it was on a larger scale and even more splendidly bedight with colour. Middle of VI. Century.

P. Orsi, *Mon. Ant.*, xxv (1919), col. 627.

(8) Syracuse, *temenos*. Mus. Syracuse.

Only the *débris* remains of the central akroterion of a youth on horseback. The principal piece represents a right thigh held horizontally, length cm. 41 × 28. It is of excellently mixed clay, rough inside and covered outside by a layer of very pure clay, mm. 4–10 thick. The flesh is painted deep cream, the overlapping *chitoniskos* is dark red with a double border of zig-zags and tongue pattern alternately red and black. From the taut muscle of the leg the figure was evidently in energetic action—a rider on horseback.

There is also a smaller fragment of the body and a little piece of the red chiton and border. There is a piece of the left leg, between knee and ankle, showing the well-developed calf and the top of the high ἐνδρομίς, painted with cream rosettes on a red ground and edged above by a cream border and below by four cream bands. Length cm. 20 × 16. Middle of VI. Century.

FIG. 72.

P. Orsi, *Mon. Ant.*, xxv (1919), cols. 626–8, pl. xvii, A, B ; *N.S.*, 1915, p. 179.

(9) S. Mauro, temple. Mus. Syracuse.

Fragment of a thigh and upper part of a man's knee, rather more than life-size. It is not entirely in the round, but in very high relief, for a fragment of the background still adheres, showing a vertical cut. This is all that has been found so far of what was evidently a group of a youth on horseback. Middle of VI. Century.

P. Orsi, *Mon. Ant.*, xx (1910), cols. 792 f., fig. 51.

(10) Metaurum.

There are rumours of the discovery of a similar group of a youth on horseback, probably belonging to another temple than the one at " *contrada Monacelli*."

(11) Gela, archaic temple. Mus. Syracuse.

Revetment of the third type. Fragments of a colossal group of a youth on horseback. It is so battered that it is only by comparison with similar compositions that the purpose of the various fragments can be discerned. So far only fragments of the horse, which was over life-size, have been verified. They are : two monstrous eyes, one with part of the brow (they are shaped like almost spherical convex discs and on one there are still traces of black paint) ; colossal right foreleg, the muscles indicated by slight relief and also by brownish lines traced on the cream skin which is further mottled in parts with brownish heart-shaped markings to represent the dappled skin ; the upper jaw with strong, square teeth. Possibly to this group belong two fragments showing part of the harness, one with little straps which pass through a ring, the other with two straps which unite under a rosette in high relief. Here the horse must have been represented as prancing forward with one foreleg projecting, an advance upon the earlier groups where the forepart of the horse was only blocked out and his legs entirely eliminated. Second half of VI. Century.

(12) Locri, earlier temple, *Marazà*. Mus. Syracuse.

Revetment of the third type. Among the architectonic terra-cottas of the early temple traces of plastic figures came to light ; a wing, the feathers marked by black lines ; the beautifully modelled claws of a bird of prey standing upon a small square base ; two fragments of the body of an animal dappled with heart-shaped markings in black on a cream ground to depict tufts of hair. Apparently here also, as at *Marafioti*, a Sphinx was represented. Second half of VI. Century.

P. Orsi, *N.S.*, 1911 Suppl., p. 39.

(13) Locri, Doric temple, *Marafioti*. Mus. Syracuse.

The fragments of the magnificent group forming the central akroterion were so numerous that it has been possible to reconstruct the whole composition. Upon the ground lies a Sphinx whose splendid female torso is in striking contrast to her slim feline body ; the juncture of the forms, however, is masked by her great wings which stretch backward and fill the space under the body of the horse. Her arms are sharply bent at the elbow and upon her upturned claws she supports the feet of the rider, a nude youth who rides barebacked right over the reclining monster. The horse steps proudly forward, one foreleg extended in the air, quite oblivious of the Sphinx below his feet. His narrow head with its long muzzle and cropped mane recalls the horses of early Attic art. First half of V. Century.

FIG. 73.

P. Orsi, *N.S.*, 1911 Suppl., pp. 39–49, figs. 33–7 ; E. Fiechter, *Jahrb. d. Inst.*, xxxiii (1918), p. 203 ; *Rev. Arch.*, xxi (1913), p. 124 ; *Arch. Anz.*, 1913, p. 169, fig. 22 ; *Rev. des ét. grecques*, xxvi (1913), p. 429, fig. in text ; Deonna, *Rev. Arch.*, 5 Série, xiii (1921), p. 137.

(14) Gela. Mus. Berlin.

Against a plain background which reaches only to the shoulders, the figure of a Gorgon running to right stands out in high relief. The head and torso are fully frontal, whilst the lower limbs are in profile. The hair hangs down on to either shoulder. She has immense eyes, a squat nose and an enormous protruding tongue which covers her whole chin. She wears a *chitoniskos*, the corners weighted down with acorns like the similar monster from Boghaz Keuei. Round her waist is a girdle of twisted serpents and she is shod with *endromides* fastened with small buckles. From her waist spring four recurved wings which form a background to the figure. Her arms are now broken off at the shoulders, but probably her two hands grasped the serpents of her girdle. End of VI. Century.

Bull. Inst., 1835, p. 30; 1836, p. 192; Kekulé, *Terrac. von Sic.*, p. 44, fig. 95; Panofka, *Terrac. des Mus. in Berlin*, pl. lxi; Micali, *Mon. ined. St. ant. popoli* (Firenze, 1844), pl. li, 10; Six, *De Gorgone*, p. 9; P. Orsi, *Mon. Ant.*, xvii (1906), col. 569.

(15) Selinus, *Propylaia, Gaggera*. Mus. Palermo.

"A small and singular slab with the archaic figure of a Medusa, with a nail hole under the left arm. Traces of red on the ground."

N.S., 1894, p. 206.

(16) Selinus, Acropolis. Mus. Palermo.

Fine akroterion decorated with a palmette in relief rising from double volutes between which is a lotus bud. The treatment is alike on both sides. The height is cm. 39 × 36, cm. 9 thick. V. Century.

(17) Medma, temple. Mus. Civico, Reggio.

Revetment of the second type. The akroterion is much damaged and measures cm. 35 × 50, but when complete it must have been nearly cm. 50 in height. It consists of a palmette whose slender leaves rise within an arch made by two branching akanthus stems which must have been crowned above by tufts of their own leaves. Although quite naturalistic in treatment, it has still some of the stiffness of early art. Beginning of V. Century.

P. Orsi, *Mon. Ant.*, xxv (1919), col. 680, fig. 249.

(18) Croton, Temple of Hera.

Revetment of the third type. Only the curving stem of the central palmette akroterion remains; it measures cm. 34. Middle of V. Century.

P. Orsi, *N.S.*, 1911 Suppl., p. 116, fig. 96; *Mon. Ant.*, xxv (1919), col. 680.

LATERAL AKROTERIA

(1) Syracuse, *temenos*. Mus. Syracuse.

Large fragments of a left wing. The inner, invisible side was not painted: on the outer surface the small, scalelike feathers at the root of the wing are painted red and black; the long, curving feathers at the end are also red and black. To this wing belongs another fine fragment, cm. 17 × 15, referable to the point where the wing joins the thorax. There are also two pieces of the tail forming three-quarters of a circle, diameter cm. 4·7: the colour is obliterated.

Only bits of the right wing still exist, but there is the front leg and paw of a seated quadruped. It is somewhat larger than life, measuring cm. 35 in height. It is hollow inside, and was evidently modelled freehand, without the aid of moulds. The clay is of a greenish tint mixed with lava particles. Over this rough core a layer of very fine red clay was spread, and finally the whole was coated with a cream slip upon which the muscles were indicated by brown lines to accentuate the very slight relief of the modelling, and there are a row of painted dots, perhaps to suggest the rough hair. The paw is pierced by cylindrical holes for the nails which fastened it to a base. One hind leg only has been preserved, stretched out almost horizontally: it measures cm. 30·5 in length from the bent joint; thus it is on the same scale as the preceding and the colouring is identical. The claws are painted black. Besides these pieces, a large fragment, cm. 21 × 21, possibly belonged to the leg where it joined the beast's belly: the play of the curale and abdominal muscles under the skin is indicated by higher or lower relief, but the outline of the muscles is mostly emphasised by double black lines. All these pieces together composed the figure of a seated Sphinx or griffin, one of the lateral akroteria. VI. Century.

FIG. 74.

P. Orsi, *Mon. Ant.*, xxv (1919), cols. 622 ff., figs. 212–14, pl. xvii, C.

(2) Syracuse, *temenos*. Mus. Syracuse.

Part of a wing, cm. 22 × 16; the feathers are rendered in plastic relief and finished in colour, now much faded. VI. Century.

P. Orsi, *Mon. Ant.*, xxv (1919), col. 624, fig. 216.

(3) Megara Hyblæa, Temple A. Mus. Syracuse.

Fragment of a wing with feathers plastically rendered and painted red, cream and black alternately. Ht. cm. 15 × 14 × 5. Middle of VI. Century.

P. Orsi, *Mon. Ant.*, xxvii (1922), col. 163, fig. 8.

(4) Megara Hyblæa, Temple B. Mus. Syracuse.

Fragments of animals which may have composed the akroteria: small paw of a Sphinx, ht. cm. 4 × 9·5; fragments of two legs (?); part of the body or tail (?); fragment of red clay representing waved locks. Middle of VI. Century.

FIG. 75.

P. Orsi, *Mon. Ant.*, xxvii (1922), col. 171, fig. 15.

(5) Gela, archaic temple. Mus. Syracuse.

The fragmentary remains of a lioness or Sphinx. There are: three life-sized paws well modelled and coloured cream with little brown markings to indicate tufts of hair; pieces of the body coloured cream and with the same brown markings; part of the belly and teats of the monster with the haunch and the curling tail which ends in a thick tuft of hair. One cannot be certain whether the monster really formed the lateral akroterion or whether it was part of the central group, serving as base to the horse and rider, as was the case at *Marafioti*. Second half of VI. Century.

(6) Caulonia, temple, *Monasterace*. Mus. Syracuse.

The head of a Siren or Harpy. The features are rather pointed, the hair is parted and waved back so that it hangs over the shoulders in a solid mass. Most of the colouring has disappeared, except the black on the hair. VI. Century.

(7) " Sicily." Paris, Mus. du Louvre (Inv. C.A., 1793).

A female head broken off at the neck, ht. cm. 15 ; face from chin to roots of hair, cm. 8. It is of coarse red clay covered with a layer of fine clay and is modelled in broad planes which ignore details, but give all the essential features. The hair is waved in scallops round the forehead and hangs in a heavy mass over the shoulders. The ears are immense and schematically rendered ; in the left one is a small disc earring. The brows are scarcely plastic ; the eyes are a bulbous swelling upon which the iris was painted. The lids were in such low relief that they are now indistinguishable. The nose is broken, but the mouth is straight, with full, closed lips. The chin and throat are plump and well rounded. She wears a low *stephané* and the object which follows the lines of her neck and shoulder seems to be a fold of drapery, a mantle, rather than part of a second figure, as has been suggested. The head is architectonic, yet it is not an antefix ; more probably it was an akroterion, a *Niké* or Sphinx like the head from Thebes, with which it has many similarities (*cf.* E. Pottier, *Mon. Piot,* vi (1899), pp. 133–42, pl. xii) ; or else it formed part of a group like the Satyr and Mænad from Olympia (*Olympia*, iii, p. 38, pl. viii). Given the provenance of the work, the former suggestion appears more credible, as so far there has been no example of an architectonic group of a Satyr and Mænad found in Sicily. If, however, it was the head of a Sphinx, it must have looked straight in front, and not turned sideways, according to M. Pottier's reconstruction of the Theban Sphinx (*op. cit.*, tail-piece), because in Sicily and Magna Græcia the archaic fictile lateral akroteria were never placed at the ends of the ascending ramp of the raking cornice, but on a base immediately behind the extreme angle of the cornice, so that they faced straight out towards the spectator. The head was purchased in 1909, and is an interesting specimen of the second half of the VI. Century.

P. Jamot, *Mon. Piot,* xix (1912), pp. 43–7, pl. iii ; A. de Ridder, *Rev. des ét. grecques,* xix (1913), pp. 429 f., fig. in text.

(8) Gela. Mus. Palermo.

The lower part of the relief is broken, but the part preserved measures ht. cm. 41 × 35. The core is of brick-red clay as hard as stone, whilst a layer of grey clay over the outer surface gives to the whole a greyish tinge. The architectonic background is plain with a projecting border at the top. Against it in high relief stands out the figure of a Harpy or Siren, her head frontally presented, her body in profile. Her hair is parted and falls in a " layer-wig " over her shoulders. Her face is a full oval with firm, round chin, bow-shaped mouth and rather large ears. Her big recurved wings fill all the left upper half of the field. Cavallari states that this relief was found at Selinus in 1882, but that cannot be correct, for it was sketched by Otto in the Palermo Museum in 1874, and the museum inventory under the number 4678 states that it came from Gela, where it was found on the seashore. V. Century.

Cavallari, *N.S.*, 1882, p. 331, fig. in text ; Kekulé, *Terrac. von Sic.*, p. 45, fig. 96 ; Koldewey, p. 104.

(9) Unknown provenance. Mus. Palermo.

This monument, ht. cm. 13, was formerly in the *Collezione Astuto*. The background is architectonic with a projecting upper border. In high relief is a winged figure running to right in the archaic manner. Her hair is parted and hangs down on to her shoulders ; she wears a *stephané*, a long chiton girt at the waist and *endromides* with recurved tongues. Her left arm is raised and the right lowered in the attitude usually adopted for one running a race or hastening. Her recurved wings spring from her waist and fill the two upper corners of the field. Early V. Century.

Kekulé, *Terrac. von Sic.*, p. 44, fig. 94.

(10) Syracuse, *temenos*. Mus. Syracuse.

The large relief, ht. cm. 56 × 50, cm. 3 thick, of a Gorgon-Medusa running " knee to earth " and clutching under her right arm the little Pegasos. Four cylindrical holes served for nails or clamps to attach the relief to a ground, but whether this was of wood or stone is unknown. The relief is developed to a depth of mm. 62. It is noteworthy that the parts surpassing the plane of the relief, that is, the head and wings of the Gorgon and the little wings of Pegasos, have a rounded edge. The Gorgon-Medusa advances in the archaic running scheme ; her head, trunk, arms and wings are presented frontally, only her legs are in profile. Her forehead is framed by six spiral curls ; she has an obtuse nose with spreading nostrils, bulbous eyes almost protruding from their orbits, and black hair hanging down in two locks, each of four " pearled " tresses. She wears a short *chitoniskos* richly embroidered, *endromides* with recurved wings from the tongues, and clasps under her right arm the little Pegasos, who has a red neck and shoulders, cream body, cream mane with black markings and red and black wings. If this relief is really architectonic and not an ἄγαλμα, it must be one of the lateral akroteria, since it is too large for an antefix at that archaic period and it cannot be the central akroterion, because that was composed of the youth on horseback, a composition with which these Gorgon-Medusa groups are always found in conjunction. Middle of VI. Century.

FIG. 76.

P. Orsi, *N.S.*, 1915, pp. 177 f., fig. 1 ; *Mon. Ant.*, xxv (1919), cols. 614–22, pl. xvi ; E. Gabrici, *Atti R. Acc. di Palermo*, serie 3, xi, p. 10, pl. ii, 5 ; B. Pace, *Mem. R. Acc. Lincei*, cccxiv (1917), p. 526, note 5 ; A. Della Seta, *Italia Antica* (Bergamo, 1921), fig. 103.

(11) Gela, archaic temple. Mus. Syracuse.

Revetment of the second type. Fragment of a Gorgon running to left ; only the piece from waist to thigh remains, but it shows that the monster wore a *chitoniskos* decorated with chequer pattern in red and black. It should be compared with the similar figure from the *temenos*, Syracuse. There is also part of the Gorgon's bent knee and part of the shin and the top of the ἐνδρομίς. Middle of VI. Century.

(12) S. Mauro, archaic temple. Mus. Syracuse.

Various mutilated fragments of a group : the lower half of a very archaic human face, rather less than life-size. As the back half is missing, one cannot say if this face belonged to a figure in the round or in high relief ; double recurved wing from a large figure : it is without plastic relief or incised outlines, and is coloured red and brownish black. The end feathers are painted alternately red and black on a cream ground. The height is cm. 29 × 23·5, and the piece is hollow, but with thick walls ; two bits decorated with imbrications (part of the *chitoniskos* drawn tightly over the hip of the Gorgon) ; a fragment, cm. 14 in length, covered with pearled strands radiating out from a centre, apparently the hair of a Gorgon ; the small head of a serpent ; the muzzle of a horse, well modelled and entirely in the round, but on a small scale. All these fragments together seem to have composed a group of the running Gorgon-Medusa, girt with a serpent girdle and holding under her arm the little Pegasos. Middle of VI. Century.

FIG. 77.

P. Orsi, *Mon. Ant.*, xx (1910), cols. 792 f., figs. 52, 53, 55, pl. vii, 2.

(13) Megara Hyblæa, temple. Mus. Syracuse.

The large paw of a lion (?). Reddish clay, cream slip. Ht. cm. 16. VI. Century.

(14) Gela, archaic temple. Mus. Syracuse.

Fragments of a lion or other monster : a portion of the nose and muzzle ; the nostrils are black, the puckered skin round the mouth is left the cream colour of the slip ; a fragment of a rough mane (?) flowing out in striated rays. VI. Century.

(15) Croton, Temple of Hera.

Revetment of the third type. A fragment of the lateral akroterion in the form of a palmette, ht. cm. 21, which rose with bold, closely united leaves, modelled in relief and coloured red and black alternately. Middle of V. Century.

P. Orsi, *N.S.*, 1911 Suppl., p. 116, fig. 98.

(16) Caulonia, temple, *Monasterace*. Mus. Syracuse.

Revetment of the third type. The lateral akroteria were in the form of palmettes consisting of a large anthemion springing from double volutes, between which is a small reversed palmette. The leaves of the anthemion are in high relief with sharp edges, coloured red, cream and black alternately. The anthemia are moulded with two wings at right angles, so as to fit the corner exactly and to be equally effective from the front or side view. VI.–V. Century.

P. Orsi, *N.S.*, 1922, p. 148.

PEDIMENT

(1) Gela, archaic temple. Mus. Syracuse.

Revetment of the first type. The triangular space within the pediment of the archaic temple was filled by an enormous Gorgoneion, ht. m. 1·05 × 1·10, worked in low relief upon a slab obtusely triangular in form. All the details are brought to the utmost degree of stylisation ; the six large spiral curls over the forehead and the series of smaller ones which indicate the beard are geometrically precise ; three " pearl-locks " on either side also end in spirals. The eyes and brows, too, form a semi-elliptical design, separated by the dart in relief running up the forehead from the root of the nose. The gaping mouth is deeply embedded in the puffy cheeks. It is surrounded by a thick roll of flesh, and is filled by two rows of even teeth, interrupted by two pairs of gigantic tusks. The pendent tongue covers the whole chin. In its original state with all the details emphasised by vivid colour, this Gorgoneion must have been most impressive. Fragments of no less than three other Gorgoneia were found. Early VI. Century.

FIG. 78.

N.S., 1907, p. 39 ; E. Gabrici, *Atti R. Acc. di Palermo*, serie 3, xi, p. 10 ; P. Orsi, *Mon. Ant.*, xxv (1919), cols. 615, 618, fig. 210.

(2) Selinus, archaic Temple C. Mus. Palermo.

At different times throughout a long series of excavations small bits were found of the great Gorgoneion which filled the tympanon of the archaic temple. This monument is the largest fictile mask yet known, and sufficient pieces have now been discovered to permit a clever reconstruction to be made which enables us to gain some idea of the original effect. The face was oval rather than round, with very little relief, for the artist relied chiefly on the contrast of colours to give an effect of relief from a distance. The hair is arranged in spirals round the forehead and in numerous closely massed "pearl-locks," possibly as many as twelve on either side, which only reach to the shoulders. The eyes are perfectly round and the gaping mouth was furnished with a double row of even teeth, interrupted by a pair of sharp tusks on either side. The beard was conventionalised into a series of little spirals which ran round the lower part of the face from ear to ear. The hair still retains a tinge of reddish brown. Early VI. Century.

E. Gabrici, *Atti R. Acc. di Palermo*, serie 3, xi, pls. i, ii; P. Orsi, *Mon. Ant.*, xxv (1919), col. 615.

(3) Hipponium.

Two pieces of a colossal Gorgoneion which, when whole, measured something more than m. 1·10 in diameter. The disc was slightly convex and the Gorgoneion was worked out in low relief. The hair round the forehead is in three rows of little curls surmounted by a diadem adorned with small writhing serpents. The eyes are almond-shaped. It does not belong to the usual type of Gorgoneion found in Magna Græcia and Sicily, but its damaged condition makes it difficult to verify the class from which it originated. Middle of VI. Century.

FIG. 79.

P. Orsi, *Mon. Ant.*, xxv (1919), col. 619, fig. 211; *N.S.*, 1922, pp. 16 f., fig. 10.

(4) Gela, archaic temple. Mus. Syracuse.

Revetment of the third type. Numerous fragments of plastic figures, less than life-size, found in the ruins of the archaic temple, confirm the supposition that the east pediment, besides the akroteria, was adorned with figurative painted terra-cottas. There are: the neck of a woman with the upper border of her chiton decorated with red and black hammer pattern; a bare foot with toes a little upturned; fragment of a shoulder (?) with drapery ornamented with black meander; another piece of the same cream drapery, also with the border of black meander; fragment with the long wavy tresses and small delicately modelled left ear of a woman. The clay is light red with a cream slip. Second half of VI. Century.

(5) Gela, *Predio Ventura*. Mus. Syracuse.

Part of a trapezoidal slab with figures in high relief. The present fragment measures cm. 48 × 44, but, when complete, it must have been almost double that size. The projecting lower border forms the ground upon which the figures advance to right. They are a woman clad in a long chiton preceded by a man wearing a *chitoniskos*. As only the lower limbs are preserved, it is impossible to divine the subject. There is also the right foot of a third person who was not in motion, but stood still with the leg rigidly vertical. The modelling is life-like, with faint traces of archaism in the slender, bony structure of the feet. The figures were moulded hollow to diminish the weight and were then touched up with a tool and attached to the base, almost as if they were stuck on. The whole relief was then rebaked and was afterwards painted, although no trace of colour now remains. The slab seems too large for a metope, for which also the trapezoidal form is not adapted ; more likely it was the pedimental decoration of a small wooden temple. Beginning of V. Century.

P. Orsi, *Mon. Ant.*, xvii (1906), cols. 570 f., pl. xlviii, 2 ; xxv (1919), col. 621, note 2.

(6) Rhegium, archaic temple. Mus. Civico, Reggio.

One of the most important finds in the excavations was a fictile slab, cm. 95 in length. It is broken at the top and right side, but in its present condition its height is cm. 70. The sides are left free, but at the bottom there is a wide projecting border. The field is adorned with two female figures in relief, dancing to right, each laying one hand upon the shoulder of her companion. Both are now headless, but they have long waved locks which hang down on to their breasts. They both wear a long chiton with an *apoptygma* which reaches to the waist. These cream chitons have black borders ornamented with little patterns in cream—meander and rows of dots ; the short sleeves are bordered with a pattern of lotus buds. There are traces of red on the long curls. The maiden on the left raises her drapery with her right hand and her companion probably repeated the gesture with her left hand. Their feet are bare. They dance forward in a most spirited manner with a rhythmic swing which gives to the scene a wonderful effect of motion. The clay is very fine and deep cream in tone and the work is beautifully executed. VI. Century.

N.S., 1884, p. 284 ; 1886, p. 242 ; Koldewey, p. 50 ; Fenger, *Le Temple Etrusco-Latin*, p. 17, fig. 68A.

METOPES (?)

(1) Metaurum, *S. Maria.* Private collection, Naples.

The fragment of a slab decorated in relief with two paws of a feline walking to right. Another slab in high relief shows two horses in profile harnessed to a biga. On another, ht. about cm. 25, only the hind-quarters of a horse are preserved. Middle of VI. Century.

N.S., 1902, p. 128, fig. 3, Nos. 1, 4, 5.

(2) Gela, *Predio Ventura.* Mus. Syracuse.

A very fragmentary slab of which practically only the wide projecting border remains intact. The original dimensions were cm. 60 × 54·5. The whole of the square field was once filled by the figure of a Gorgon-Medusa in high relief, moving to left in the archaic running scheme. Her face was framed by " pearl-locks " and she wore a *chitoniskos* girt at the waist and high boots with recurved tops. Her recurved wings extended into the upper corners of the field and are quite plain, for the feathers were indicated in colour only, not plastically. Under her right arm she held the little Pegasos, traces of whose tail and tiny hoofs are visible on the left border. The composition is similar to that of the Gorgon-Medusa from the *temenos*, Syracuse, and it is therefore probable that the other hand was held downwards and open, with stiffly extended fingers. The figure was moulded hollow, worked up with a tool and applied to the background. The light-toned clay mixed with volcanic particles was covered with a thin layer of very pure clay to receive the colour. VI. Century.

FIG. 80.

P. Orsi, *N.S.*, 1901, p. 309; *Mon. Ant.*, xvii (1906), cols. 568–9, pl. xlviii, 1.

(3) Selinus, *Propylaia, Gaggera*. Mus. Palermo.

Fragmentary slabs with figures in relief. One consists of a projecting lower border forming the ground upon which are the bare feet of two persons walking to right. In front of them is the leg of a third standing figure.

Another fragment shows a man, from waist to thigh, in impetuous movement to right. He wears a short chiton with wavy folds.

A third bit contains only part of an arm and hand which grasps the right arm of another figure clad in a chiton with short sleeves.

The fourth slab has the head of a Gorgon. VI.–V. Century.

N.S., 1894, pp. 206–8, figs. 5, 6; P. Orsi, *Mon. Ant.*, xxv (1919), col. 621.

(4) Gela. Mus. Syracuse.

Within an architectonic frame is a fragmentary scene of worshippers who come to present offerings to a goddess seated upon a high throne to left. All that remains of her is her head covered by a veil and a lofty *polos*. Before her stands a woman with long hair hanging over her shoulders; she raises her right hand in which she holds her offering (an ear of corn ?). The arm and hand of another figure, a priestess, who stands between her and the goddess, are stretched out to touch that of the worshipper, evidently to take the offering and present it to the goddess. The architectonic framing suggests that this slab may have been a metope, but considering the subject, it may have been merely a votive relief. The clay is light red. All the right side is broken away. What now remains measures cm. 36 × 47·5. Beginning of V. Century.

FRIEZE

(1) Metapontum, small shrine. Mus. Naples.

A long narrow slab with figures in high relief representing a hero and the *ἅλιος γέρων*. The slab has a projecting border decorated with tongue pattern in red and black at the top and a narrow border at the bottom which the figures partly overlap. The action is all to right, the left side of the relief being filled only by the long fishy tail of the *ἅλιος γέρων* and by the extended legs of the hero, who floats or swims besides his companion and evidently clasps the *ἅλιος* γέρων with both arms (now broken). He wears a *chitoniskos* and his legs are bare. He has reddish-brown hair and a close beard. Broken: the crown of his head, both arms, left ankle and foot. Only the fishy tail of the ἅλιος γέρων is preserved, and his right arm which he lays over the hero's back, as if helping him along rather than repulsing him. His drapery formed a *diploïs* with many folds, thus concealing the juncture of disharmonious forms. The flesh of both protagonists is dark red. No colour is now visible on the ground of the relief, but it seems to have been dark. The slab measures about cm. 12 × 25.

Cf. E. Petersen, *Ann. d. Inst.*, 1882, pp. 73–89.

RELIEF

(1) Akragas. Mus. Palermo.

A slab of which only the left side is preserved, decorated in very high relief with a scene of a lion rending a bull. The lion springs from the left upon the bull and bites him in the back. The bull sinks on his forelegs. The treatment is quite realistic, for the bull's head is lowered and his nose is squashed against the ground. The clay is red. Ht. preserved about cm. 30. The back of the slab is smoothed and very slightly curved; in the middle there are traces of a buttress or support which extended the whole length of the lower half of the slab which still exists. This support suggests that the relief served as an akroterion, for which, however, its quadrilateral shape does not seem appropriate. It cannot be identified with certainty as architectonic and may have been an ἄγαλμα. VI. Century.

INDEX

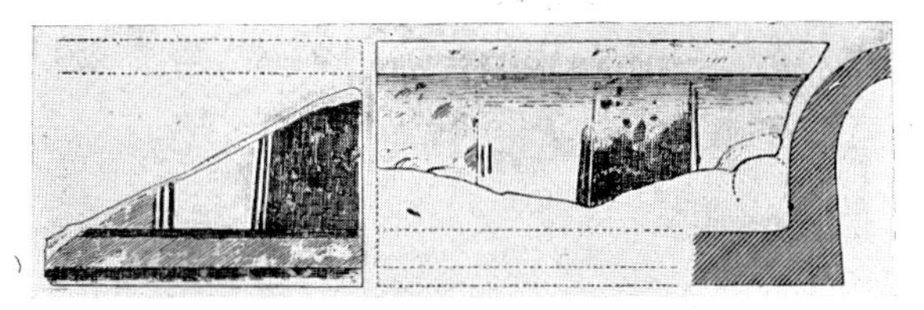

FIG. 1.—LATERAL SIMÆ, SYRACUSE, *temenos*.
(*Mus. Syracuse.*)

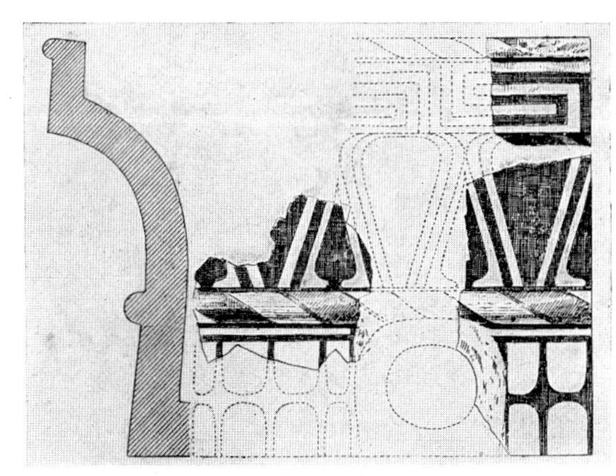

FIG. 2.—LATERAL SIMÆ, SYRACUSE, *temenos*.
(*Mus. Syracuse.*)

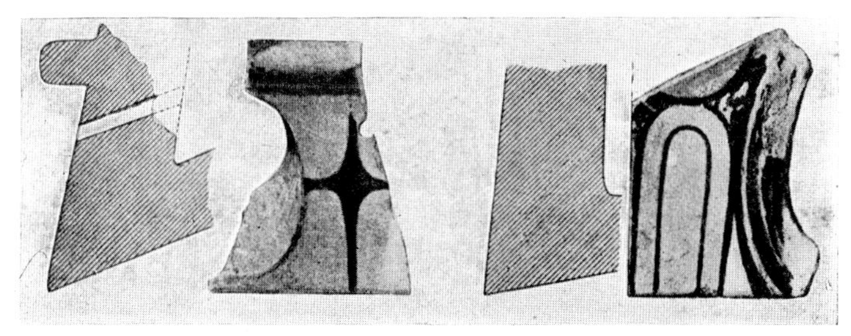

FIG. 3.—LATERAL SIMÆ, MEGARA HYBLÆA, TEMPLE A.

FIG. 4.—LATERAL SIMÆ, MEGARA HYBLÆA, TEMPLE A.

(*Mus. Syracuse.*)

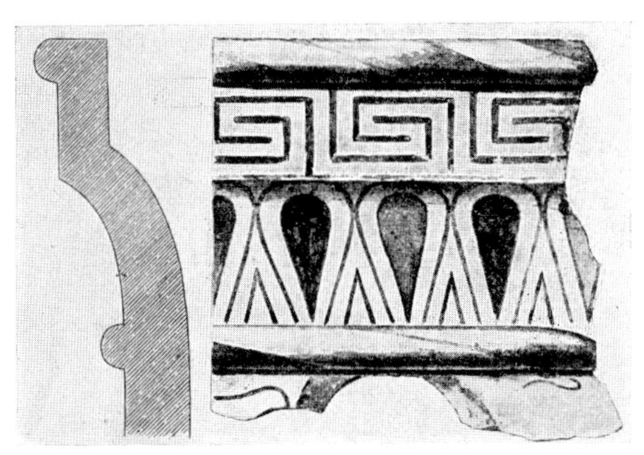

FIG. 5.—LATERAL SIMÆ, CROTON, TEMPLE OF HERA.
(*N.S.*)

25

FIG. 6.—LATERAL SIMÆ, CAULONIA, SMALL SHRINE.
(*Mon. Ant.*)

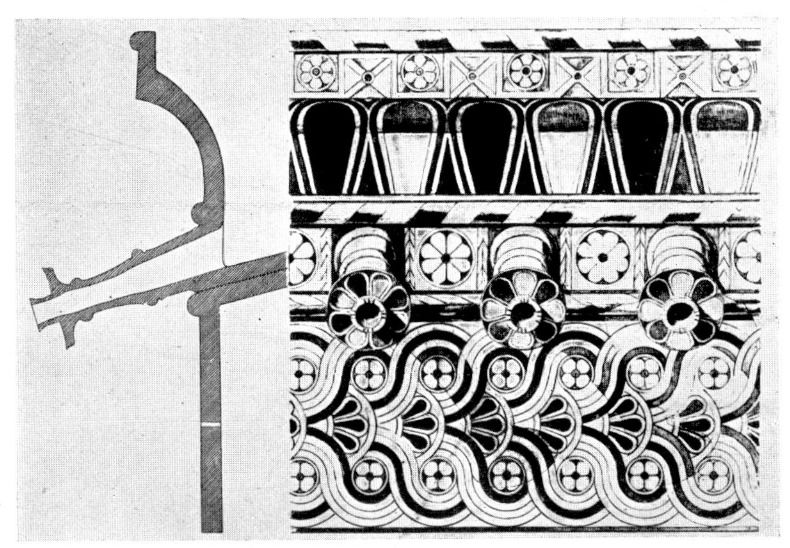

FIG. 7.—LATERAL SIMÆ, SYRACUSE, *temenos.*
(*Mus. Syracuse.*)

FIG. 8.—LATERAL SIMÆ, S. MAURO, ARCHAIC TEMPLE.
(*Mus. Syracuse.*)

Fig. 9.—Lateral Simæ, Caulonia, *Monasterace.*
(*Mus. Syracuse.*)

Fig. 10.—Lateral Simæ, Locri, temple, *Marafioti.*
(*Mus. Syracuse.*)

Fig. 11.—Lateral Simæ, Caulonia, temple.
(*Mus. Reggio.*)

Fig. 12.—Lateral Simæ, Caulonia, temple.
(*Mus. Reggio.*)

FIG. 13.—LATERAL SIMÆ, CROTON, TEMPLE OF HERA.
(*N.S.*)

FIG. 14.—LATERAL SIMÆ, HIPPONIUM, TEMPLE, *Coltura del Castello.*
(*Mus. Reggio.*)

FIG. 15.—LATERAL SIMÆ, CAULONIA, TEMPLE, *Monasterace.*
(*Mus. Syracuse.*)

FIG. 16.—LATERAL SIMÆ, METAPONTUM, TEMPLE OF APOLLO.

FIG. 17.—LATERAL SIMÆ, METAPONTUM, TEMPLE OF APOLLO.
(*Mus. Naples.*)

FIG. 18.—LATERAL SIMÆ, METAPONTUM, TAVOLE PALADINI
(*Mus. Potenza.*)

FIG. 19.—CRESTING, CROTON, TEMPLE OF HERA. (*N.S.*)

FIG. 20.—RAKING CORNICE, GRANMICHELE, TEMPLE. (*Mus. Syracuse.*)

FIG. 21.—RAKING CORNICE, MEGARA HYBLÆA, TEMPLE A. (*Mus. Syracuse.*)

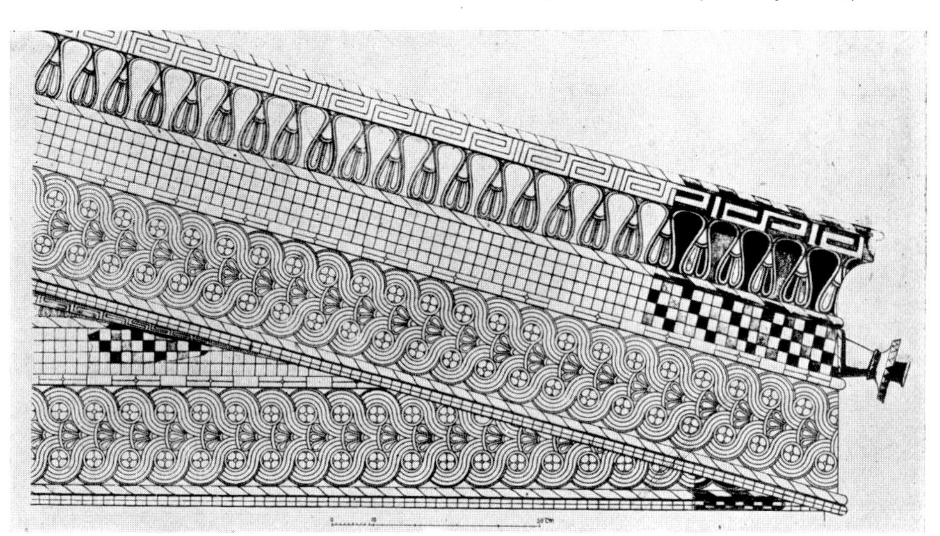

FIG. 22.—RAKING CORNICE, SYRACUSE, *temenos.* (*Mus. Syracuse.*)

FIG. 23.—RAKING CORNICE, SYRACUSE, *temenos.* (*Mus. Syracuse.*)

FIG. 24.—RAKING CORNICE, S. MAURO, TEMPLE. (*Mus. Syracuse.*)

FIG. 27.—RAKING CORNICE, MEDMA. (*Mus. Reggio.*)

FIG. 25.—RAKING CORNICE, SYRACUSE, *temenos.* (*Mus. Syracuse.*)

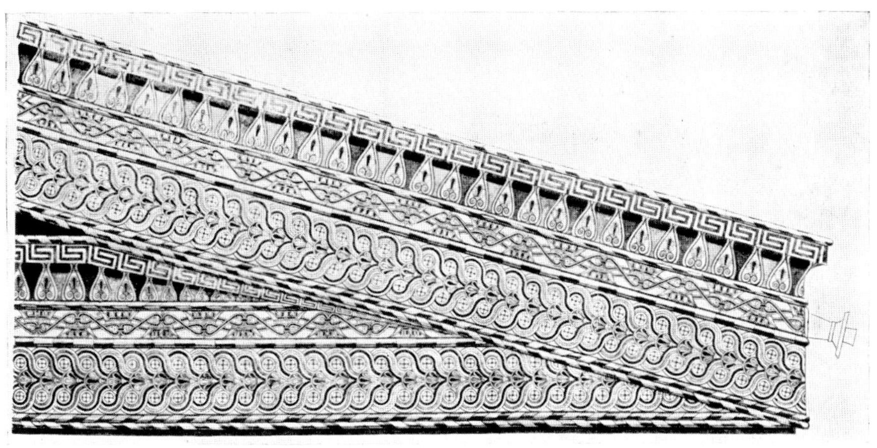

FIG. 26.—RAKING CORNICE, SYRACUSE, *temenos.* (*Mus. Syracuse.*)

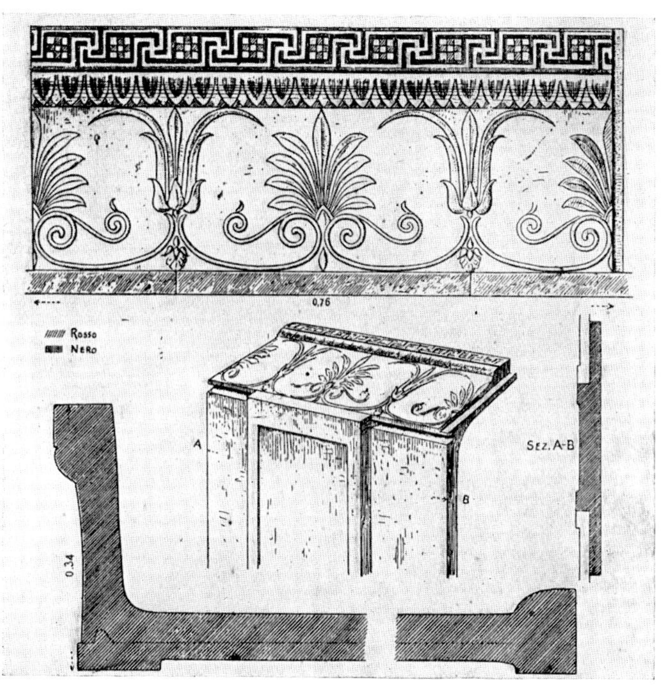

Fig. 28.—Raking Cornice, Locri, temple, *Marafioti.*
(*Mus. Syracuse.*)

Fig. 29.—Raking Cornice, Caulonia, temple.
(*Mus. Reggio.*)

Fig. 30.—Raking Cornice, Selinus, Acropolis.
(*Mus. Palermo.*)

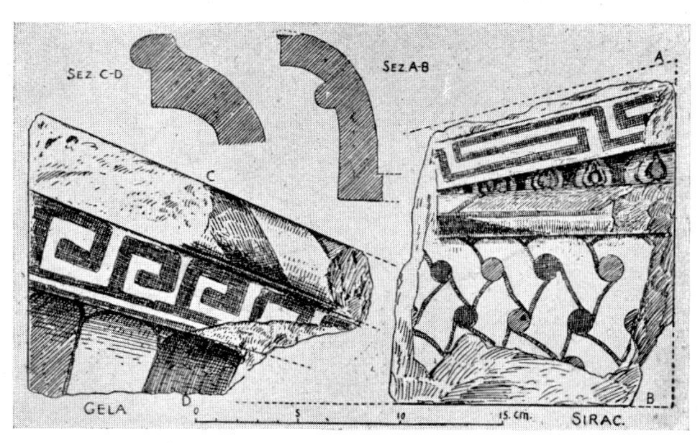

FIG. 31.—GEISON, GELA. FIG. 32.—GEISON, SYRACUSE, TEMPLE OF APOLLO.
(*Mus. Syracuse.*)

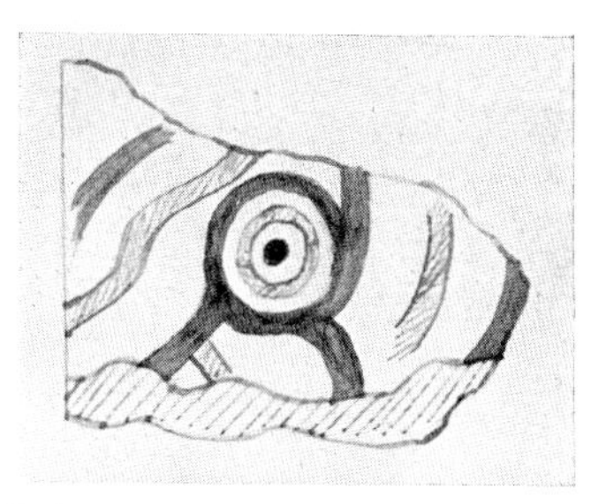

FIG. 36.—GEISON, LOCRI, TEMPLE, *Marazà.*
(*Mus. Naples.*)

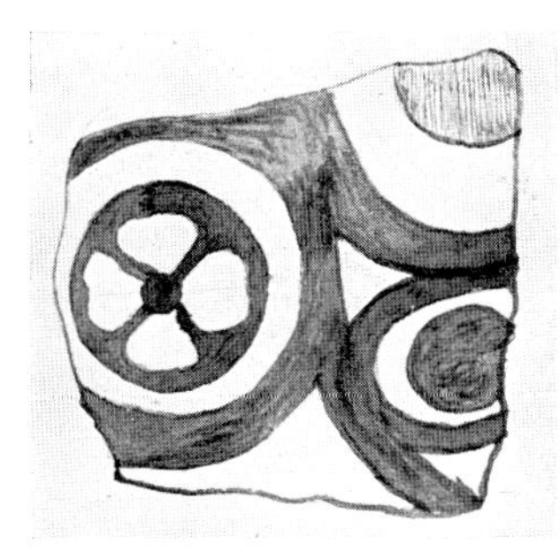

FIG. 33.—GEISON, MEGARA HYBLÆA, TEMPLE A.
(*Mus. Syracuse.*)

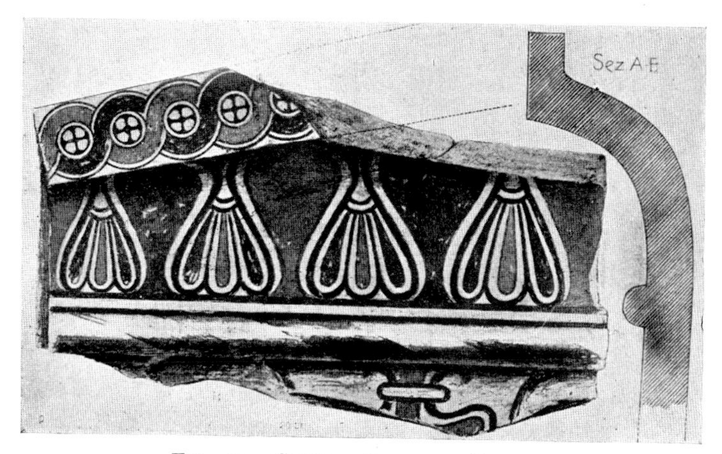

FIG. 37.—GEISON, RHEGIUM, ODEON.
(*Mus. Reggio.*)

FIG. 35.—GEISON, UNKNOWN PROVENANCE.
(*Paris, Louvre.*)

FIG. 34.—GEISON, MEGARA HYBLÆA, TEMPLE A.
(*Mus. Syracuse*).

Fig. 38.—Geison, Syracuse, *temenos*. (*Mus. Syracuse.*)

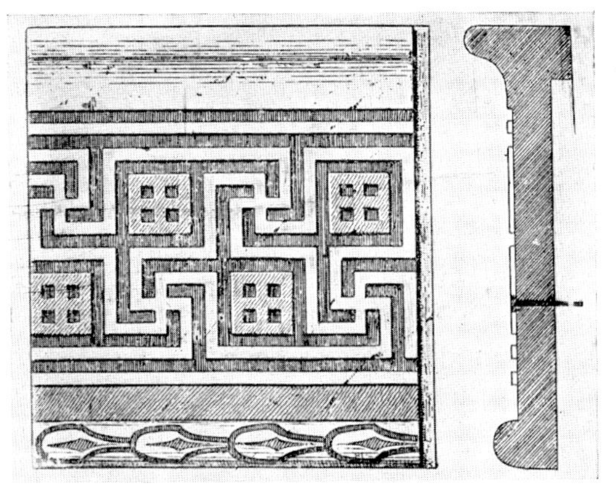

Fig. 41.—Geison, Locri, *Marafioti*. (*Mus. Reggio.*)

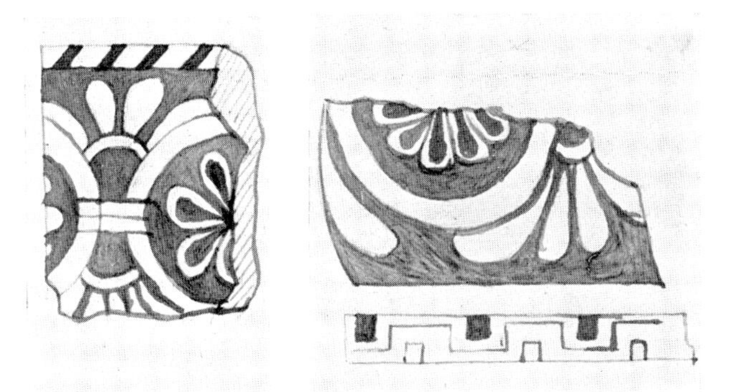

Fig. 39.—Geison, Locri, *Marazà*. (*Mus. Naples.*)

Fig. 42.—Geison, Medma. (*Mus. Reggio.*)

Fig. 40.—Geison, Syracuse, Olympieion. (*Mus. Syracuse.*)

Fig. 43.—Geison, Croton, Temple of Hera. (*Mus. Reggio.*)

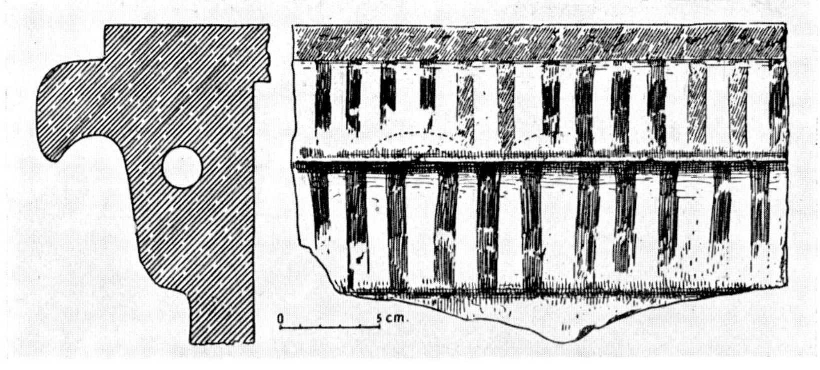

Fig. 44.—Simæ, Croton, Temple of Hera.

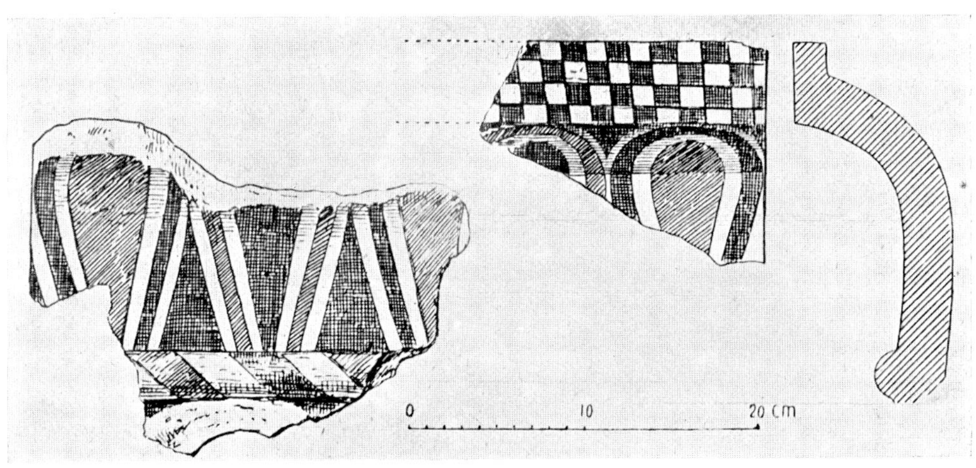

Fig. 45.—Simæ, Syracuse, *temenos*.
(*Mus. Syracuse.*)

Fig. 47.—Simæ, Metapontum.
(*Paris: Cabinet des Médailles.*)

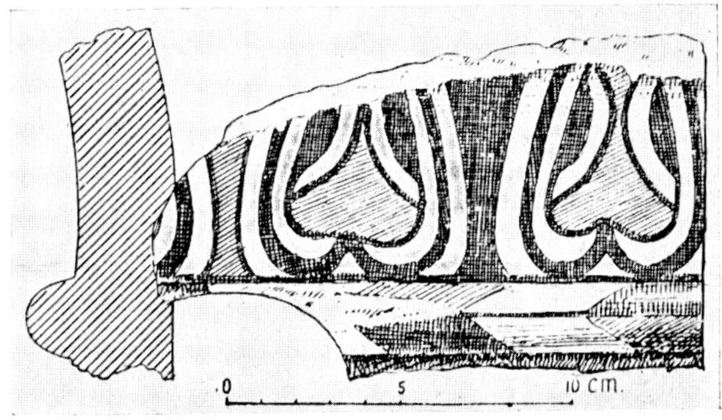

Fig. 46.—Simæ, Syracuse, *temenos*.
(*Mus. Syracuse*)

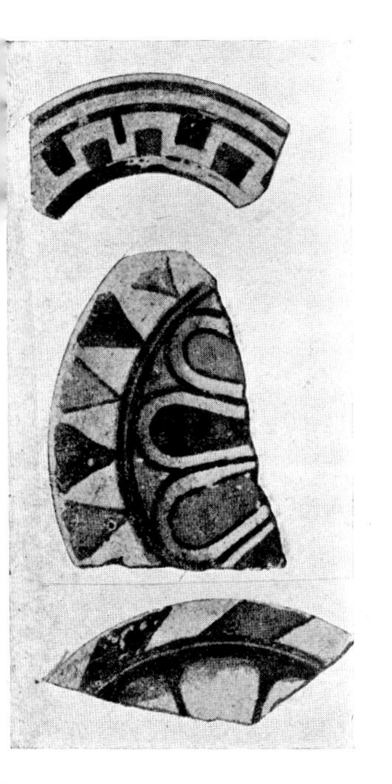

FIG. 48.—WATERSPOUTS, MEGARA HYBLÆA, TEMPLE A.
(*Mus. Syracuse.*)

FIG. 50.—LIONS' HEADS SPOUT, MEDMA.
(*Mus. Reggio.*)

FIG. 51.—LIONS' HEADS SPOUT, MEGARA HYBLÆA, TEMPLE A.
(*Mus. Syracuse.*)

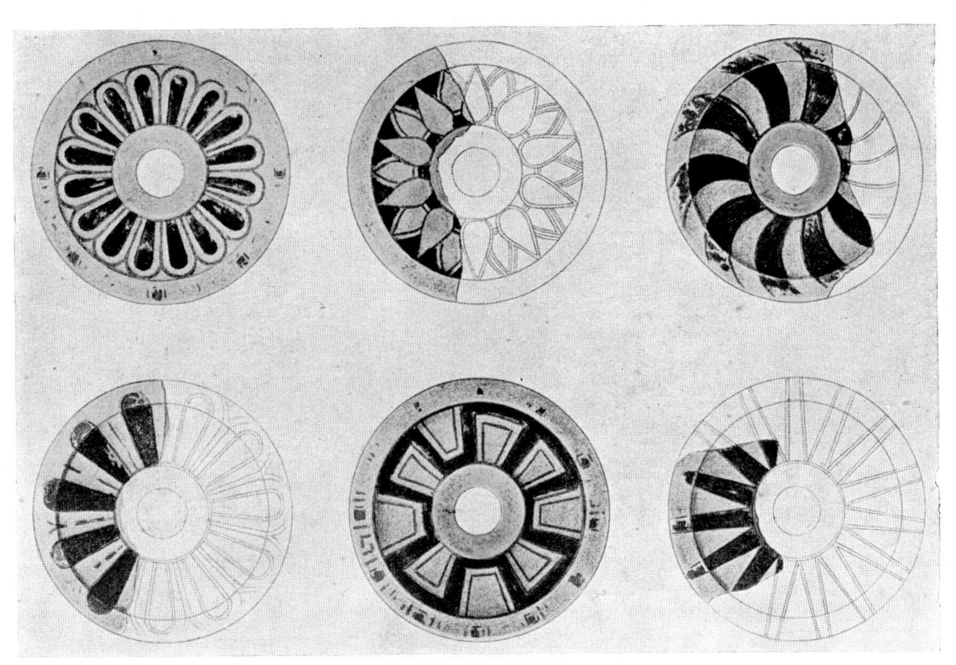

FIG. 49.—WATERSPOUTS, S. MAURO, TEMPLE.
(*Mus. Syracuse.*)

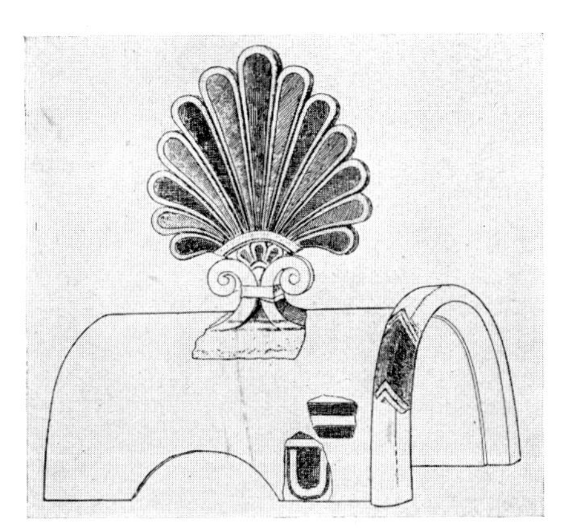

FIG. 52.—PALMETTES OF THE RIDGE-POLE, S. MAURO.
(*Mus. Syracuse.*)

FIG. 53.—PALMETTES OF THE RIDGE-POLE, SYRACUSE, *temenos*.
(*Mus. Syracuse.*)

FIG. 54.—KALYPTERES, GELA, TEMPLE.
(*Mus. Syracuse.*)

FIG. 55.—ANTEFIX, TARENTUM.
(*New York Mus.*)

FIG. 56.—ANTEFIX, TARENTUM.
(*Marseilles: Coll. Vlasto.*)

FIG. 57.—ANTEFIX, TARENTUM.
(*Trieste: Mus. Civico.*)

FIG. 58.—ANTEFIX, TARENTUM.
(*New York Mus.*)

FIG. 59.—ANTEFIX, TARENTUM.
(*Marseilles: Coll. Vlasto.*)

FIG. 60.—ANTEFIX, TARENTUM.
(*Trieste: Mus. Civico.*)

FIG. 61.—ANTEFIX, TARENTUM.
(*New York Mus.*)

FIG. 62.—ANTEFIX, TARENTUM.
(*Trieste : Mus. Civico.*)

FIG. 63.—ANTEFIX, AKRAGAS.
(*The Hague.*)

FIG. 64.—ANTEFIX, MEDMA.
(*Mus. Reggio.*)

FIG. 66.—ANTEFIX, TARENTUM.
(*Trieste: Mus. Civico.*)

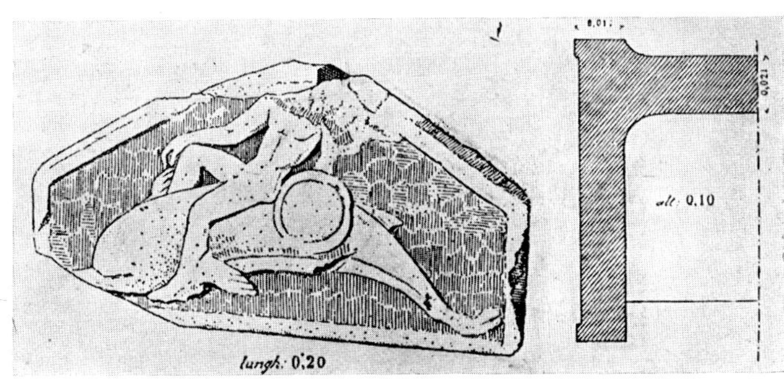

FIG. 68.—ANTEFIX, CAULONIA, *Collina del Faro.*
(*Mus. Civico.*)

FIG. 65.—ANTEFIX, MEDMA.
(*Mus. Reggio.*)

FIG. 67.—ANTEFIX, METAPONTUM.
(*Paris: Cabinet des Médailles.*)

FIG. 69.—AKROTERION BASES, CAULONIA, *Collina del Faro.* (*Mus. Reggio.*)

FIG. 71.—CENTRAL AKROTERION, CAMARINA.

FIG. 70.—CENTRAL AKROTERION, METAPONTUM. (*Paris: Cabinet des Médailles.*)

FIG. 73.—CENTRAL AKROTERION, LOCRI, TEMPLE, *Marafioti.* (*Mus. Syracuse.*)

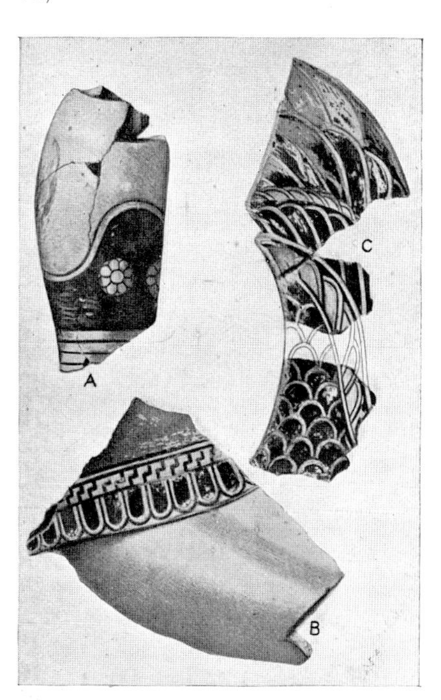

FIG. 72.—A and B, CENTRAL AKROTERION, SYRACUSE, *temenos.*

FIG. 74.—C, LATERAL AKROTERION, SYRACUSE, *temenos.*

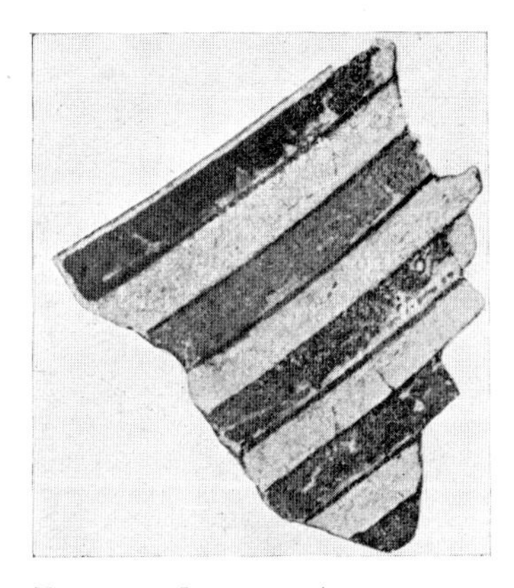

FIG. 75.—LATERAL AKROTERION, MEGARA HYBLÆA, TEMPLE B.
(*Mus. Syracuse.*)

FIG. 77.—LATERAL AKROTERION, S. MAURO.
(*Mus. Syracuse.*)

FIG. 76.—LATERAL AKROTERION, SYRACUSE, *temenos.*
(*Mus. Syracuse.*)

FIG. 78.—PEDIMENT, GELA.
(*Mus. Syracuse.*)

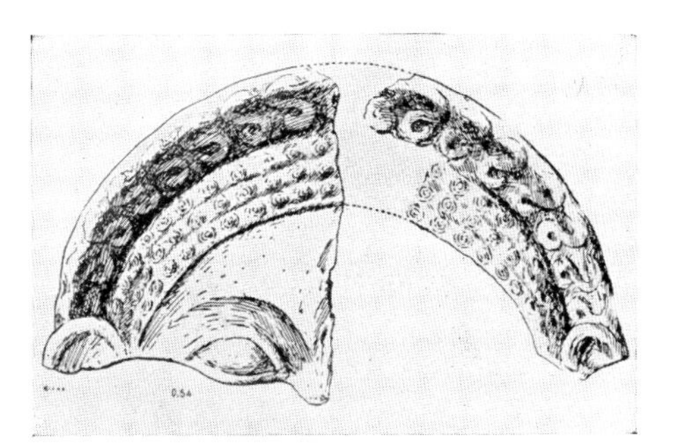

FIG. 79.—PEDIMENT, HIPPONIUM.

FIG. 80.—METOPES (?), GELA, *Predio Ventura.*
(*Mus. Syracuse.*)